THE
SOFT
WAR

OTHER GROVE PRESS BOOKS
BY TOM BARRY AND DEB PREUSCH:

The Central America Fact Book

The Other Side of Paradise
(with Beth Wood)

THE SOFT WAR

The Uses and Abuses of U.S. Economic Aid in Central America

by TOM BARRY and DEB PREUSCH

GROVE PRESS
New York

Published by Grove Press, Inc.
920 Broadway
New York, N.Y. 10010

Library of Congress Cataloging-in-Publication Data
Barry, Tom, 1950–
    The soft war.
    Bibliography: p.
    Includes index.
    1. Economic assistance, American—Central America. 2. United States—Foreign relations—Central America. 3. Central America—Foreign relations—United States.
I. Preusch, Deb. II. Title.
HC141.B375   1988   338.91′73′0728   87-13238
ISBN 0-8021-0003-1

The Inter-Hemispheric Education Resource Center, P.O. Box 4506, Albuquerque, New Mexico 87196, is a non-profit organization that produces reports, books, and slide/tape shows on Mexico, Central America, and the Caribbean.

Designed by Irving Perkins Associates

Manufactured in the United States of America

First Edition 1988

10 9 8 7 6 5 4 3 2

Acknowledgments

During the more than two years that we worked on this book, we talked to hundreds of people, both in the United States and in Central America, about the escalating soft war. Without their cooperation, it would have been more difficult to understand the dimensions of nonmilitary intervention in Central America. In particular, we thank the women and men in U.S. government offices who answered our steady stream of questions.

The book benefited enormously from the comments of those who read sections of the manuscript. We thank: Russ Bellant, William Bollinger, Karen Branan, Betsy Cohn, Martha Doggett, Mark Fried, Steven Goose, Joy Hackel, Fay Hansen, Peter Kornbluh, Deborah Levenson, Richard Martinez, Reggie Norton, Charlie Roberts, Janet Shenk, Hobart Spalding, Bob Stix, Carl Toth, Al Weinrub, and Mike Zielinski.

Our warmest thank yous go out to the staff, associates, and supporters of the Resource Center. We thank Beth Wood, a coauthor of the first Resource Center book on Central America *(Dollars and Dictators),* for her careful editing of the book and her commentary on its information and analysis. Chuck Hosking also provided excellent editing assistance. We thank Mary Ann Fiske for keeping the office running during difficult times and Pat O'Meara for maintaining our computers. Resource Center staff who helped with word processing and research were Liz Calhoon, Sally Gwylan, Barbara Bush-Stuart, and Beth Sims. For their financial help, we thank Kit Tremaine, Carol Bernstein Ferry, Michael Kelley, Linda Hoaglund, and National Community Funds.

Finally, we again want to thank Grove Press and its editor-in-chief, Fred Jordan for their continued belief in the importance and marketability of books from the Resource Center.

Tom Barry
Deb Preusch
February 20, 1987
Guatemala City

Contents

Introduction

"Would anyone of you, fathers, give his son a stone, when he asks you for bread? Or would you give him a snake, when he ask you for a fish?"

—Matthew 7:9

In the name of democracy and development, the U.S. government has a long history of offering stones and snakes to the people of Central America. When they have asked for development assistance, Washington has often responded with support for U.S. investors and the national elites. When they have asked for justice and democracy, Washington has funded pacification and counterinsurgency programs.

While public attention has focused on the military side of U.S. intervention, there has been little debate about the uses and abuses of U.S. economic aid. In the first half of the 1980s, U.S. economic assistance to Central America increased by an amount five times as great as U.S. military aid. The dollars slated for nonmilitary programs like economic stabilization, rural development, democratization, and food aid far exceed those going for military hardware and training. For every dollar of direct military aid the U.S. government sends to Central American countries, it sends three dollars of economic aid. This is the soft side of the new U.S. presence in Central America.

It is not too surprising that the public concern has centered on the military aspects of U.S. intervention in Central America. For the most part, U.S. citizens commonly regard economic aid as a form of charity and as evidence of their country's humanitarian and magnanimous spirit. Most liberals and conservatives share the conviction that U.S. nonmilitary aid fosters political stability by satisfying the basic needs of the population of the underdeveloped world. Increased economic aid to Central America has received backing from Republicans and Democrats alike.

Economic aid from the United States to Central America is intervention with a smile. Unlike military aid, economic assistance frequently comes with a friendly face. The Agency for International Development (AID), a branch of the State Department, administers most foreign economic assistance. AID officials often have a background of liberal schooling and employment; many are former Peace Corps volunteers. In its literature, upbeat and positive, AID displays photo after photo of smiling recipients: a small farmer who has received agricultural credit, a mother grateful for food handouts for her children, a student with a scholarship to study in the United States, and a union member graduating from an AID-sponsored training course.

The smiles and friendly faces associated with economic aid hide the frequently strategic and self-interested nature of foreign assistance programs. In this book, we look at the underside of Washington's economic and humanitarian aid programs in Central America. We ask where these billions of dollars in economic aid have been going. What is being done in the name of charity? Are the poor truly being helped? Is actual development occurring as a result? Or is this U.S. beneficence simply making the elites richer while giving the poor majorities nothing more than stones and snakes?

On setting out to investigate the role of the United States' economic aid in Central America, we expected to find evidence that a substantial portion was furthering U.S.'s own political, military, and financial interests. But we were shocked to find the extent to which U.S. foreign aid to Central America works against the interests of the poor. We did see smiling faces and find grateful families. Yet the more we looked—

both in Washington and in the seven countries of Central America—the more evidence we found to support our conclusion that the poor majorities of this troubled region would be far better off without U.S. economic aid. Instead of solving the region's problems, the flood of U.S. economic and humanitarian assistance into Central America is fueling the political and economic crisis.

The Soft War is divided into two parts. Part One, Development and Stabilization, explores AID's various development strategies for the region. The first chapter examines the rhetoric of economic aid programs over the past several decades, reviewing the objectives and the failures of the Alliance for Progress and showing how the mistakes of the Alliance strategy are being repeated today. The next chapter focuses on the various ways economic aid programs attempt to stabilize the region rather than to set it on the path of self-sustaining development. The third chapter takes a critical look at the myths and magic of AID's programs of private-sector support, which provide economic assistance to the region's economic elites. The final chapter in Part One examines AID's approach to agricultural development.

Part Two, Pacification and Counterrevolution, presents the results of our investigation into the political uses of U.S. economic aid. We lead off this section with a discussion of the military doctrine of Low Intensity Conflict (LIC), which calls for increased use of humanitarian aid, military civic action, and development programs in conflictive areas. The next three chapters look at the place of nonmilitary instruments of intervention in Guatemala, El Salvador, and Nicaragua. In the first two countries, economic aid programs have closely paralleled military counterinsurgency campaigns. In the case of Nicaragua, we describe the various ways that nonmilitary measures, including assistance programs, have been used to destabilize the government and further the cause of counterrevolution.

In the final chapter in Part Two, we focus on the activities of the American Institute for Free Labor Development

(AIFLD), a private organization that receives support from the federal government to keep the region's labor movement under U.S. control. The book's conclusion summarizes the uses and abuses of U.S. economic aid while suggesting ways this assistance could be better used.

U.S. ECONOMIC AID, FY 1946–1987
BY COUNTRY AND PROGRAM
($ million)

Country program	*1946–1979*	*1980–1985*	*1986*	*1987 estimate**
Belize				
Development Assistance	1.5	19.1	6.9	7.3
Economic Support Funds	—	24.0	1.9	2.3
PL480	2.9	—	—	—
Peace Corps	5.3	7.2	2.4	2.3
Total	9.7	50.3	11.2	11.9
Costa Rica				
Development Assistance	158.2	105.2	10.9	12.8
Economic Support Funds	—	476.6	120.6	127.7
PL480	19.4	93.6	16.5	16.2
Peace Corps	15.3	10.5	2.6	2.8
Total	192.9	685.9	150.6	159.5
El Salvador				
Development Assistance	123.8	307.3	83.9	75.5
Economic Support Funds	—	714.2	177.0	236.7
PL480	36.7	227.5	54.4	47.2
Peace Corps	12.3	0.5	—	—
Total	172.8	1249.5	315.3	359.4
Guatemala				
Development Assistance	256.0	105.1	36.9	33.3
Economic Support Funds	33.7	22.5	47.9	98.8
PL480	59.2	63.2	21.2	24.3
Peace Corps	16.2	13.0	2.9	3.2
Total	365.1	203.8	108.9	159.6

Country program	1946–1979	1980–1985	1986	1987 estimate*
Honduras				
Development Assistance	213.8	219.3	44.3	40.9
Economic Support Funds	2.4	283.0	61.2	136.4
PL480	37.8	78.6	18.5	17.0
Peace Corps	17.0	18.9	5.2	5.1
Total	271.0	599.8	129.2	199.4
Nicaragua				
Development Assistance	226.9	20.8	—	—
Economic Support Funds	8.0	62.8	—	—
PL480	25.5	19.6	—	—
Peace Corps	7.5	0.2	—	—
Total	267.9	103.4	—	—
Panama				
Development Assistance	279.6	62.7	18.8	19.3
Economic Support Funds	28.2	50.0	5.7	—
PL480	20.9	6.7	0.1	0.1
Peace Corps	6.9	—	—	—
Total	335.6	119.4	24.6	19.4
ROCAP**				
Development Assistance	283.3	97.6	53.2	42.1
Economic Support Funds	—	81.8	43.4	13.1
PL480	—	—	—	—
Peace Corps	—	—	—	—
Total	283.3	179.4	96.6	55.2

Country program	1946–1979	1980–1985	1986	1987 estimate*
CENTRAL AMERICA TOTAL				
Development Assistance	1543.1	937.1	254.9	231.2
Economic Support Funds	72.3	1714.9	457.7	615.0
PL480	202.4	489.2	110.7	104.8
Peace Corps	80.5	50.3	13.1	13.4
Total	1898.3	3191.5	836.4	964.4

*At the time of printing, fiscal year 1987 had not yet ended; therefore, additional funds could have been appropriated for each account.

**ROCAP—Regional Office for Central America and Panama. In 1985, AID created another regional office called Central America Regional. This office is managed out of Washington (ROCAP is based in Guatemala) and basically handles scholarship programs. From 1985 on, ROCAP figures include the Central America Regional allocations.

SOURCES: AID, *U.S. Overseas Loans and Grants and Assistance from International Organizations,* July 1, 1945–September 30, 1983; and July 1, 1945–September 30, 1985; AID, *Fiscal Year 1988 Summary Tables, Revised February 1987.*

PART ONE

*Development
and
Stabilization*

CHAPTER 1

Promises and Illusions

"The United States appears to be destined by Providence to plague America with misery in the name of Liberty."
—Simon Bolívar, hero of Latin American wars of independence in the early 1800s.

In most Central American countries, the headquarters or missions of the Agency for International Development (AID) are located within sight of the U.S. embassies. Generally less imposing than the fortresslike embassies, AID missions do not display signs or U.S. flags for identification. Yet like the U.S. embassies, AID plays a central role in the politics and economies of Central American countries.

Since 1980, AID missions in Central America have doubled and tripled their staff, becoming what amounts to shadow governments in some countries. The AID headquarters serve as centers to plan economic policies, manipulate politics, and chart pacification campaigns. Going in and out of the heavily guarded doors of the AID offices are agronomists, police trainers, economists, development experts, intelligence agents, and an array of special consultants. The seven-fold increase in economic aid to the region during the 1980s has been called the "rain of dollars" in some countries. In Honduras, a new crop of luxury restaurants and clubs sprang up almost overnight to cater to the needs of the new wave of AID employees, consultants, and contractors.

3

The red-white-and-blue AID emblem is popping up all over the isthmus. You see it deep inside La Mosquitia where AID has built a bridge to ease transportation problems for the Honduras-based contras. The emblem is stenciled on the bags of U.S. food aid distributed in the militarized areas of the Guatemalan highlands. It appears on the jeeps used by agronomists and population planners, and can be seen on signs posted outside community centers built with AID funds in the "pacified" areas of El Salvador.

AID has been active in Central America since 1961, when the Kennedy administration created the agency to administer the U.S. economic aid and food assistance program. In recent years, an unprecedented amount of AID dollars has poured into the region. The six small countries that now receive aid (Belize, Guatemala, Honduras, El Salvador, Costa Rica, and Panama) account for over 20 percent of AID's worldwide program. This high geographical concentration of economic aid is not explained by the poverty of the region (which is comparatively better off than many countries in Africa) but rather by its geopolitical significance to Washington.[1]

Over the years, many justifications have been given for the U.S. foreign aid program. Economic aid has been presented as an expression of Christian charity, a stimulation to trade and investment, a weapon in the Cold War, a way to keep friends and influence enemies, an outlet for agricultural surpluses, and part of the U.S. defense program. The Foreign Assistance Act of 1973 defines the objective of foreign aid as "the encouragement and sustained support of the people of developing countries in their efforts to acquire the knowledge and resources essential to development and to build the economic, political, and social institutions which will improve the quality of their lives." A more realistic description of the objectives of U.S. foreign aid was supplied by President John F. Kennedy in 1961, when he said, "Foreign aid is a method by which the United States maintains a position of influence and control around the world and sustains a good many countries which would definitely collapse or pass into the Communist bloc."[2]

Year after year Congress approves increased foreign aid programs in the belief that in one way or the other they serve the national interest. Economic aid is seen as an instrument of a U.S. foreign policy formulated to extend and protect the country's economic and political interests. AID has described itself as "a tool of U.S. foreign policy" and an "economic arm of the State Department."[3] The geographical priorities of AID are determined not by the urgency or severity of a country's need for assistance. Rather, AID's priorities are set by the State Department and its definition of what is the "national interest" of the United States. The problem here is not that U.S. economic aid is self-serving (something one would expect), but that the definition of the U.S. national interest is too narrow and shortsighted. A more enlightened definition of the U.S. national interest would not necessarily run contrary to the interests of Central Americans.

The tremendous increase in economic aid to Central America raises questions about its purpose and effectiveness. Before examining the current uses and abuses of U.S. economic assistance, let us first look at the origins and history of economic aid programs in Central America. While aid now earmarked for the isthmus far outweighs that of the past, Central America has been a special target of such assistance for over 25 years. U.S. aid programs have shown little success in developing the region. But rather than learning from previous mistakes, the failings of past aid programs are only compounded in current AID practices.

THE ORIGINS OF U.S. FOREIGN AID

The politics of U.S. economic aid began at the close of World War II. Having survived the war unscathed, the United States offered reconstruction assistance to war-damaged Western

Europe through the Marshall Plan. At the same time that European nations were beginning to receive U.S. aid, Latin American governments were also petitioning Washington for support.

The leading U.S. proponent of economic aid to Latin America was Nelson Rockefeller. During the war years and the late 1940s, Rockefeller served as the coordinator of Inter-American Affairs and as chairperson of President Truman's International Development Advisory Board. Rockefeller, a member of a family with extensive investment throughout Latin America, might seem an improbable figure to be pressing for development aid. Yet the Rockefeller family felt that aid would link the region more closely to U.S. foreign policy, spur economic growth, and preempt nationalist and revolutionary struggles.

Small amounts of aid were granted, mostly in the form of technical assistance. However, the larger program sought by Rockefeller and Latin American politicians was rejected by the Truman and Eisenhower administrations on the grounds that there was no pressing threat to U.S. interests in the region. Outside Europe, most U.S. aid went to countries like Greece and Turkey, which border the Soviet Union. Washington's concern with Latin America increased, however, as the 1950s progressed and the Cold War started to cast its shadow over the hemisphere.

It was in Guatemala where Washington first felt its hemispheric hegemony slipping. The progressive, elected government of Jacobo Arbenz adopted a nationalist program that was regarded in many quarters as a challenge to U.S. economic and political interests. A 1954 military coup—planned and financed by the Central Intelligence Agency (CIA)—installed a government more compatible with U.S. security interests and with the unbridled financial clout of U.S. companies like United Fruit.[4] After the coup, the Eisenhower administration pumped economic aid into Guatemala, promising to turn the country into a "showcase of capitalist development."

Five years later, the Cuban revolution of 1959 shook the

foundations of U.S. foreign policy in Latin America. Out of the rubble of past policies emerged a new Latin American foreign policy that regarded internal insurgency, not external aggression, as the main challenge to U.S. interests in Latin America. The State Department was alarmed that Che Guevara's prediction of "one, two, three, many revolutions" would prove an accurate political forecast for Latin America. The nations of Central America, among the poorest and most repressed in the hemisphere, were considered the most likely targets of leftist revolution.

Promise of the Alliance

The Cuban revolution presented an alternative path of political and economic development to Latin Americans who saw their own future blocked by recalcitrant and repressive oligarchies. Apparent to all those who bothered to look was that major changes were needed if Latin American countries were to become modern nations with more broadly based economies and political systems. Violent class revolution modeled after Cuba was now more widely regarded as the way to effect those changes.

After a period of initial shock, Washington responded to the new state of affairs in Latin America with its own plan for the region's future. The Alliance for Progress announced by President Kennedy in 1961 was an attempt to direct and control economic and political progress in Latin America while preempting violent class revolutions. As an alternative to revolution, Kennedy offered mild reforms and the promise of capitalist progress. He said that the Alliance would be a joint effort in which all American nations would "mobilize their resources, enlist the energies of their people, and modify their social patterns so that all and not just a privileged few share in the fruits of progress."

Kennedy proposed a ten-step program for the Alliance that included such measures as increased training and technical assistance, commodity agreements, aid for economic integration, and collective defense arrangements. With the Alliance, the 1960s were to be the decade of progress. Kennedy predicted that by 1970, "the need for massive outside help will have passed," and every American nation would be "the master of its own revolution and progress."⁵ Under the guidance of the Alliance, a revolution would take hold of Latin America, but it would be a peaceful revolution ushered in not by guns but by foreign aid.

The heyday of the Alliance for Progress occurred in the early 1960s during the Kennedy presidency, although the phrase continued to be used by the Johnson administration to describe the foreign aid program in Latin America. While talk of the Alliance became less common in the 1970s, the patterns and philosophy of foreign aid established during the Alliance years were carried over into that decade. All Latin American countries received U.S. foreign aid, although the programs had their biggest impact on the small and acutely underdeveloped countries of Central America.

Kennedy cautioned the region's elite that they must "lead the fight for those basic reforms which alone can preserve the fabric of their own societies." He called for the oligarchs to "do their part," warning that "those who make peaceful revolution impossible will make violent revolution inevitable."⁶ While that warning has proved prophetic in Central America, Kennedy's advocacy of peaceful revolution was a product more of his liberal idealism than of any understanding of social dynamics in the third world. It would have been similar to asking Ford or U.S. Steel in the 1920s to open up their factories to unions in order to avoid bitter class conflict. The oligarchs of Central America were not about to give away their land, pay more taxes, or give popular leaders a voice simply because the United States asked them to do so, and they were not farsighted enough to realize that some minor concessions offered immediately would ensure the long-term survival of their class dominance.

After the first outpouring of promises to the Latin American

poor, Washington adopted what it considered a more pragmatic approach to development. AID officials like Teodoro
Moscoso, who served as the coordinator of the Alliance, moved
quickly to reassure the traditional power brokers in Central
America. "In supporting the Alliance, members of the traditional ruling class will have nothing to fear," clarified Moscoso.
Rather than land reform, Moscoso said he "preferred to speak
in terms of modernizing agriculture." Toning down the implicit
challenge to the landed oligarchs, he emphasized that the U.S.
government was not necessarily advocating "taking land away,
dividing it up, and redistributing it." Instead, Washington was
more interested in the "orderly reorganization" of the agricultural sector by increasing credit, farm-to-market roads, and
extension services.[7]

Modernization, not reform, soon became the theme of the
Alliance and AID. The AID missions in Central America were
more interested in modernizing national planning agencies than
in prodding nations to follow progressive development plans.
They helped to increase the use of fertilizers and pesticides
rather than work for distribution of idle land to landless *campesinos.* In agriculture, the focus of economic aid shifted from
land redistribution to expanded production.

Central American oligarchs were not the only ones who felt
alarmed by President Kennedy's call for a peaceful revolution
of economic reforms. North American corporations also felt
threatened, and they joined the opposition to proposals for
agrarian reform and progressive tax laws. The corporate lobby
in Washington not only resisted the reform orientation of the
Alliance for Progress but also used its influence to ensure that
economic aid programs served corporate interests. Bowing to
this pressure to forge closer links between economic aid and
corporate profits, President Kennedy in 1963 told Congress
that "the primary new initiative in this year's program relates
to our increased efforts to encourage the investment of private
capital in the underdeveloped countries."

Corporate groups like David Rockefeller's Business Group

for Latin America demanded that Alliance funds be used for projects that would create a better investment climate in Central America. The corporate lobby made certain that the structure of the Central American Common Market (CACM), which the United States helped design and fund, reflected their interests. Due to corporate pressure, economic aid to Central America came with strings that tied it to the U.S. business community. Recipient nations were required to spend most of the aid money on U.S. goods—an obligation that remains true today.

Many economic programs established in the 1960s ran directly counter to the region's own development needs. AID encouraged the increased export of unprocessed agricultural commodities and promoted expanded U.S. investment, even though these activities often resulted in U.S. companies driving local firms out of business. Economic aid agreements established between AID and recipient governments contained clauses prohibiting governments from imposing restrictions on foreign investment, profit remissions, and import trade.

Alliance with Security Forces

While the promise of economic reform was pushed aside due to pressure from international and local business interests, Kennedy's political promise—*"progreso, sí; tiraña no"* (yes to progress, no to tyranny)—was also broken. When push came to shove, Washington found it easier and safer to ally itself with military regimes than to back the cause of political reformers.

Instead of supporting efforts to diminish the power of the military and the police, the U.S. government reinforced the region's security forces. The rationale offered for strengthening the security apparatus was that economies could develop, investment flourish, and democracies flower only in politically stable environments. Armies and police, trained and financed by the United States, would provide that stability. "If the Alliance for Progress is to have its chance," advised Defense Secretary Robert McNamara, "governments must have the effective force required to cope with subversion, prevent terrorism, and deal with outbreaks of violence."[8]

In 1969, at the end of the first decade of the Alliance for Progress, Nelson Rockefeller, after returning from Latin America on a mission for President Nixon, called for yet stronger support of security forces. "Without some framework for order," warned Rockefeller, "no progress can be achieved." The United States should "give increasing recognition to the fact they many new military leaders are deeply motivated by the need for social and economic progress. They are searching for ways to bring education and better standards of living to their people while avoiding anarchy or violent revolution." A U.S. policy to provide training and equipment to the police and military "will bring about the best long-term hope for the . . . improvement in the quality of life for the people." In Latin America, the military is "the essential force of constructive social change," concluded Rockefeller.[9]

It was not their purported concern for socioeconomic progress that endeared the security forces to Washington, but their political power, discipline, and dependability. As President Kennedy asserted: "Governments of the civil-military type of El Salvador are the most effective in containing communist penetration."[10] In fact, Washington encouraged the region's military and police to become involved in their country's economic and political affairs. Training courses introduced the military and police to such concepts as nation building and civic action, while advocating that they establish civil affairs divisions and increase their participation in government. Not surprisingly, the power of the Central American security forces increased rather than diminished during the 1960s and 1970s.[11]

In most countries, moderate reformers not leftist guerrillas were the main victims of the newly equipped and newly trained security forces. Labor union leaders, progressive politicians, and *campesino* cooperatives—the very people who were trying to implement the politics of reform—were arrested or kidnapped. From 1960 to 1979, 11 military coups occurred in Guatemala, El Salvador, Panama, and Honduras.[12] The Somoza family kept a tight rein on Nicaragua, and the power of the military expanded in all the above nations.

Models of Development Aid

One has only to look at the countries that AID once called its models of developing countries to understand the agency's concept of development. The Latin American countries that received the best marks from AID during the 1960s were Nicaragua and El Salvador—nations marked by repression and dictatorship and where anti-imperialist sentiment now runs strong. During the Alliance for Progress years, AID did not search for governments embarking on a reformist path but instead favored countries where authority was concentrated and governments easier to work with. The fiscal conservatism, state support for export agriculture, and desire for infrastructure improvements that characterized the Nicaraguan and Salvadoran regimes matched AID's own priorities. In contrast, Costa Rica frustrated AID officials, who felt that economic advances were being stifled by too many expenditures on social services.[13]

The close relationship between the U.S. and Salvadoran governments began soon after the 1961 military coup in El Salvador. The military and oligarchy loosely interpreted the Alliance for Progress charter as being reflective of their principles and objectives. As one study of Alliance programs in Central America noted: "Nowhere in Latin America did a regime give such strong support to the Alliance for Progress" and the "assistance agencies responded with generous financial support for the economic development of El Salvador."[14] President Johnson called the military-controlled nation "a model for other Alliance countries."[15]

Nicaragua was also praised by the United States as a model of government cooperation with economic development agencies. In 1965, AID said that Somoza's Nicaragua was "making substantial social and economic progress"—an assessment that it held until the Somoza regime began to crumble in 1978.[16] The World Bank in 1966 also praised Nicaragua: "Its record has been very good in the past and we are confident that its possibilities are good. We have always been impressed with the stability of Nicaraguan currency and fiscal administration and we have always viewed its low external debt with great satisfaction."[17]

Broken Promises, False Hopes

Rebellion and revolution were contained in Central America for two decades after the Cuban revolution. However, tremors of change began to reverberate through the region again in the late 1970s, when the Nicaraguan people overthrew the Somoza dictatorship and revolutionary movements challenged the military regimes in El Salvador and Guatemala. This political upheaval precipitated a second wave of economic and military aid to the region.

But what were the results of previous foreign aid programs? Did they improve conditions in the region, spur economic development, and channel social changes into peaceful rather than violent paths? While the economic aid that has poured into Central America after 1979 has been truly enormous, the amount of aid given to the region during the previous quarter century was also a hefty sum for such a small region. From 1954 (the year of the Guatemalan coup) to 1979, Washington pumped about $2 billion of nonmilitary aid into Central America, and U.S.-supported international financial institutions (IFIs) injected another $4 billion.

The agricultural sector, where AID had focused much of its attention, was an example of the agency's detrimental priorities. Instead of helping Central American countries increase the production of food for local markets to ensure their "food security," AID and the IFIs encouraged Central American countries to expand their production of cotton, sugar, and beef for export and financed infrastructure projects to facilitate such agroexport production. In addition, AID, in the late 1960s, encouraged countries to diversify their cash crops beyond the traditional coffee and bananas, promoting nontraditional items like flowers and winter vegetables. This emphasis on agroexport production mainly benefited the large landowners rather than the peasants who cultivated beans and corn on small plots. One result of the agroexport strategy promoted by AID was the region's expanding need to import basic foodstuffs.

Foreign aid did facilitate economic growth. During the 1960s and 1970s, Central America's per capita income doubled, and the regional economy moved forward at the rate of 5 percent a year. There were more than statistics to show this progress. By the end of the 1970s, Central America boasted a network of modern highways, a sizeable electricity-generating capacity, and a new industrial sector. Increased credit supplied by foreign aid modernized the agricultural sector, sparking a tremendous growth in the use of pesticides and mechanized farm machinery. AID programs paid for thousands of bureaucrats, politicians, and technicians to travel to the United States for their education. Economic aid created an array of government and regional agencies that still manage national bureaucracies.

Although there was strong economic growth, the region became burdened by two negative features of that growth: balance-of-trade deficits and a skyrocketing public debt. Central America's trade deficit increased threefold, and its external public debt increased thirty-threefold, between 1960 and 1979. While not wholly responsible, foreign aid institutions were largely culpable for these indicators of unstable economic growth since they had fomented increased imports and encouraged these countries to emulate the consumption patterns of the developed world. These foreign aid institutions had also encouraged the underdeveloped countries of Central America to borrow development funds from external sources rather than seeking to raise the money locally through increased taxation.

Behind the rosy economic indicators were societies in the same underdeveloped state. During the years of economic growth, distribution of land and income worsened, and the number of those living in absolute poverty was higher than ever. Unemployment deepened, and the number of people living without adequate shelter rose dramatically. Foreign aid had sparked economic growth but had not ushered in the promised reforms. As a result, the benefits were not broadly shared but went as before to the privileged classes. New highways, hydro-electric dams, and luxury hotels were evidence of the region's economic take-off. Yet the worsening poverty and hunger that was the lot of most Central Americans told a different story about development.

During the Alliance for Progress years, economic aid did have some positive impact on the poor. Health and education programs sponsored by such organizations as Pan American Health Organization, AID, and the IDB did improve some social conditions. Between 1960 and 1979, illiteracy declined, infant mortality dropped, and access to health care improved. Literacy and health levels, however, remained substantially below those of developed countries. Slight improvements in health and education did not translate into jobs for the mushrooming urban population, more land for *campesinos,* or better income distribution. While it was more likely that the poor could read or had access to a medical clinic, many basic needs remained unsatisfied.

THE SECOND FRONT OF U.S. INTERVENTION

The victorious march of the Sandinistas into Managua on July 19, 1979, marked the beginning of a new era in the U.S. foreign aid program for Central America. Never before had U.S. hegemony in the region been so seriously threatened. Shortly after the triumph of the anti-Somoza forces in Nicaragua, the Carter administration, fearful of "losing" another Central American country, arranged a new aid package for El Salvador while at the same time attempting to use U.S. aid dollars to keep the Sandinista government tied to the United States. The Democrats and Republicans agreed that the U.S. national interests were at stake in Central America, creating bipartisan backing for the Reagan administration's call for rapid increases in military and economic aid to the region. Before 1980, annual U.S. economic aid to Central America was counted in the millions, but it now measures in the billions.

The Reagan administration likened its own aid program in Central America to the Alliance for Progress. Indeed, there were similarities. Like Kennedy's plan, Reagan's initiatives came in direct reaction to revolution. Kennedy was responding to the revolution in Cuba; Reagan reacted to the revolution in Nicaragua and guerrilla struggles in El Salvador and Guatemala. Like Kennedy, Reagan promised that economic and political progress would be achieved peaceably without violent class confrontations. Like the Alliance, the new surge in economic aid programs has come with a shield of military assistance.

But major differences do exist between the current economic aid program and those of previous decades. Never before has U.S. development strategy been so uncompromisingly oriented to export production (both manufacturing and agricultural) and committed to the private sector (both U.S. and local). Under Reagan, the "trickle down" principle of development was elevated to new heights. Socioeconomic reforms as a method of insuring that lower classes obtain access to income and land have been completely discarded. AID now pushes for "reforms" that increase trade and investment incentives for business owners.

The biggest difference, however, is the way in which today's aid programs are more closely related to broader counterrevolutionary goals. While the Alliance for Progress was situated within a counterinsurgency framework, its programs were more preventive than related directly to strategic objectives. There were exceptions. In the mid-1960s, AID projects complemented military efforts to decimate a guerrilla movement in Guatemala; and in the 1970s AID supported Somoza's counterinsurgency campaign against the Sandinistas. For the most part, though, AID programs during the 1960s and 1970s were of a less overtly political character.

In contrast, the ongoing aid program in Central America has been eminently political. AID activity in the 1980s has reflected the three main U.S. foreign policy goals in the region: 1) the destabilization of Nicaragua and support of counterrevolutionary forces there, 2) the defeat of revolutionary guerrilla armies in El Salvador and Guatemala through counterinsurgency campaigns, and 3) reestablishment of uncontested U.S. political and economic hegemony throughout the region. Military aid to Central America has functioned as the sharp edge of this foreign policy, with economic aid serving as the second front in the battle to control Central America.

The second front is the soft side of intervention. It relies on a wide array of tactics and nonmilitary instruments to secure its objectives. AID is the quartermaster of this other war in Central America, although supplies and personnel also come from the Pentagon, the corporate community, and private organizations.

The Variety of Nonmilitary Aid

Washington selects from a wide variety of nonmilitary aid to supply the second front in Central America. The two largest categories of economic aid are bilateral and multilateral. Bilateral aid is that which goes directly to one government from another (in this case, from the United States). Multilateral aid refers to concessional (low-interest) loans given to governments by IFIs like the World Bank and IDB. Because of its relatively large commitments to the IFIs, the United States is in the position to persuade them to grant aid to favored countries like El Salvador and Costa Rica while denying it to a less-favored country like Nicaragua.

In this book, we are mostly concerned with bilateral aid. AID administers three categories of bilateral economic aid: development assistance, Public Law 480 (PL480) food aid, and Economic Support Funds (ESF). To qualify for this aid, countries are obliged to sign an agreement (called a Memorandum of Understanding) that requires that the assistance be used in certain ways set down by AID. In addition, Washington often uses these memorandums as leverage to force recipient nations to change their economic and political policies. Another little-known aspect of aid agreements is the way AID specifies the manner in which local currency generated from either the sale of food aid or the exchange of dollars is to be spent. The conditions specified by these agreements make them a powerful instrument of U.S. foreign policy.

Bilateral assistance does not stop with AID. Through agencies like the Export-Import Bank (Eximbank) and the United States Information Agency (USIA), Washington also offers trade and investment insurance, commodity credit, scholarships, training for labor organizers, and financial support for political and business organizations.

A hybrid subcategory of bilateral aid is humanitarian assistance, a term that has traditionally meant relief to refugees and victims of natural disasters. The definition of humanitarian assistance, however, has been distorted by government and private programs that purport to have humanitarian intentions but actually are politically motivated. Congressional funding of humanitarian assistance for the contras and the opening of a humanitarian assistance office in the Pentagon illustrate the extent to which the term is being used to mean nonlethal support for military campaigns.

Pacification and stabilization are two other terms used to describe economic aid programs in Central America. Pacification usually refers to attempts to control and possibly win over rural communities through the distribution of humanitarian assistance (mainly food, clothes, and medicine) in the context of counterinsurgency conflicts. Pacification is often described as "winning hearts and minds." Stabilization is the term AID uses for its efforts to prop up economically allied governments in the third world. It does this by providing the national treasuries and business communities with ESF dollars. Neither stabilization nor pacification can rightly be labeled a development strategy. They are strategies to control political and economic crises.

THE INEVITABLE CONSEQUENCE

The flood of U.S. aid into Central America since 1980 has been accompanied by a flurry of promises. President Reagan pledged that the aid would set the region on the road to "self-sustaining development." The economic assistance and trade incentives offered by Reagan's Caribbean Basin Initiative (CBI) were supposed to spur economic growth by increasing regional exports of nontraditional crops and light manufactures. AID promised that the Central American economies would soon advance at a rate of 4 percent to 6 percent annually. The National Bipartisan Commission on Central America (commonly known as the Kissinger Commission) in 1984 proposed a copious program of economic and military aid (most of which was later approved by Congress) as a solution to the region's socioeconomic and political ills.*

While Congress and most U.S. citizens have objected to Washington's increased military involvement in Central America, there has been little concern about the vast sums of economic aid committed to the region. Republicans and Democrats alike continue to foster the illusion that U.S. economic aid attacks the

*In August 1984, Congress approved initial financing for a five-year, $8.4 billion program of assistance to Central America to address the region's fundamental economic, social, and political problems. The Central America Democracy, Peace and Development Initiative (CAI) included more than 40 recommendations of the National Bipartisan Commission on Central America. Financing for the program includes $6.5 billion in appropriated funds and $2 billion in credit guarantees and certain programs of the Department of State, USIS, and the Peace Corps.

root causes of poverty and violence. The history of U.S. economic aid programs, however, proves that to be a false proposition. Broken promises and dashed hopes are its legacy. As in the past, U.S. aid to Central America contributes to economic dependency, underdevelopment, and political injustice. With this aid, the U.S. government is backing short-term stability instead of social progress, and reaction instead of reform. As presently structured, the variety of U.S. nonmilitary aid programs cannot be considered part of the solution to the unfolding crisis in Central America. Far from being instruments of peaceful revolution, U.S. economic aid programs help make peaceful revolutions impossible and violent ones inevitable.

CHAPTER **2** Stabilization Not Development

> *"Our economy is like a junkie waiting for the next hit from Uncle Sam."*
> —A Salvadoran businessperson

Washington views Central America as if it were a string of old buildings on the verge of collapse due to unsettling conditions. The first to crumble was the Somoza regime in Nicaragua. Tumbling down with Somoza came the entire framework of U.S. control in Nicaragua. Since 1979, the tremors of political change have coursed through the region, shaking the foundations of traditional power structures. Economic crisis has also undermined the stability of governments and oligarchies. Falling agroexport prices, the worsening debt crisis, and world recession have shaken the pillars of power in Central America. The cracks in the region's governmental, social, and financial structures grow wider and deeper each year.

The U.S. government's main economic solution to this crisis has been stabilization aid. Determined to prevent the ruin of another allied government, it has commissioned AID to patch up the cracks, repair the structural damage, and buttress the foundations of the U.S. client states. From Guatemala to Panama, stabilization—not development—has been AID's number one priority since 1980. About 75 percent of AID funds flowing to Central America have been slated for stabilization. At first, AID promised Congress that the region's need for these funds would diminish by 1986. However, the political and economic crisis has worsened each year, creating the need for ever increasing sums just to keep governments from bankruptcy and collapse.

The White House and politicians of both parties give the U.S. public the impression that U.S. economic aid is tackling the root causes of poverty and rebellion in Central America. In fact, the overwhelming portion of nonmilitary aid goes not to poor people or to development projects. Instead, this aid is used to pad government budgets, ease balance-of-payments crises, and subsidize business activity. Stabilization is not a solution to Central America's deep-seated economic and political problems. Rather, AID's stabilization plan is a defensive strategy to protect and support traditional power structures.

Economic reforms have been a major part of AID's stabilization programs. Besides pumping money into favored governments, Washington uses its aid as leverage to make demands of recipient governments. When AID now talks about reforms, it is referring not to structural reforms that redistribute political and economic power but to measures designed to strengthen the agricultural, industrial, and financial elites. On the grounds that the private sector is the principal source of economic growth and democratic sentiment, AID advocates lower taxes for investors, reduced government involvement in the economy, and more subsidies to exporters. These are what AID calls "growth-promoting" reforms.

While AID stabilization programs in Central America are ostensibly economic measures, they represent a political response. Other countries and regions battered by similar financial problems have not received similar attention. At the same time the United States is stabilizing its "friends" in Central America, it has pursued a campaign of destabilization against Nicaragua.

THE TOOLS OF STABILIZATION

The main symptoms of economic instability in Central America from the perspective of the U.S. capitalist economy are: 1) scarcity of dollars (and other foreign exchange) to pay for imports and to meet debt payments, and 2) expanding government budget deficits. AID's stabilization aid addresses both of these problems through two sources: Economic Support Funds (ESF) and PL480 (Title I) food assistance. Before 1980, these forms of economic aid were relatively rare in Central America. Together, the amount provided by these two assistance programs jumped nearly sixtyfold from $11 million in 1979 to nearly $650 million in 1986. An examination of the nature of the ESF and Title I stabilization programs is essential to a full understanding of the dimensions of U.S. intervention.

ESF grants and loans are a special type of foreign aid given to countries where the U.S. government feels its security interests to be threatened. Both the Defense Department and the State Department include ESF funding requests in their congressional presentations of security assistance programs. However, once authorized by Congress, ESF assistance is administered by AID. Unlike development assistance, which also falls under AID management, ESF monies usually do not fund specific projects but are targeted for general financial support of "strategic allies."*

---

*Economic Support Funds were known in the 1960s as Security Supporting Assistance, much of which was sent to Southeast Asia and South Korea. The Middle East became the most prominent security consideration in the 1970s, and money previously earmarked for South Vietnam, Laos, and Cambodia was rechanneled to Egypt and Israel. The International Security Assistance Act of 1978 gave ESF its present name and now over 30 countries receive ESF monies. Strategic importance for the United States supersedes poverty or economic strife as a qualification for this aid. Israel and Egypt lead the list, followed by Pakistan, Turkey, Costa Rica, El Salvador, Sudan, Jamaica, Philippines, Grenada, and Honduras. While levels for bilateral development

According to the State Department, "This Fund has meant the difference between survival and collapse for several countries, notably for those in Central America."[1] AID regards ESF as "a flexible means of providing assistance to countries of particular security and political importance to the United States."

Most ESF assistance to Central America is in the form of what AID calls Cash Transfers. The funds are simply moved from the U.S. Treasury to accounts kept by recipient governments in the Federal Reserve Bank in New York. Cash transfers have an immediate stabilizing effect. They allow countries to continue to import essential items like fuel and medicine as well as luxury goods needed to keep the upper classes content. ESF money also provides the economic foundations for the militarization of Central America by allowing countries like El Salvador and Honduras to increase military budgets at a time when internally generated revenues are steadily declining.

The second stabilization tool, food assistance, might seem an unlikely way to shore up U.S. allies, but that is the primary use of the PL480 program. One of its two main dispensing mechanisms, the Title I program, is designed to provide balance-of-payments and budgetary assistance. The commodities go directly to the governments and are then sold in their national markets to processors. Such commodities reduce the need for governments to expend scarce foreign exchange on food imports while at the same time generating a source of local currency from sale of this surplus.[2] In contrast, Title II food assistance is distributed free or as part of food-for-work programs managed by governments in coordination with the U.N.'s World Food Program (WFP) or private voluntary organizations like CARE. Referring to its program in Central America, AID noted that Title I assistance "increases, sometimes substantially, the magnitude of the total assistance pack-

---

assistance have declined or remained the same for most countries around the world, ESF allocations have more than doubled since 1980.

age we are able to offer governments, and thus increases our ability to influence their decisions."[3]

Reshaping Government Policies

Economic aid comes with many strings. Not only does AID determine how its dollars are to be used, but the agency also uses its aid packages to pressure recipient governments to change their policies and practices. When dependent on U.S. funds, governments are less likely to criticize the United States and more likely to yield to its foreign policy demands. "ESF levels may be set higher than economic needs alone may warrant to communicate political messages," stated the U.S. General Accounting Office (GAO).[4]

In return for tremendous sums of economic aid, governments like Costa Rica and Honduras have been persuaded to adopt policies that are not in their best long-term interests. As one Costa Rican businessman told the *Christian Science Monitor,* "They [Americans] are giving us more than $1 million a day, and that has to be paid back with something."[5] In the cases of both Costa Rica and Honduras, that quid pro quo includes U.S.-sponsored military buildups and permission for the Nicaraguan contras to use land within their borders. President Oscar Arias of Costa Rica told *Forbes* magazine that "as long as there are [Sandinista] commandantes in Nicaragua, we'll be able to get $200 million more or less" in economic aid.[6] That opinion was echoed by Roberto de la Ossa, director of the Central America Institute for International Affairs in Costa Rica, who said, "The Sandinistas are our best industry."[7]

Changes in economic policy are also part of the stabilization package. In its 1983 regional plan, AID announced that, "We will be seeking policy changes and reform more aggressively than before. . . ." With each ESF or Title I program comes a Memorandum of Understanding that specifies reform measures to be undertaken by the recipient government. Generally, these ensure increased government support for the private sector, the promotion of export production, and the imposition of austerity measures (such as those demanded by the International Monetary Fund).

Besides creating new economic agendas for recipient governments, AID's Memorandums of Understanding often contain clauses that obligate countries to abide by austerity guidelines laid down by the IMF or World Bank. "ESF is a good type of assistance because it's very flexible," noted Larry Cohen, a U.S. Embassy official in Tegucigalpa. "With it, we strong-armed the [Honduran government] into paying some multilateral debts."[8] Frequently, AID warns Central American nations that its continued support is contingent on their submission to IMF austerity plans. It also stipulates its own austerity measures, which have included: divestiture of public-sector enterprises, removal of price controls on basic goods, higher utility rates and gasoline prices, increased employee contributions to social security, imposition of higher sales taxes, cutback of government social services, modification of progressive labor codes, and termination of rent control and other constraints on the private housing market.

Another little-known condition of economic aid is something AID calls "policy dialogues," which are meetings between AID officials and government ministers. In the course of these meetings, AID insists that it should be given access to complete financial information about the internal affairs of the government, including access to its complete budget and the records of the nation's central bank. AID says these regular discussions allow the agency to provide "inputs to policy formulation, planning, and the design and implementation of management and administrative systems."[9] Not only do Central American governments have to submit to dialogues with AID but also with other U.S.-sponsored organizations, including private-sector groups. A recurring theme of policy dialogues is AID's insistence that there be "improved private-public sector coordination"—meaning more government responsiveness to business demands for reduced import tariffs, lower export taxes, more credit, better control of labor, and expanded infrastructure. This private-sector orientation benefits the largest traders, industrialists, and bankers as well as U.S. transnational corporations (TNCs).

The conditions imposed by the economic aid agreements restrict each government's range of political and economic options, and in a very real way undermine the sovereignty and democratic process of each country. AID tells the government what bills to introduce into the legislatures and often withholds the release of promised economic assistance until the bills are passed. Reacting to this pressure, legislators in Costa Rica charged AID with practicing "economic blackmail." Yet despite widespread resentment, Central American governments feel compelled to yield to AID's demands. With one-third or more of their budgets dependent on AID funds and without their own alternative development plans, these client states may protest from time to time, but it is unlikely that they will reject AID's offerings in the name of self-determination and national dignity.

WHERE DOES THE MONEY GO?

The billions of dollars pouring down on the region have not made much of a difference in the lives of most Central Americans. Because the main purpose of AID's assistance is stabilization not development, few new clinics, housing projects, or schools have been built. Most aid is used for less concrete purposes: to cover deficits, to provide credit, to promote more investment. As Peter Bielack, information officer at the U.S. Embassy in San Salvador, explained: "You can't see most of our aid because over half of it goes to the private sector."[10]

Not only is much of AID's assistance invisible to most Central Americans, but even AID itself has a hard time tracing where its money has gone. When AID sends ESF money to

recipient governments, it does so without any advance require-
ment for proof of actual use of the foreign exchange. The money
is usually transferred to the country's national bank account in
the Federal Reserve Bank in New York, where most of it stays
to be used to buy U.S. goods.[11]

AID has little control over which U.S. imports are bought
with its money, leaving that decision largely up to recipient
governments. It is not uncommon to find that, along with necessary items like fuel and medicine, countries use the dollars to
import luxury cars, toys, VCRs, and cosmetics for the upper
crust. AID does encourage governments to place a higher tax
on the import of luxury items, but both AID and the countries
of the region say that any attempt to ban the import of luxury
goods would encourage smuggling.[12]

A major shortcoming of ESF cash transfers is the trust
placed in corrupt recipient governments. AID favors cash
transfers because they involve little administrative work and are
quickly dispensed. But the Central American governments lack
the capacity to monitor adequately such massive sums of economic assistance. Moreover, as one government-commissioned
accounting survey team pointed out, the problem goes beyond
inadequate price checking. Political influence and payoffs guarantee access to U.S. aid dollars, and generally the large traders,
entrepreneurs, and the national oligarchy reap both the legal
and illegal benefits of cash transfers. "A key question," said an
AID-commissioned report by Arthur Young & Associates, "is
whether there is sufficient political will or desire to enforce
administrative controls."

An unstated objective of aid is to fill the gap caused by capital
flight from Central America. The problem began in the late
1970s, when coffee growers, who had been enjoying high export
prices, were putting their profits into stable foreign accounts
rather than reinvesting them at home. The Sandinista victory
in 1979 followed by the eruptions of guerrilla rebellion in El
Salvador and Guatemala sparked a new exodus of capital.

From 1979 to 1981, at least $1.5 billion left the region.[13] Capital flight continues, although at a reduced rate. Despite the massive flight of capital to foreign banks, thanks to AID's cash transfers, there is no scarcity of private-sector credit in Central America. The chieftains of the private sector have removed their own capital for safekeeping in Miami banks while, in their home countries, they rely on the easy credit and foreign exchange that AID provides.

War-Related Cash

In El Salvador, where ESF monies are intricately involved in the war effort, there are several variations of the ESF program. Along with the ESF cash transfers to aid the country's balance of payments, AID also uses ESF grants to rebuild infrastructure destroyed by the war. When the guerrillas blow up a bridge or destroy a communications station, AID arranges for the almost immediate reconstruction of those facilities. The other distinguishing feature in El Salvador is that AID permits a portion of ESF-generated local currency to be used directly for the government's operating expenses.

A 1985 study by three members of the Arms Control and Foreign Policy Caucus of the Congress took exception to the Reagan administration's labeling of ESF cash transfer programs as being aid "for economic and social development." The study said that "it is crucial to distinguish between U.S. aid programs intended to reform and develop El Salvador's economic and political system (and thereby remove the underlying causes of the war), and those programs such as the Cash Transfer, intended simply to maintain the status quo prior to the economic collapse brought on by the war." The stabilization program relates to the war in the following ways: 1) it helps fill budget deficits aggravated if not caused by the war, and 2) it indirectly sustains the expansion of the armed forces by allowing the government to shift its budget priorities toward the war effort.

Other conclusions reached by the congressional study include:

- Cash Transfers strengthen the political power of those who are most resistant to the concept of reform and social change, namely the international trade sector of the country's business community.
- Stabilization aid serves as a disincentive to a negotiated end to the war because it permits the government to resist economic pressures that would have otherwise forced it to the bargaining table.
- Economic aid has brought only artificial stability in that economic activity other than that directly sustained by the aid continues to decline.[14]

LIMITS OF STABILIZATION

In the broadest terms, AID can claim some success in its strategy of stabilization. Without the more than $2 billion of economic aid in the first half of this decade, the U.S. government would surely be having a more difficult time maintaining its grip on Honduras, Costa Rica, and El Salvador. Tensions between the private sector and government would be more intense, bankruptcies would be more frequent, and many more business owners and professionals would have abandoned Central America. But real stability, let alone economic progress, is not within sight in Central America. After a half decade of large-scale stabilization assistance, AID's goals are still paper dreams.

Economic decline since the late 1970s has set much of the region back 20 years. Optimistic AID evaluations cite any positive growth rates—as little as zero to 3 percent—as evidence that the economy is advancing. But the region's economic progress rate falls far short of the rate of population growth. In El Salvador, per capita income levels are comparable to the early 1960s. Intra-regional trade has dropped precipitously in recent years. Since 1980, trade in the Central American Common Market has been cut in half.

On the one hand, there is not enough money available to stabilize the economies. Although substantial, the stabilization funds flowing to Central America have fallen far short of covering the losses caused by capital flight, disinvestment, and war damage. The aid cannot cover the full costs of militarization and the ever-increasing debt burden. As Eduardo Lizona, the president of the Costa Rican Central Bank said, "The aid is merely a finger in the dike. We're recycling money from the U.S. government and paying it out [debt payments] to U.S. banks."[15]

Another major difficulty with AID's stabilization program for Central America is the agency's assumption that real political and economic stability ever existed in the region. Any stability enjoyed in previous decades was characterized by gross economic injustices and usually maintained by military repression. Because of AID's failure to push for needed socioeconomic reforms, its alliance with the region's elite, and its support for austerity programs, the agency is actually aggravating the Central American crisis. Cutbacks in social services, loss of government jobs, bankruptcy of local industries producing for local and regional markets, and higher food and utility prices are increasing social tension and economic dislocation.

AID accepts the fact that stabilization policies may mean a decreased standard of living for the poor, but sees this only as a temporary state of affairs. Once the private sector starts booming and exports increase, AID rationalizes, the resulting economic growth will trickle down and bring improved conditions for everyone. The agency's Strategy Statement for Honduras notes that the government's "implementation of a stabilization program will probably lower living standards and may well increase unrest among the country's already impoverished people in the short term." In reference to Costa Rica, AID said, "It is not certain how Costa Ricans will react to a protracted period of high unemployment, eroded purchasing power, periodic food shortages, and cutbacks in public services" that will result from the policy changes the agency demanded.[16] Echoing these concerns, the State Department, in its evaluation of U.S. economic strategy in Central America, said that the changes AID seeks "require considerable political preparation and entail serious economic dislocation. These reforms would be difficult to carry out in peaceful and secure societies; they are especially hard to manage in ones that are caught up in the turmoil of armed insurgencies."[17] Economic stabilization programs forced upon Central American governments have proved politically destabilizing.

Stabilization aid results in neither stability nor development. It is a crisis management tool, not a remedy for the profound economic and social problems that afflict the region. AID's strategy is to throw money at a problem instead of addressing its root causes. This rain of dollars invites waste, corruption, and dependency rather than encouraging more efficient and self-sustaining governments. As long as they can count on aid, government leaders can more easily ignore popular pressure for reforms. Originally, Washington said that ESF commitments to Central America would be a short-term fix. The dismal economic prospects for the region combined with U.S. determination to block popular political solutions to the crisis may mean that it will be raining dollars in Central America for a long time to come.

CHAPTER **3** Expensive
Magic

*"Privatization can liberate developing
economies. . . ."*
—AID Administrator Peter McPherson

When Ronald Reagan moved into the White House, the economy of Central America was on the skids and leftist revolution on the rise. But President Reagan was optimistic because he had the solution to the region's problems. He promised to let loose the "magic of the marketplace" in Central America. A strengthened, unrestricted private sector would pull the region out of its desperate economic straits, he said, while putting Central Americans on the road to democracy.

Most U.S. departments and agencies with foreign dealings— including AID and the departments of State, Commerce, Treasury, Agriculture, and Labor—were enlisted in the drive to strengthen the third world's private sector. AID formed a Private Enterprise Bureau (PRE), and both the Peace Corps and the United States Information Agency climbed on the bandwagon by creating private-sector offices. Never before had the private-sector orientation of foreign aid been so enthusiastically enforced.

With the business approach to economic aid so prevalent, the language of development changed to keep up with the times. At the AID Missions in Central America, officials talked of rural entrepreneurs when they meant farmers. To give aid a more businesslike ring, it was called "functional economic assistance." AID Administrator Peter McPherson told the House

33

Committee on Foreign Affairs that his agency promoted "contraceptive social marketing" as a way of "increasing distribution of population commodities." When asked to translate that statement, McPherson said that "social marketing" meant "retail sales."[1]

PRIVATE-SECTOR INVESTMENT

The theory of privately led development came into vogue during the Reagan administration, but it is hardly an innovative idea. President Eisenhower, for example, ordered AID's predecessor agency, the International Cooperation Agency (ICA), to be "doing whatever our government properly can do to encourage the flow of private American investment abroad. This involves, as a serious and explicit purpose of our foreign policy, the encouragement of a hospitable climate for such investment in foreign nations."[2] During a congressional hearing, a spokesperson for the Congressional Research Service politely highlighted this fact: "With no pejorative connotation intended, what we see is a re-emphasis of earlier policies that have fallen into disuse at various times."[3] Using economic aid to improve the business climate, support private development banks, promote nontraditional exports, build industrial parks, and provide technical assistance to the private sector was the overriding development philosophy of the Reagan administration. But it had all been tried before in Central America with less than favorable results—if the region's poverty, social inequities, and political upheaval are any indication.

The Caribbean Basin Initiative (CBI) set the tone for other U.S. economic aid programs to Central America. The CBI called for the elimination of import duties for certain products from the region, a U.S. tax exemption for new U.S. investors in the Caribbean Basin (which was deleted from the final bill because of U.S. labor opposition), and financial assistance aimed to enhance the region's business climate.[4] Along with the recommendations of the Kissinger Commission in 1984, the administration's Central America Democracy, Peace, and Development Initiative, proposed in 1985, stressed the importance of bolstering the private sector. The overall purpose of the CBI was to improve the economic and political stability of strategically important countries by increasing exports, attracting U.S. investors, and strengthening local business. Lawrence Theriot, director of the Department of Commerce's CBI Center, said in 1985 that "success under the CBI will come to those countries willing to seize the opportunities." To alert the Central American business community about these opportunities for investment and trade, AID sponsors international teleconferences; the USIA publishes notices; and the Foreign Commercial Service maintains regular contact with investors and traders.

The Kissinger Commission recommended the creation of a regional organization to promote economic development. Such an organization is in the process of being formed. The Central America Development Organization (CADO) promises "to engage the private sector to identify activities that will most increase productivity at the cutting edge of local production." If the organization goes ahead as planned, a quarter of U.S. economic aid to Central America will flow through CADO. While described as a regional organization, Washington will control the purse strings of CADO, which excludes Nicaragua. The Reagan administration stipulated that CADO include executives from U.S. corporations and U.S.-funded organizations, and AID will have the ultimate authority in funding decisions. This assistance will "provide a continuous and coherent approach to the development of the region" and will "make political, economic, and social development recommendations for each country and the structure of their economies."

The Bureau for Private Enterprise (PRE), created in 1981, is another government-financed tool for overseas business. PRE says its overriding goal is "to build stability and meet basic human needs in countries fighting hunger, poverty, and poor health"—all of which it supposedly does by propping up national business elites and facilitating U.S. investment. Its specific goals are to "create a climate that encourages investors, remove government roadblocks to investment, call for the privatization of government-owned firms," and "build private financial institutions."[5] PRE focuses on the countries of Central America and other regions of special geopolitical interest.

PRE is part foundation, part investment banker, and part think tank. A portion of PRE's funds are allocated for investment purposes, providing some of the start-up capital for joint ventures between local and U.S. corporations. As PRE says, "Nurturing robust business activity in developing nations takes capital." Its research division formulates policies and programs that AID incorporates into its policy dialogues with governments.

Because public-sector corporations are regarded as a major obstacle to private-sector expansion, PRE advocates the "privatization" of these firms. As a result of this pressure, public corporations have been turned over to business in Honduras, Panama, and Costa Rica. PRE manages a "privatization fund" for AID that allows country missions to prepare and implement privatization agreements. So hot is this concept that in 1986 AID sponsored an International Conference on Privatization. AID Deputy Administrator Jay Morris said during the conference that the agency aimed to carry out at least two privatizations of government-owned businesses in most recipient countries by the end of 1987. "We're talking about a new approach to development," said Morris, "one based on a central role for the entrepreneur." At the same conference, AID administrator McPherson declared that "statism has failed," and called for the dismantling of state bureaucracies in the third world.[6] Not only government-run businesses but also government services are under attack by AID. AID feels that the private sector should take over health care, and PRE has funded "private for-profit health delivery."

Insuring trade and investment is an important component of the U.S. strategy to stabilize Central American economies and boost the region's private sector. While the costs of insurance are not included in the official economic aid figures for the region, they are nonetheless an added burden for U.S. taxpayers. The Overseas Private Investment Corporation (OPIC) and the Export-Import Bank (Eximbank) insure U.S. trade and investment around the globe; and they now operate under a special presidential mandate to pay special attention to Central America, even to the extent of skirting their own guidelines.

Eximbank offers insurance and financing to U.S. exporters for their trading deals.[7] A government agency, Eximbank issues loan guarantees and insurance to foreign governments and businesses to facilitate the purchase of U.S. goods. If a Central American importer does not pay up, Eximbank will. In the last 40 years, Eximbank has provided over $4 billion in financing to Central America. Since 1979, however, when the region's economy went into a downspin, the rate of trade financing has also slumped. The bank's lending criteria simply have not permitted it to extend loans where the risks are too high. To remedy this problem, the Reagan administration created a new financing facility called the Trade Credit Insurance Program (TCIP), which uses ESF funds and is managed by Eximbank. Recommended by the Kissinger Commission, this new program allows Eximbank to bypass its traditional lending criteria. ESF funds from AID will cover all defaults under this new program. One dollar is set aside for every $5 in credit as a bad debt reserve.

OPIC insures foreign investors against losses due to wars, revolutions, civil strife, expropriation, and inconvertibility of currency. If a third world country expropriates a mining company's investments, the firm can recoup any losses by appealing to OPIC, the world's largest government-sponsored political risk program.[8] OPIC not only insures investments but also sponsors "investment missions." On these tours, OPIC officials escort prospective U.S. investors around Central America, show them the free zones, and inform them of all the incentives offered to foreign investors. As a result of ten investment missions, OPIC's Robert Jordan said that the agency identified more than 200 investment "possibilities." But there has been little to show in actual new investment. Typical of recent OPIC investors are Cat-Ketch Cayman (to expand yacht assembly operations in Honduras), Helechos de Costa Rica (to expand a fern farm), Trophy de El Salvador (to export melons), and Kimberly-Clark (to expand its toilet paper assembly operations in Honduras).

If a corporation is thinking about investing in Central America, many U.S. agencies are ready to assist. Washington pays for feasibility studies to determine if prospective investments will be profitable, puts up part of the capital, pays for the training and sometimes the housing of workers, and constructs the industrial parks for assembly plants. The U.S. also pressures governments to reduce their taxes and guarantee that investor profits can be quickly returned to the United States. In addition U.S. investors can count on the backing of the U.S. embassies if they run into trouble with their host governments. In recent years, Washington has threatened to withhold economic aid from Costa Rica, Honduras, and Panama until the those countries settled disputes involving U.S. investors.

Volunteers for Profit

AID's private-sector fixation extends to its support of what are known as private voluntary organizations (PVOs). In Central America, where over 60 percent of the population cannot afford the basic necessities of life,[9] AID asks PVOs to assist projects that support the private businessperson. Rather than building health clinics, helping farmworkers, or assisting small farmers to harvest more corn and beans, an increasing number of PVOs are found working with well-to-do business owners, promoting agroexport production, and aiding business associations.

The International Executive Service Corps (IESC) is a PVO established by David Rockefeller. Called "shirt-sleeve ambassadors," IESC volunteers are retired corporate executives who advise companies doing business in the third world. Each year IESC (using U.S. government funds) grants free business advice to such companies as Jardines del Recuerdo (an upper-class cemetery in Costa Rica), Costa Rica's Chamber of Industries (an organization that promotes foreign investment), Procesadora de Alimentos (a division of United Fruit in Costa Rica), *El Diario de Hoy* (a right-wing newspaper in San Salvador), and Hotel Honduran Maya (a prominent luxury hotel in Tegucigalpa), as well as Coca-Cola franchises, textile factories, and candy companies throughout the region.

The Pan American Development Foundation (PADF) is another PVO primarily concerned with business development. Over the last twenty years PADF has used AID funds to establish business organizations and financial institutions in Central America. In addition to AID support, the foundation depends on financial help from major U.S. corporations with foreign operations. PADF creates "development foundations" in Central American countries to make credit available to the private sector. In Nicaragua, for example, PADF founded the Nicaraguan Development Foundation (FUNDE) during the Somoza era. Washington has counted on FUNDE to mount private-sector opposition to the Sandinistas. Many other PVOs like Technoserve, Partners of the Americas, Partnership for Productivity, and Winrock International are devoted to business development, but even humanitarian-oriented organizations like CARE are now using AID funds to encourage entrepreneurship.

Also joining the private-sector campaign is the Peace Corps. In today's Peace Corps, more and more volunteers are helping businesses improve their productivity and profitability. In 1982, the Reagan administration called upon the Peace Corps to cooperate with the CBI program by assisting the private sector. The Peace Corps opened up its own Office for the Private Sector in Washington to facilitate communication with U.S. investors who might benefit from volunteer services. In its CBI Starter Kit, the Commerce Department informs prospective investors that the Peace Corps is ready to help them in Central America.

For those firms interested in nontraditional exports, over 150

Peace Corps volunteers in the Caribbean Basin are assisting in the "production and marketing of food and vegetable crops to fill seasonal gaps in the North American and European markets."[10] Volunteers even help set up joint ventures between U.S. agroindustries and local producers. Peace Corps director Loret Miller Ruppe told Congress that the agency has formulated a "complete in-service training model . . . to train volunteers how to do prefeasibility studies" for new business investment.[11]

The Peace Corps is disproportionately represented in Central America; in 1984, President Reagan called for a 50 percent increase of Peace Corps workers in the region. Over 400 Peace Corps volunteers are assigned to Honduras, the country with the highest Peace Corps presence in the world. In addition to their business involvement, new volunteers participate in the U.S. ideological offensive. To better prepare them for that role, volunteers now receive lectures on "the menace of Communism" and briefings from members of the National Security Council (NSC).

Building a Business Lobby

In keeping with AID's business orientation, the U.S. government pays the bills for nearly 20 private-sector associations throughout Central America. The United States views an organized business community there as essential to democracy and as a strong deterrent to leftist political tendencies. Private-sector organizations in the region, particularly those funded by Washington, can usually be counted on to back U.S. foreign policy. The two driving forces behind this push to prop up business groups in Central America are AID and the National Endowment for Democracy (NED).

President Reagan created NED in 1984 to channel funds from the United States Information Agency to the U.S. Chamber of Commerce, which in turn passes on the aid to the Center for International Private Enterprise (CIPE). CIPE was established in 1984 for the purpose of "strengthening private enterprise institutions throughout the world." It does this by supporting or creating "private voluntary business organizations" that take an "active part in economic and public policy."

CIPE, which includes a representative of the right-wing Heritage Foundation on its board of directors, propagates a conservative agenda. It has collaborated with the Center for Strategic and International Studies at Georgetown University to study foreign policy and the role of elections in Central America. In Panama, CIPE offers seminars on "free enterprise" and "competition"; in Costa Rica, it trains local chamber members to run business organizations. NED and CIPE are even active in Nicaragua where they work with conservative and anti-Sandinista business organizations like FUNDE and the COSEP (Superior Council of Private Enterprise).

In order to enhance its business philosophies, CIPE sponsors seminars for Central American business owners conducted by the International Policy Forum (IPF). IPF, which was founded about the same time as NED and CIPE, aims "to support democracy and to promote international communications and cooperation among pro-free enterprise leaders." Its president is Morton Blackwell, who moved over to IPF from a White House position as Special Assistant to the President for Public Liaison where he worked closely with former NSC adviser Lt. Colonel Oliver North. The Chamber of Free Enterprise in Guatemala, an organization formed by AID in 1985, used its CIPE grant to host a seminar for Guatemalan and Salvadoran business owners on the subject of "Understanding Politics." The seminar encouraged increased participation in the political process by the business community through direct mail operations, development of key interest groups, and better use of the media.

AID too has helped create an extensive network of private-sector organizations throughout the isthmus. Not only do business leaders generally share AID's economic philosophy but they also espouse the same political principles. For this reason, AID says it is "nurturing public and private institutions such as trade associations, chambers of commerce, business training facilities, and financial institutions that support free enterprise and free investment."[12]

AID sees the organizations it funds as a way to circumvent the public sector. Many of them now serve as what AID calls "one-stop investment centers" that function outside government regulations and bureaucracy to further the interests of the private sector. Instead of transferring its "development" grants and loans to Central American governments, AID funds are now often given directly to private-sector organizations. AID has used these business associations to formulate and lobby for economic stabilization plans and to pressure Central American governments to pass pro-business economic reforms. In addition, the agency funds programs to train government officials "to support overall AID-development objectives, emphasizing export and investment promotion."

Invariably, the AID private-sector groups support measures that are opposed by workers and peasants, such as cutbacks in government spending for social services, more restrictive labor laws, and an end to price controls. In Costa Rica, the consumers' organization, National Patriotic Committee (COPAN) protested that the country's sovereignty was threatened by the growing influence of AID-supported business lobbies. COPAN objected that the Coalition for Development Initiatives (CINDE), which has received millions of dollars from AID, serves as an unofficial government economic planning ministry representing the interests of the right-wing and the economic elite.[13]

AID's support for business organizations extends to groups based in the United States. Caribbean/Central America Action, which is funded by AID, represents most major U.S. investors in the Caribbean Basin and promotes increased foreign investment in the region. Most local affiliates of the American Association of Chambers of Commerce in Latin America (AACLA) receive AID money. One of the largest recipients of AID funds in Honduras, HAMCHAM or the

Honduras-American Chamber of Commerce (which represents about 180 firms, mostly from the U.S., doing business in Honduras), uses AID money to transport local entrepreneurs to the annual CBI conference in Miami, to print brochures like the *Businessman's Guide to Honduras,* and to "act as a liaison between the private sector and the government." HAMCHAM's slogan links the private sector with freedom: "La empresa privada produce libertad."

There are political as well as economic reasons why AID chose to create its own network of business associations in Central America. In addition to wanting organizations that would advocate its economic agenda for the region, the agency hoped to use the network to form a more centrist political base among the business community. AID felt that its interests—and those of the private sector—would be better served by business organizations that were not so closely affiliated with the extreme right wing and traditional agroexport oligarchy. Unable to find existing groups to fit its needs, AID used its considerable financial resources to create new ones or to resurrect and refashion dying or dormant associations.

THE CIRCLE OF AID

Congressional members hope foreign assistance will meet basic needs, spur economic growth, attract investment, and reform recipient governments while acting as an effective instrument of U.S. foreign policy. But the most commonly expressed congressional concern can be summed up as "What good does all this aid do our constituents?"

With military aid, the answer is easy. Virtually all of it is spent to buy U.S. weapons and services. Congress has discovered that a surprisingly large percentage of economic aid also comes back home. In fact, most AID funds never really leave the United States.

When Representative Stephen Solarz raised the issue about the benefits of economic assistance to the United States during

Congressional budget hearings, AID administrator McPherson presented figures showing that about 70 percent of U.S. aid bounces back to this country to pay for goods (like fertilizer and road equipment) and services (mainly consultants). What's more, McPherson also told Solarz that 25,000 U.S. jobs result from each $1 billion of foreign aid, meaning that each year the worldwide program creates or maintains "somewhat over 100,000 jobs" within the United States.[14]

The self-interested nature of U.S. economic bilateral and multilateral aid was the subject of a recent report by international trade consultant Vicki Hicks. She said that, "Aid is usually closely tied to the donor country. That is, the funds are used to buy goods and services from the U.S. In fact, money spent by multilateral banks on U.S. goods and services greatly exceeds our contributions to them."[15] Economic aid, both bilateral and multilateral, also serves U.S. financial interests by increasing the ability of governments and the local private sector to pay back foreign debts.

Lots of Hoopla, But Little Money Down

All the hoopla and ballyhooing about investment in Central America have produced little in the way of results. Since 1980, the investment and trade picture has deteriorated alarmingly. Washington is offering a feast of incentives, exemptions, and credit to new investors, but nobody's coming to dinner.

With few exceptions, the only new U.S. businesses investing in Central America are small, privately held firms exporting vegetables, flowers, and other nontraditional exports. (Traditional exports are those like coffee, cotton, sugar, bananas, and tobacco that historically account for most of the region's exports.) These companies have set up farms in Central America to cultivate cocoa, passion fruit, cantaloupe, citrus, and shrimp. In its 1985 summary of investment in the region, the CBI Business Information Center in Washington acknowledged that there had been "no earthshaking results," but pointed out a few success stories, such as a new yacht assembly plant in Honduras.

The Commerce Department in 1985 claimed that U.S. efforts in the Caribbean Basin had resulted in 268 new export-oriented business operations and 32,000 new jobs.[16] But these statistics are suspect. It appears that the calculation of jobs created involved mostly indirect employment. Fruta del Sol, an AID-funded vegetable firm operating in the Comayagua Valley in Honduras, was listed as providing 1,200 jobs, when in fact the company employs only a dozen or so workers. Apparently, the report included the number of farmworkers who pick the cucumbers for the farmers that sell to Fruta del Sol. Most of those farmworkers are women and children employed temporarily for less than $2 a day.

The results of U.S. attempts to increase regional exports are also less than earthshaking. A 1985 study by the Overseas Development Council (ODC) concluded that the CBI countries have been less successful than many other countries in increasing their exports to the United States. In 1984, the first year of the CBI, exports from Central America (excluding Nicaragua) grew by just under 10 percent. This represented a rather weak performance in light of the 26 percent trade increase with the U.S. market from all sources in 1984, and the 17 percent increase from all developing countries. Any increase in imports to the United States from the Caribbean Basin, said the report, could not be attributed to the CBI. It noted that the only significant increases were in traditional agroexports, such as tobacco from Guatemala and Honduras and citrus products from Belize, Costa Rica, and Honduras.[17]

Despite the promotion of exports from Central America to the United States, they are declining. In 1985, a substantial portion of the decline in Central America-U.S. trade came in the very goods enjoying CBI duty-free status. At the same time, Central America purchased more U.S. imports, further aggravating the region's trade balance crisis. The Commerce Department blames the decrease in exports on the depressed market for traditional items like coffee, sugar, and bananas. And experts say that the prospects for those three commodities remain poor for the rest of the decade. According to the CBI Business Information Center, the difficulties experienced by traditional commodities have overwhelmed the small increase in nontraditional exports.

Besides agricultural products, the main nontraditional items being promoted by Washington are electronic goods and garments. The electronics assembly operations are waning in Central America despite access to the duty-free trade provisions of CBI. Even before the withdrawal of Texas Instruments from El Salvador, the region's electronics exports were in rapid decline. The garment industry, although it does not enjoy CBI trade benefits, has shown a substantial increase in the 1980s.

The value of assembling brassieres, underwear, shirts, and jeans for the U.S. market is questionable. Like the so-called electronics industry in Central America, the garment business there is not a true industry. Rather it is a finishing-touch operation that contributes little or no taxes and has no linkages to other local businesses. Commerce Department statistics show that 71 percent of the value of electronic items and garments imported from the Caribbean Basin comes from U.S. parts shipped to the region for assembly.[18] In other words, when Costa Rica ships $100 worth of garments to the United States, it only gets back $29—and a good portion of this $29 goes into the coffers of the U.S. corporations that oversee the assembly operations. The only real contribution of these assembly industries are the sweatshop jobs they provide at $2–4 a day. "Cost-competitive labor" is the region's "major asset," according to the CBI Center director.[19]

Like Humpty Dumpty

The private sector in Central America is a lot like Humpty Dumpty before the "big fall." Foreign investors are nervous, local businesses are going bankrupt because nobody has the money to buy their goods, international market prices are depressed, and those with extra capital prefer to keep it in Miami banks. By giving business special care and hoping that some benefits trickle down to the majority of the population, the marketplace magic of the United States is being used to keep the private sector from tumbling from its precarious perch.

Prospects are not propitious. All the king's programs and subsidies have failed to steady the wavering private sector in Central America. Many agroexporters and industrialists have shut down because of adverse conditions on the international, regional, and national markets. The per capita GDP, which has dropped back to the level of the early 1970s for most countries, can no longer even keep up with population growth. Domestic consumption, exports, and national production, as well as local saving and borrowing, have dropped to lower levels than in 1980. Private investment dropped between 40 and 65 percent between 1980 and 1985.

Up and down the isthmus, the private sector is on the offensive. Backed by the United States, business organizations are demanding lower taxes, deregulated commodity prices, and easier credit. As a result, the burden falls on the public, which faces higher sales taxes and fewer government services. Reduced private-sector taxes and reductions in government expenditures for social services might provide temporary relief for business, but these actions do not address the conditions that caused the crisis. On the contrary, reduced expenditures and less control over the distribution of national wealth worsen the deterioration of national and regional markets.

MYTHS AND MAGIC

Referring to his development approach to Central America, President Reagan said, "The success of our overall policy is directly linked to what the private sector can accomplish."[20] If the business elite prevails, the reasoning goes, then the region will come to enjoy development and democracy. This foreign

policy strategy, which is not distinctive to the Reagan administration, is a costly endeavor that is based on the following
myths:[21]

- Stimulation of the private sector is the best way to help all
  members of society, including the poor.
- Political freedom is a by-product of the economic freedom of
  private property and free markets.
- Free enterprise, operating in free markets, distributes resources
  in an efficient and just manner.
- Governments are constraining business through high taxes, ob-
  trusive regulations, and competing enterprises.
- Central American governments maintain a high degree of in-
  volvement in the economy.
- The private sector expands as the public sector shrinks.
- Economic development stems directly from business activity.

Political scientist Richard Newfarmer challenges the first
two myths, by noting that neither in the United States nor in
Central America has personal political freedom been a by-
product of free enterprise. "It is quite clear historically," asserts
Newfarmer,

> that a strong private sector does not assure that personal freedom
> will follow. One need only recall the painful evolution of democ-
> racy in the United States—through slavery, abolition, workers'
> rights to collective bargaining, women's suffrage, the Civil Rights
> Act—to realize that political empowerment and participation do
> not follow in lock step to a free private sector.[22]

Since 1821, when the Central American elite declared the
region's independence from Spanish colonialism, the private
sector has invested and traded wherever and however it wanted.
This 165-year history of unfettered activity certainly has not
resulted in an equitable allocation of resources. Only the rich
enjoy economic freedom and easy access to education, health
services, and good housing. The poor peasants and workers
have little social mobility because they have no free choice in
occupational activity or discretionary income. As Newfarmer

states, "Only when the bottom 40 percent can escape from absolute poverty can free markets and economic freedom have any relevance."[23]

In its policy dialogues, AID obliges governments to cut back their expenditures and reduce their control of the private sector. Yet Central American governments account for only 20 percent of the GDP (Gross Domestic Product), about the same level as the U.S. government and far less than other capitalist countries like France, Great Britain, or Mexico. In Central America, business pays a disproportionately low share of government expenses. Fearful of confronting the private sector with requests for higher taxes, governments have instead raised taxes that fall on consumers and made up the difference by borrowing money overseas.

In underdeveloped countries, like those of Central America, a strong public sector is even more important for growth than in developed economies. Not only does a government need to consider the welfare of its citizens, but it also is called upon to invest in areas of the economy passed over by the private sector because they are regarded as unprofitable (public transportation) or because they require too much capital (communications). Many studies have shown that private-sector development in third-world nations actually depends on public-sector activity. From the time of Adam Smith, as Newfarmer points out, "public-sector expenditures tend to increase the capitalist sector's growth" if kept to under one-third of the GDP. Without government infrastructure projects, there would be very little private-sector activity. Foreign loans contracted by the government also help Central American businesses from going bankrupt.

On the basis of private-sector myths, the money of U.S. taxpayers is being liberally handed out to oligarchs, financiers, and U.S. investors in Central America. Over a billion dollars of economic aid has poured into the region to promote private-sector growth, but the results are hard to find. In fact, more businesses have shut down than have opened or expanded.

Exports from the region have not increased, but continue to shrink despite an array of incentives and subsidies offered to agroexporters. Neither have tax-breaks, tariff-exemptions, nor AID's meddling in government policies resulted in any surge in U.S. investment. Instead many U.S. investors have pulled out of Central America. Using government funds to promote private-enterprise projects in Central America is a waste of taxpayer revenues. After three decades, it is time for this expensive undertaking to be exposed for the phony magic it really is.

CHAPTER **4** Plantation Development

"We are looking at moving subsistence-oriented agriculture toward high commercial value agriculture and at linking campesinos *to the export process."*
—Anthony Cauterucci,
AID/Honduras director.

The society and economy of Central America are rooted in agriculture. Half the population works in the sector, and over 80 percent of the extra-regional exports are agricultural commodities. Outside the metropolitan areas, there are few factories or commercial centers. The industries that do exist are related to the region's main agroexports. Smoke plumes rise from blackened sugar mills, women and children sort coffee beans in *beneficios,* and laborers load 100-pound bundles of cotton onto trucks headed to nearby ports. In the fertile fields along the coast, cattle graze in lush pastures, farmworkers stoop over to pick cotton bolls, and crop dusters loop back and forth spraying deadly doses of pesticides on farms and farmworkers alike. If you move inland away from the tropical coastlands, the terrain turns mountainous. Here on rocky, eroded slopes, *campesinos* grow corn and beans—the staple foods of Central America.

The region's dual structure of agriculture—agroexport crops cultivated on plantations covering the best land, and basic foods for local consumption cultivated on tiny plots of the least fertile land—defines the agricultural economy and is the main cause

51

for the region's underdevelopment. A narrow group of land-holders, mill owners, and traders benefit from this structure, while the majority of the population are included only as poorly paid farmworkers and marginal farmers.

The peasantry, by providing cheap food from their small plots and cheap labor to the agroexport plantations, is the foundation of the region's agricultural economy. While this division of land and labor makes good economic sense from the point of view of the plantation owners, it is inherently unstable. The dollar or two a day that agroexport growers pay their seasonal work force does not cover the basic needs of peasant families; this shortfall creates the conditions for rural rebellion. When they finish their temporary work on the agroexport plantations, many *campesinos* return to their small plots in the interior of the country. Historically, the corn and beans they cultivate have sufficiently supplemented their wage income to ensure minimal subsistence. But as the agroexport economy expands and the population grows, less and less land is available to provide the cheap food the agroexport economy counts on to feed the underpaid population.

What should the role of economic aid be in these circumstances? Should aid be used to industrialize Central America, moving it away from its age-old dependence on a land-based economy? Or should U.S. assistance help modernize agricultural production? Is it better to encourage the expansion of the most profitable sector of the economy (agroexport production) or to concentrate on bettering the lot of the marginal peasant sector?

AID has responded to the underdevelopment problem in Central America with an array of programs, including food assistance, small farmer support, agricultural credit, agrarian reform, integrated rural development, basic-needs support, and export diversification. Yet after several decades of aid, the conditions of poverty, malnutrition, and powerlessness remain much the same. In large part, AID's lack of success is not due to bureaucratic bungling or government waste and corruption, but is the direct result of the agency's own economic priorities and political motivations.

TOYING WITH AGRARIAN REFORM

In Central America where elites control most of the land and income, agrarian reform is a necessity. With the Alliance for Progress, President Kennedy advocated a series of peaceful agrarian reform programs for Latin America as a way to avoid revolutionary upheaval. The charter of the Alliance called for:

> Programs of comprehensive agrarian reform leading to effective transformation, where required, of unjust structures and systems of land tenure and use, with a view to replacing latifundia and dwarf holdings by an equitable system of tenure so that . . . the land will become for the man who works it the basis of his economic stability and dignity.

The inspiring rhetoric of the Alliance, however, was just an empty promise.

Local oligarchs as well as U.S. investors, notably the banana companies, vigorously opposed all programs that expropriated idle land. In 1962, the U.S. Congress, reacting to angry complaints of the Latin American oligarchy and backing off from the spirited language of the Alliance, said "the primary objective of agrarian reform . . . should be at all times increased agricultural productivity" and that "land reform is not a tenure problem but a problem of improved farming practices generally."[1] This conservative approach permeated the programs backed by AID in Central America. As an editorial in *El Imparcial,* the right-wing newspaper in Guatemala City, observed: "At last they [U.S. political leaders] are beginning to realize the danger of the so-called peaceful revolution by the Alliance for Progress. Rapid reform creates more political and social problems than it solves."[2]

What AID calls agrarian reform is a far cry from what was initially proposed by the framers of the Alliance for Progress.

Over the years, the agency has shied away from programs that effectively challenge "unjust structures and systems of land tenure and use." Instead AID has sponsored colonization projects to resettle landless peasants on isolated and previously uncultivated frontier land. The military and the oligarchy have endorsed colonization projects as a way to open up new lands for pastures and plantations. When resettled peasants have completed clearing the land and foreign aid has financed the construction of new roads into the agricultural frontier, generals and oligarchs frequently have ordered the peasants off their plots, pushing them further into the rain forests.

Land titling is another AID substitute for agrarian reform. In Central America, where land is passed from generation to generation without the legal titles, the lack of documentation is certainly a major problem. Because they cannot prove they legally own their farms, small growers have a difficult time obtaining agricultural credit and frequently are shoved off their farms through legal chicanery. AID has financed land-titling projects to solve these problems, but such projects do nothing to alter the structures of land tenure. Titling programs do not benefit the many landless and near-landless farmers. Instead, AID's assistance is usually intended for the very small sector of commercial-level farmers who, in addition to growing enough food for their families, have enough acreage to produce agroexports like coffee.

Another sorry substitute for real agrarian reform is AID's land-sales programs. These projects do facilitate the selling and buying of land by acting as an intermediary between large property owners wishing to sell and small landowners or landless peasants who want to buy land. AID arranges mortgages with low-interest rates and guarantees the sellers payment for their property.

Over the past quarter century, AID has supported these token reform programs as a way to ease rural tensions. Yet as the population increases, the emphasis on agroexport production continues and the agricultural frontier shrinks, social tensions over land issues in Central America have intensified. In Nicaragua, the Sandinista guerrillas (FSLN) attracted a rural base with their call for the expropriation of Somoza family landholdings. In El Salvador, landless and near-landless *campesinos* filled the ranks of the leftist mass organizations that surged in the late 1970s. The success of the Sandinistas and the momentum of Salvadoran leftists served to persuade AID in 1980 to sponsor an agrarian reform program in El Salvador.

AID's agrarian reform for El Salvador was designed to co-opt support for the guerrillas while pacifying peasant communities. It represented a sharp departure from the modest land transformation programs sponsored in other Central American countries. The reform mandated extensive land expropriations, and was a slap in the face of the oligarchy. But in other ways, the land reform in El Salvador was well within the tradition of other AID-sponsored rural programs.

Agrarian reform is a necessary precondition for development in Central America. In a 1978 *Agricultural Development Policy Paper*, AID acknowledged this fact, stating that: "A highly skewed distribution of land among agricultural producers . . . will adversely affect both improved equity and increased production, thereby rendering a broadly participatory agricultural production strategy virtually impossible to implement." Nonetheless AID has been reluctant to use its resources to push forward agrarian reform programs. The vigorous opposition by local oligarchs and U.S. investors to land reform is one reason for AID's hesitation to support land redistribution programs. AID is also concerned that substantial reform could open the gates to revolution. While recognizing the problems of distorted land tenure in Central America, AID has, since the early 1960s, tried to evade the politically sensitive issue of land distribution through programs that promote agroexport production, support "integrated rural development," and provide for the short-term "basic needs" of the rural poor.

MORE, ALWAYS MORE AGROEXPORTS

The Spanish colonial system in Central America crumbled at the beginning of the 19th century, but the agroexport production system that developed under Spain's mercantile empire has remained the dominant element in the economy of Central America. First cacao and indigo were exported to meet the European taste for chocolate and demand for dyes. When in the 19th century, Europeans acquired a craving for coffee, growers in Central America responded by opening up new plantations on the volcanic uplands, which until then had been occupied by Indian communities. At the turn of the century, U.S. investors cleared tropical forests to make way for vast banana estates, converting entire regions of Guatemala, Honduras, Costa Rica, and Panama into enclaves controlled by corporations like United Fruit and Standard Fruit.

After World War II, the industrial world's postwar recovery opened up new markets for Central America's agricultural commodities. With foreign aid from both bilateral and multilateral sources, governments began to modernize agroexport production in the 1950s and 1960s. For the first time, governments established agricultural ministries, road departments, and schools to train agronomists—all oriented toward increasing agroexport production as the region's financial base. Economic aid was also channeled into regional industrialization through the Central American Common Market. But the plans for industrialization and regional trade were not accompanied by a reorganization of the region's dual structure of agricultural production.

AID and the multilateral lending institutions have long been concerned about the region's economic dependence on a few largely unprocessed agricultural commodities. To reduce that dependence, foreign development planners have recommended diversification. AID itself has a long record of supporting programs aimed at increasing the variety of agroexports by encouraging items like beef, vegetables, and flowers. During the 1960s, the cattle industry in Central America grew dramatically as a result of programs sponsored by AID, the World Bank, and IDB to improve breeding practices, to construct USDA-approved packing houses, and to clear land for pastures. As a result, beef has become one of the five traditional exports from Central America (along with coffee, bananas, cotton, and sugar). The beef export boom increased the wealth of large landholders and packinghouse owners (many of whom are U.S. investors), but at a terrible cost. Tens of thousands of peasant families were pushed off their land and rain forests were leveled by the cattle industry—all to satisfy the demands of fast-food chains like Burger King.

Diversification into nontraditional agroexports like broccoli and carnations is a major theme of AID development programs in the 1980s. AID advocates the increased export of winter vegetables and other nontraditionals as a solution to the region's declining agroexport income and a way to ease the land tenure crisis. The agency says that Central America needs a "long-term strategy that relies heavily on increasing nontraditional exports."[3] AID has taken its campaign to large and small farmers alike. For large landowners, nontraditional agroexports are presented as an alternative to traditional crops (like cotton and sugar) that have been hit hard by declining prices and shrinking markets. Financing, investment support, and technical assistance are provided to U.S. investors and local oligarchs for ambitious agribusiness projects. For owners of small- and medium-sized farms, AID recommends changing from corn to vegetable production as a way to increase their income without increasing the extent of their landholdings.

Since 1970, AID has channeled over $60 million in Central America development assistance to a consortium of U.S. corporations called the Latin America Agribusiness Development Corporation (LAAD). LAAD is one of the few private-sector business organizations that has successfully used government funds to increase investment in Central America. Corporate members of this AID-financed consortium, which includes Bank of America, Castle & Cooke, Ralston Purina, and Borden, are interested in investing in nontraditional agribusiness projects throughout Latin America (with most investments in Central America). To justify its support of LAAD, AID contends that the business consortium provides jobs for landless peasants and provides marketing outlets for small farmers while increasing exports and economic growth. In its proposals to AID, LAAD says one of its main goals is "improving the standard of living of the Central American poor."

Using AID funds, LAAD finances the production and processing of mainly nontraditional exports destined for U.S. corporate buyers. While many of LAAD's projects have succeeded as business investments, it is difficult to justify them as development projects. Statements found in the first AID-funded evaluation of LAAD pinpoint problems that continue to plague the consortium's current projects in Central America. The 1974 evaluation noted that LAAD's investments had not produced additional food for those who really needed it. Instead, the crops are "destined for upper middle, upper class consumption, or for export."[4] In its 1977 annual report, LAAD boasted of the flourishing business of a Guatemalan frozen food company that shipped frozen broccoli and cauliflower "grown by Indian communities." But later investigations into this Guatemalan company called ALCOSA revealed it to be a subsidiary of Hanover Foods. While the vegetables were being grown in largely Indian areas, the better-off mestizo farmers grew the crops and hired the Indians as temporary farmhands. A 1977 evaluation by an AID contractor found that only the "opportunistically entrepreneurial" members of the community had received the contracts from ALCOSA. The net result was "an increase in economic inequality."[5]

AID says that LAAD works with small- and medium-sized businesses. A recent evaluation of AID activities in Central America, however, revealed that the average size of LAAD loans was $462,500. A half-million-dollar loan is not the kind of investment that small- and medium-sized entrepreneurs in the region even consider.[6] Loans were given to a sesame exporter and a cardamom trader in Guatemala, a frozen beef exporter in Honduras, a tropical flower company in Costa Rica, two shrimp exporters and a poultry firm that produces chicken for fast-food restaurants in Panama.

One justification offered by AID for its financial support of LAAD and similar investment projects is that they create jobs. A 1983 AID-contracted evaluation of LAAD revealed that in a recent 2-year period, LAAD loaned close to $4 million to 8 agribusinesses but generated only 126 direct jobs. The loans were used to refinance and improve the technology of agroexport firms.[7] So few are the direct jobs created by this type of loan that AID acknowledged in a 1984 LAAD project paper that "job generation" might have to be interpreted as increases in the income of commercial farmers who contract with LAAD.[8] Money used to buy a new pickup truck for a well-to-do farmer might then be counted as a job or two in this innovative evaluation method.

The real benefit, says AID, comes from the temporary jobs resulting from these agroexport projects. But AID does not even require that businesses using AID funds pay a minimum or life-sustaining wage. In 1984, LAAD claimed that 80 percent of the labor-intensive jobs resulting from new AID financing agreements would be held by women. In a typical AID-financed project producing vegetables for export, Central American women and their children pick vegetables out in the field or work in packing sheds.

AID's emphasis on nontraditional agroexports is highly consistent with its private-sector oriented development philosophy. Like the more traditional exports, nontraditionals earn foreign exchange, allowing countries to pay their external debts and continue their imports of agricultural inputs like pesticides and tractors. Nontraditional agroexport production also opens investment opportunities for U.S. corporations, thereby keeping the region economically tied to the United States.

AID also regards nontraditional agroexport production as a nonconfrontive solution to the land tenure crisis in Central America. It is the agency's opinion that small farmers lacking enough land to support their families by cultivating corn and beans do not necessarily need more land to increase their incomes. At the AID Mission in Honduras, Tom King said, "We're moving the *campesinos* away from being prisoners of basic crops." In Costa Rica, AID's David Gardella told us that small farmers have to change over from basic grains cultivation to export crops "because you never know what the price is going to be" for corn and beans.[9] The AID Mission in Guatemala has adopted a development plan that "looks toward stimulating the production of high-value, labor-intensive crops thereby diversifying away from the traditional corn and beans."[10] Instead of supporting substantive agrarian reform programs or encouraging increased production of basic grains to ensure regional food security, AID tells peasant farmers that they can better their lives by harvesting broccoli and strawberries rather than corn and beans.*

For the past 15 years, Guatemala has been the focus of AID's promotion of nontraditional exports. Aside from military repression, one of the most serious problems facing the country is the steady decline in the rate of food production—which means a corresponding rise in food imports.[11] The statistical evidence of a shortage in staple goods can be readily seen in the increasing hunger and malnourishment of the Guatemalan poor. Most of the AID projects to promote nontraditional exports have been concentrated in the Altiplano, home of the country's large Indian population.

Indian farmers, agricultural extension agents, and even AID consultants criticize the illusory nature of the agency's develop-

---

*Food security means both the availability of sufficient food and the economic means to acquire it. Food security requires a national system that satisfies the basic needs of even the poorest social strata.

ment plan for the Altiplano. Edmund Silvestre Montego, the government's director of agricultural services for one Altiplano sector, complained that there was no internal market for non-traditional vegetables in Guatemala and that the small external market was extremely fickle. "Brussels sprouts is a good example of the problems with diversification," he said. "The people here don't eat them, so when ALCOSA (the Hanover Foods company that has been supported by AID) decides that it doesn't need any more of them, the brussels sprouts are just fed to the animals." Montego said that nontraditionals would be a good idea only if sales were guaranteed. As it is, most small growers cannot afford to take risks. "Because most people don't know how to cook these vegetables, there is no local market for [them]. And the international market seems to open up only when there is a frost or a heavy rain in Florida or California." The large financial commitments by AID, he said, have not guaranteed success of these ventures.[12]

Consultant Bill Ross, who works for an AID project office in the Altiplano, agreed that the main problem was finding markets for the nontraditional exports. "Even those farmers," he said, "with irrigation systems and who live next to the main highway to Guatemala City are having trouble making a go of it." Yet AID is paying for the construction and maintenance of "farm-to-market" dirt roads that reach deep into the mountainous Altiplano. Ross said that even if the soil in the northern highlands were suitable for the cultivation of nontraditional vegetables, it probably would not be feasible for the subsistence farmers living there to diversify given their precarious economic circumstances.[13] Noel Garcia, an agronomist with the Institute for Inter-American Cooperation on Agriculture (IICA) called AID's agricultural plans "utopian."

This idea of diversifying production in the highlands sounds good but just doesn't work. Imagine the small farmer with less than two acres trying to grow snow peas for the U.S. market. He is going to lose because he cannot afford to take the risk since the market is not firm. Most Guatemalans have neither the money nor the desire to eat many vegetables. This means depending on whether U.S. importers are buying a lot of vegetables that year. Growing vegetables is not a solution. It is just AID's way of not facing the real problems of land tenure, repression, and the lack of rural organizing.

The Guatemalan army agrees with AID that nontraditional agroexport production is the way to develop the Altiplano. (See Chapter Six.) The diversification of crop production fits well into the political circumstances of the highlands. Using the framework of this agricultural plan, the military can implement pacification. Farm-to-market roads are used for better military control; rural development funds are used in pacified villages and the military tries to break down the culture of the Indians by forcing them to grow vegetables for export instead of corn to sustain themselves and their culture.

AID insists that agricultural production should be more "outward looking."[14] But this ignores the basic history lesson of Central American economic development. The domination of export-oriented production has been the major obstacle to development, not its solution.

Nontraditional export promotion is a dead-end development option. Early in this century, the United States told Central America that banana exports would put the region on the path to development. In the 1950s and 1960s, the region was told that it could beat economic dependency by diversifying the agricultural sector to include cotton, cane, and cattle. And for more than twenty years, AID has hailed the export-oriented production of vegetables, flowers, and shrimp as the solution to Central America's economic woes. In recent years, AID has spent tens of millions of dollars to promote winter vegetable production, but vegetables still account for only 2.5 percent of the region's total agroexports while the five main agroexports constitute nearly 95 percent.

RURAL DEVELOPMENT AND
THE SMALL FARMER

For AID and most other foreign aid institutions, agricultural development in Central America means the development of agroexport production. The purpose of assistance to the agricultural sector is to increase production and profits, thereby sparking economic growth and development. Within this framework, where development is defined as commercial development, it follows that the best way to develop is to assist those growers who have sufficient resources to increase their production and who have commercial experience. Research, credit, extension services, infrastructural support, and marketing assistance are offered to those who can literally profit the most from this development assistance. For the most part, then, the prime beneficiaries of agricultural development programs have been large-scale growers.[15]

Foreign aid continues to provide support for large-scale capitalist agriculture in Central America as well as facilitating alliances between local agrarian capitalists and foreign investors. Since the early 1970s, AID and other foreign donors have expanded their definition of agricultural development to include "rural development," "small farmer development," and "basic needs" projects. Large growers can still count on support from AID's agricultural development projects, especially when they are interested in diversifying export production. But in the last 15 years, development assistance programs for agriculture have been stressing the need to reach the small farmers and to provide for the basic needs of the poor rural population. Collectively, these programs are often known as "integrated rural development."

Essentially, there are two main components of integrated rural development strategy: 1) strengthening agrarian capitalism among small- and medium-sized growers, and 2) providing for the "basic needs" of landless and near-landless *campesinos.* While the new direction of development assistance has undeniably upgraded the life of some peasants, it has not challenged the dual structure of the agricultural economy. In fact, these new rural development programs have worked to rationalize and stabilize the inequitable system of land tenure, land use, and rural labor. Integrated rural development is an attempt to reduce pressure for revolutionary land reforms, thereby preserving the main characteristics of the present agricultural economy.

Invariably, AID's rural development projects claim to help the small farmer. Although AID does not offer a definition of its intended beneficiaries, in practice the small farmers that AID reaches with its rural development programs are not the truly small farmers of Central America. The small-scale growers that AID works with are generally those who either already have commercial experience or those peasants who have the resources to become commercial farmers. Left on the margin of AID's "small farmer" projects are the rural majority of landless and near-landless peasants. Oftentimes, the farmers that these AID projects benefit are actually the largest and most well-to-do landowners in the community.

There are both economic and political reasons for rural development projects. By providing technical assistance and other help to "small" farmers, AID hopes to strengthen the wobbly agroexport system while opening up new markets for U.S. agricultural inputs like seeds and pesticides. Rural development projects are also designed to create a network of small agrarian capitalists. Agrarian economist Alain de Janvry contends, "The dominant objective is political—to buffer class conflict in the rural sector and to reduce the possibility of a class alliance between the peasantry and the urban proletariat." This is done through the "creation of a pampered conservative rural petty bourgeoisie of peasant origin."[16] While semiproletarianized peasants (the ones that need to look for seasonal work on agroexport estates) are a potentially revolutionary class, AID regards self-sufficient and commercial-level growers as a conservative and potentially counterrevolutionary force in rural Central America.

Rural development programs aim to reinforce an upper stratum of peasantry who see their interests linked to those of larger capitalist growers and to the international market. The assistance reaches only a small minority of peasant farmers, generally those with more and better land and those who have easier access to markets and transportation. Without an effort to organize and educate the most disadvantaged peasants, agricultural credit and technical assistance commonly flows to the most privileged—those with the most land, best political connections, and better education.

The assistance fortifies their dominant position and results in the increased impoverishment of the rest of the community. Those who have the resources and capability to benefit from small farmer projects often seek to increase their landholdings as a result of these projects. As a rule, land is available only from less-privileged peasants forced to sell because of debts or other hardships. In this way, class divisions within rural communities often widen. After several years of experience with rural development programs, AID itself concluded in an agricultural policy paper that the provision of inputs like credit and technology was probably "exacerbating the plight of the poor in situations where land tenure practices are inequitable."[17] There have, however, been no substantive changes in AID's approach to rural development.

Rural development programs have met only limited success. They have integrated an upper stratum of small farmers into commercial agriculture, usually for export. These programs have also raised the expectations of many others, who harbor hope of one day escaping their status as poor peasants. By raising these hopes for vertical mobility without land reform, rural development programs help diffuse political tension. However, the successful implementation of rural development programs also causes greater poverty, landlessness, and hopelessness among other peasants, who see land and resources flowing to a few privileged small farmers. This impoverishment leads to increased pressure for land reform and demands for higher wages for farm labor—social pressures that are politically and economically destabilizing to the dual structure of the agricultural system. To counteract this social tension, foreign aid agencies deliver supplies and services to meet the short-term basic needs of the poor majority.

The Band-AID Approach

Although they may be regarded as too marginal to be commercially viable, AID does help the peasantry's lower stratum with its basic-needs programs. The provision of medical assistance, housing, and food does provide survival support to the destitute *campesinos,* but these services do nothing to alter the conditions that keep this population poor and hungry. It is a strategy of institutional charity dependent on foreign aid to underwrite a government welfare system. Like the rural-development strategy, the basic-needs strategy has both political and economic aspects. Politically, charity programs like food-for-work and medical care projects serve to pacify the poor and to make them dependent on the government. They inculcate a welfare mentality and promote individualism while undermining community organizing and more radical solutions to underdevelopment.

Basic-needs programs are also economically stabilizing. They decrease the upward pressure for wage hikes by providing supplemental income and supplies. The basic-needs strategy serves to keep wages at their below-subsistence level, a situation that keeps peasants and workers at the edge of survival, but which keeps profit levels high for the capitalist classes. These welfare programs also serve to patch up the agricultural economy's dual structure by enabling peasants to continue producing cheap food for the domestic market. Programs to satisfy basic needs are band-aid solutions for poverty and underdevelopment, but they do serve to maintain the status quo in Central

America. It is for this reason that governments, the military, and foreign aid institutions are all so supportive of the basic-needs strategy.

FOOD AID WITH A U.S. MENU

The PL480 or Food for Peace program in Central America is not for the hungry, nor is it for peace. It is a program for stabilization, pacification, and war. Since 1979, U.S. food assistance to Central America has increased dramatically. The amount of food aid delivered to the region in the 1980s accounts for nearly 80 percent of the total food assistance to the region since the PL480 program was established by Congress in 1954.

Central Americans certainly need improved diets. In most countries, seven out of ten children are malnourished; and the minimum wage (which most workers do not get) does not even cover the cost of a family's basic food requirements. The picture is further complicated by the region's declining per capita food production. But U.S. assistance is not addressing these problems. Instead, it is actually contributing to the region's decreasing food security.

Increases in food assistance to Central America are the result of Washington's preoccupation with a perceived national security threat in the region. During the Vietnam War, South Vietnam received more food aid that any other country around the globe—even though many countries in Africa were experiencing drought and famine. Currently, most U.S. food aid goes to South Korea, Egypt, Central America, and other places where U.S. geopolitical interests are considered most strategic.

On the occasion of its 30th anniversary, President Reagan called PL480 "one of the greatest humanitarian acts ever performed by one nation for the needy of other nations."[18] The president greatly overstated the altruistic aspects of U.S. food assistance. The underlying objectives of the PL480 program are far from selfless. In fact, the program was established not to relieve world hunger but to dump surplus farm commodities.[19]

In addition to serving as a government-subsidized outlet for surplus food (mainly wheat and corn), PL480 was also designed as an instrument of foreign policy. As Hubert Humphrey, one of the authors of the program, acknowledged in 1957:

> People may become dependent on us for food. I know that is not supposed to be good news. To me that is good news, because before people can do anything, they've got to eat. And if you are looking for a way to get people to lean on you and be dependent on you, it seems that food dependence would be terrific.[20]

The leading representatives of the U.S. farm sector, especially the giant grain companies like Cargill, have been strong advocates of the PL480 program. That is because about 40 percent of U.S. flour exports are channeled through PL480.[21] The U.S. Department of Agriculture (USDA) boasts that the PL480 program has been instrumental in developing commercial markets for U.S. commodities, especially wheat. Many Central American consumers are now accustomed to eating wheat-flour products and this has created a "need" for them to import wheat through commercial channels. Commercial wheat imports have skyrocketed in the last several decades, increasing twentyfold in the case of Costa Rica.

Basic-grain farmers in Central America, however, do not share the U.S. enthusiasm for PL480. The flood of food assistance into Central America lowers market prices or local produce to the detriment of the peasant farm sector. Competing against third-world farmers through a U.S.-government subsidized export program is probably not in the best long-term interests of the U.S. farm sector either. If Central American peasants received a good price for their basic grains, their incomes would increase commensurately. Studies of developing countries show that most additional income earned by rural communities is spent on improving their diet, with a large part of the increased food expenditures covering purchases of imported processed food. Groups like the North American Farm Alliance have recognized the damage that the PL480 program is causing overseas and have drawn parallels between the plight of small farmers in Central America and those in the United States.

The conclusion that the Food for Peace program does not necessarily contribute to development or the elimination of hunger has been made in reports published by both the GAO and the USDA. A USDA report found that food aid "contributed indirectly to the developing countries' growing dependence on grain imports by permitting them to postpone needed agriculture programs."[22] The GAO reached a similar conclusion and also noted that U.S. food assistance "has helped to depress prices [and] shifted public tastes, especially those of urban consumers, away from locally grown foods towards imported ones."[23] Despite these findings, food aid is increasing rapidly in Central America due to the region's political situation and because of large grain surpluses in the United States.

Besides serving as a vehicle for dumping surplus commodities and creating commercial markets for U.S. farmers, food aid works in diverse ways to prop up governments, strengthen the private sector, and pacify the poor. We saw in Chapter Two how Title I of the PL480 program helps stabilize governments by reducing their need to purchase food imports on commercial terms. About 81 percent of the food aid going to Central America falls under the Title I program—up from 12 percent in 1979. The dollars saved can be used to maintain or increase the import levels of other goods like weapons and luxury items, as well as socially necessary imports like medicine.

The local currency earned by governments when they sell Title I food on local commercial markets seldom supports programs that increase a country's capacity to feed itself. Instead, AID directs governments to channel this money into projects that advance the economic and political agenda of Washington—an agenda that usually coincides with that of the region's elite. The three main uses of this local currency in Central America are private-sector support, government budgetary support (stabilization), and pacification.

AID's practice of channeling local currency from Title I sales to the private sector was boosted by the Food Security Act of 1985, which encourages the programming of at least 25 percent of locally generated currencies for "private enterprise development." Most of the private-sector projects financed by this method involve the expansion of the agroexport economy, thereby worsening the food security crisis in Central America. As discussed previously, AID also allows governments, notably El Salvador, to use this money to fill budget deficits. In addition, Title I local currency is used to pay for pacification campaigns in Guatemala and El Salvador (See Chapters Six and Seven).

When U.S. citizens think of food assistance as a distribution of food to the malnourished, they are thinking of the Title II program. Only about one-fifth of U.S. food aid to Central America falls into the Title II category. Under Title II, commodities are distributed by PVOs, by the U.N. World Food Program (WFP), and less commonly by government agencies. The food is distributed either through supplementary feeding (like school lunches and maternal and child health programs), refugee and disaster relief, or food-for-work programs. In the first two categories, items are handed out free, while in food-for-work programs the recipients are required to work on projects determined by the government. Another related program is known as Section 416 of the Agriculture Act of 1949, which makes available surplus dairy products. The use of Section 416, like the other components of the U.S. food assistance program in Central America, has increased dramatically during the 1980s.

While this humanitarian food aid does reach poor people, it does little to solve problems of malnutrition and food shortages. Governments use food-for-work programs to serve national economic and political objectives, which in Central America rarely coincide with the pressing needs of the poor. Hunger and malnutrition are symptoms of underdevelopment. Treating the symptoms with food aid provides temporary relief, but does not address the causes of poverty. Food handouts constitute charity, not a vehicle to self-reliance and food security.[24] Only in emergency relief situations is this kind of assistance effective. The inappropriateness of Title II food as a development tool is one problem with this program. Another more serious concern is the way Title II food assistance is being used as an instrument to pacify and control rural communities in Central America.

In the future, the U.S. food assistance program to Central America is projected to increase beyond its current high levels. Under the Food Security Act of 1985, a new program called Food for Progress allows the special use of "America's agricultural abundance to support countries that have made commitments to agricultural policy reform during a period of economic hardship."[25] The term "policy reform" refers to measures to increase agroexport production and to spur agribusiness investment by giving added incentives to the private sector. Food for Progress combined with already existing efforts by Washington to use food aid for its stabilization and pacification objectives has caused what one AID official in Guatemala called an "explosion" of U.S. food assistance in the region.

BEYOND THE PLANTATION

AID's agricultural and food programs reinforce the region's agroexport economy and its attendant inequities. What exists is a plantation economy characterized by concentrated land tenure, widespread rural poverty, and repressive social structures. It is a system that has dominated the region for four centuries. In insisting that the Central American countries become more "outward-oriented," AID has ignored the fact that the region's main obstacle to development has been the selfsame foreign-controlled and export-oriented agricultural economy that U.S. policy promotes.

Moving beyond plantation development requires bold steps by Central Americans themselves, including widespread organizing by farmworkers and small growers. It means involving *campesinos* in the development planning process, and it necessitates a national and regional commitment to food security. Foreign aid could play an important role in helping the region move toward such broad-based agricultural development. As it is, however, most U.S. economic aid programs directly or indirectly keep Central Americans down on the plantation.

PART TWO

Pacification and Counterrevolution

CHAPTER **5** Low Intensity
Battlefield

> *Central America is the experimenting grounds*
> *for low intensity conflict. If it succeeds in*
> *Central America, it will be applied worldwide.*
> —Paul Harvey,
>   syndicated radio commentator

A few years ago only military theorists and specialists in small wars were familiar with the concept of low intensity conflict (LIC). Today, even casual listeners of conservative commentator Paul Harvey have been introduced to the military doctrine of low intensity conflict and the related concepts of "total war" and "violent peace."[1] The current laboratory for LIC theories is Central America. General Paul Gorman, former chief of the U.S. Southern Command (SOUTHCOM)*, said that "low intensity conflict is the form of political violence that we are most likely to encounter in my part of the world."[2]

Low intensity conflict refers to battlefields with little direct U.S. military involvement. LIC operations are those that fall short of conventional or nuclear war. While middle-level and high intensity conflict involve massive deployment of U.S. troops and weaponry in heavy or prolonged combat, low intensity warfare makes sparing use of U.S. soldiers.

LIC doctrine is an extension and refinement of the theory of counterinsurgency warfare that emerged in the early 1960s.

*SOUTHCOM, the U.S. military command responsible for U.S. military operations in Latin America and the Caribbean, is headquartered in the Panama Canal Zone.

Many of the instruments of counterinsurgency warfare—military civic action, interagency coordination, pacification, special operations, internal civil defense, and military assistance and training—have been given new attention by LIC proponents. But LIC doctrine is more than just a new name for counterinsurgency theory. While incorporating the major elements of counterinsurgency warfare, LIC stresses the following principles:

- Avoidance of direct or prolonged U.S. combat involvement.
- Limited use of firepower.
- Ability to coerce or control the population through psychological and political operations, and through the distribution of economic aid.
- Capability for peacekeeping, terrorist/counterterrorist activity, and rescue operations.
- Use of surrogate forces.
- Support for pro-U.S., anti-communist insurgents that will roll back the advance of socialism.
- Need for a well-coordinated public-relations campaign—through public diplomacy and media manipulation—that will develop public support for protracted low-intensity wars.

LIC advocates see the combat deployment of U.S. troops only as a last resort. In many ways, this reluctance to intervene militarily in the third world is the result of the U.S. experience in Vietnam. LIC strategists acknowledge that any commitment of U.S. ground troops in the third world is likely to be counterproductive, given that direct military intervention erodes domestic and international support for U.S. foreign policy and can increase internal resistance.

While LIC doctrine represents the national and international limits of U.S. military might, it is emphatically not isolationist or moderate in its view of the U.S. role in world affairs. On the contrary, LIC proponents advocate increased U.S. intervention around the globe to prevent the establishment of anti-U.S. governments and to roll back the advances of anti-imperialist and socialist elements. It is an aggressively anticommunist and imperialist doctrine that recommends an array of interventionist tactics short of sending in the GIs.

According to the U.S. Army's *Operational Concept for Low Intensity Conflict,* "Low intensity conflict represents the most likely form of conflict the U.S. Army will be involved in for the remainder of this century." In the view of LIC proponents, the United States (and everything for which it stands) is currently under attack by diverse and devious forces virtually everywhere on the planet. Guerrilla wars, terrorist assaults, drug trafficking, domestic turmoil in the third world, and even media criticism of U.S. foreign policy are all symptoms of this overall attack on U.S. security and values.

National security is placed within an ideological as well as geopolitical framework. The United States is considered to be the global guardian of political democracy and private enterprise. Any threat to those values, no matter how remote from U.S. borders, is taken as a threat to U.S. national security. "We must not break faith with those who are risking their lives on every continent . . . to defy Soviet-supported aggression," said President Reagan. "Support for freedom fighters is self-defense."

LIC doctrine has redefined and expanded the concept of war. Military theorists like Lieutenant Colonel David Caldon of SOUTHCOM express the ominous nature of this constant LIC warfare:

> We are at war today in the Caribbean Basin. It is not a war in the conventional sense. It is unconventional and is irregular in that there are no "battle lines" where the economic infrastructures, social traditions, and political systems are eroded from within through external support by both military and paramilitary means.[3]

The ideological battle is often described by champions of LIC doctrine in medical terms. Insurgency is a virus or a cancer that must be surgically removed or fought with anticommunist antibodies. Reagan administration spokesperson Patrick Buchanan called Nicaragua "a malignant tumor" threatening the health of the hemisphere. According to the logic of this political/medical analogy, there can be no negotiation with a cancer. LIC adherents see symptoms of communist infection everywhere: in trade union organizing, political dissension, peasant organizing, liberation theology, and guerrilla movements. The editors of *Special Operations in U.S. Strategy*, a book published jointly by the National Defense University and the National Strategy Information Center, frame their entire discussion of special operations in this medical analogy:

> A serious illness can be difficult to detect because the initial symptoms are confused with those of commonplace diseases. Some types of aggression likewise defy an early, accurate diagnosis. These species of political-military virus or ideological infection resist early detection and can lead to large scale war if they are not identified and countered in their early stages.[4]

The instruments of low intensity conflict are then prescribed as the bitter medicine needed to counter the spread of ideological disease.

To meet this perceived global threat, LIC theory recommends a combination of unconventional military operations and political warfare. Instead of sending off planeloads of U.S. boys to fight in foreign jungles, LIC global military defense relies more on Rambo-style raids, covert activities, quick operations like the one in Grenada, support for surrogate forces of "freedom fighters," and counterterrorist strikes. Uncovered during the Iran scandal of early 1987, a directive from President Reagan that authorized CIA efforts to kidnap suspected terrorists is indicative of this new "preemptive surgery" emphasis. When it comes to actual deployment of U.S. troops, "Get in, get out" is the motto of this new interventionism.

Besides military adventurism, LIC doctrine also stresses the importance of the "war on minds." As many of its advocates say, "Controlling minds is more important than controlling territory." Or as Colonel John Waghelstein, the former chief of the U.S. MilGroup in El Salvador, put it, "The only territory you want to hold is the six inches between the ears of the peasant."[5] The war for those six inches involves the extensive use of nonlethal instruments of intervention, including humanitarian assistance, economic aid, and propaganda. These can be applied both covertly and overtly as part of four overlapping categories of nonlethal or political intervention:

Psychological Operations (Psyops): Planned dissemination of information to create attitudes and behavior favorable to the achievement of political and military objectives.

Public Diplomacy: Attempts to explain and to implement U.S. foreign policy to national and foreign citizens through information and disinformation campaigns and through the formation of U.S.-controlled institutions.

Military Civic Action: Military operations designed to improve the public image of the military through social service and infrastructure development programs.

Pacification: Government and military programs that, in the context of counterinsurgency wars, attempt to pacify and control rebellious or potentially rebellious populations.

TOTAL WAR

The advocates of U.S.-sponsored low intensity conflict say that all resources should be tapped in the struggle against communists and terrorists. LIC has been described as "total grassroots war" that encompasses the "total environment—a fusion of economic, political, and military intelligence."[6] As Richard Armitrage, Assistant Secretary of Defense for International Security Affairs, stated: "The United States has a broad range of ways in which it can assist those groups struggling against communist regimes. The issue is which of these and which combinations of political, economic, information, humanitarian, and military hardware are appropriate."[7]

LIC doctrine defines economic aid and humanitarian assistance as weapons, making little distinction between the roles of different government agencies like the Agency for International

Development, the CIA, the United States Information Agency, and the Pentagon. Psychological operations—used both to prime the U.S. public for LIC intervention and to pacify third world populations—are an essential component of LIC warfare.

The U.S. Army says that LIC "transcends the normal concept of peace and war" and that in low intensity conflict the "principles of war" are a guide for both civilian and military leaders.[8] Under Secretary of Defense for Policy Fred Ikle added that U.S. citizens must accept a world of "small wars in many regions."[9] LIC theorist Sam Sarkesian warned that we must change the "American way of war" and accept the fact that there are "few clear lines between war and peace."[10] Former UN Ambassador Jeane Kirkpatrick suggested that the U.S. public has to change its attitude that "peace is a norm and that war and violence are abnormal."[11] This new world environment is described by LIC advocates as a state of "violent peace."

Army Guidelines for LIC

A firm basis for the developing LIC doctrine is found in various Army manuals on the topic. The *1981 Field Manual on Low Intensity Conflict* officially placed LIC strategy within military operations. That manual is now regarded as a bridge between the dated counterinsurgency theory and the latest formulations of LIC strategy. It presents LIC as an expression of the Internal Defense and Development (IDAD) theory of counterinsurgency that evolved in the 1970s, giving thorough treatment to pacification and civic action.

The 1981 manual outlines the need for national IDAD pacification campaigns that consolidated civilian and military institutions. These campaigns are designed to be administered by national and local coordination committees that would deploy military, paramilitary, and economic resources to strengthen the targeted nation. Psychological operations are employed to "make population and resource control measures more acceptable to the population." Local self-defense patrols and other paramilitary forces are organized to guarantee the security of pacified areas. The field manual considers U.S. special forces "ideal for IDAD operations," particularly for civil affairs and psychological operations. An essential component of this LIC pacification strategy is AID; the plan calls economic aid and humanitarian assistance programs "an integral part of collective security efforts."

It is highly likely that the 1981 field manual provided the conceptual underpinning for pacification campaigns in Guatemala and El Salvador. Both countries introduced national security and development plans, adopted programs of psychological operations, and supported their pacification campaigns with AID and U.S. private economic assistance. In Guatemala, the military's Inter-Institutional Coordination Committees bore a striking resemblance to the coordination and consolidation committees described in the Army manual.

Another Army field manual on operations *(FM 100–5)* provides overall guidance for low intensity conflict with its articulation of following four "Airland Battle" principles:

Initiative: This means action, not reaction to the enemy through two kinds of intelligence operations: a) identification of root causes of conflict and its main antagonists, and b) removal of both the causes and the popular support for the conflict. This second type of LIC intelligence relies on the military's Civil Affairs and PSYOPS (Psychological Operations) departments.

Depth: Because the struggle is not restricted to battlefields, LIC involves the coordination "across the entire spectrum of operations from national development, PSYOPS and Civil Affairs, to tactical combat operations." The goal is to "erode or eliminate the base of popular support" by integrating political, economic, and social programs with military operations.

Agility: LIC strategy must be flexible, and "tactical operations must be supportive, as well as complementary, of ongoing political, economic, and social reforms."

Synchronization: All participants should have "a total understanding of U.S. national objectives." This includes: civilian and military resources; tactical and non-tactical; and U.S., host nation, and joint U.S. forces.[12]

In October 1985, the U.S. Army Training and Doctrine Command at Fort Monroe, Virginia circulated draft copies of the updated LIC doctrine, *Military Operations: U.S. Army Operational Concept for Low Intensity Conflict.* The document sets forth the Army's role in LIC and proposes the following definition for U.S.-supported LIC:

A limited political-military struggle to achieve political, social, economic, or psychological objectives. It is often protracted and ranges from diplomatic, economic, and psycho-social pressures through terrorism and insurgency. Low intensity conflict is generally confined to a geographic area and is often characterized by constraints on the weaponry, tactics, and level of violence.

Bringing the War Back Home

In low intensity conflict, the targets include not only leftist guerrillas and socialist states but also U.S. and third world residents. To ensure the success of a U.S.-sponsored LIC, its proponents support psychological operations and public diplomacy aimed at the U.S. public and the Central American population. "I think the most critical special operations mission we have today is to persuade the American people that the communists are out to get us," warns J. Michael Kelly, Assistant Deputy Secretary of the U.S. Air Force, "If we can win this war of ideas, we can win everywhere else."[13] Likewise, George Tanham, former president of the Rand Corporation, says, "Our most pressing problem is not in the third world, but here at home in the struggle for the minds of people."[14]

This war to win the hearts and minds of the U.S. public has taken the form of an intensive public relations campaign to cure the population of the Vietnam Syndrome and stoke the interventionist spirit. Computerized maps that turn blood red, charges of Sandinista drug trafficking, conjuring up international anti-U.S. terrorist conspiracies, and alarmist predictions that Central American revolutionaries will transport their battles to U.S. border cities like San Diego have all been part of this psychological warfare.

Two examples of the new reliance on public diplomacy were the Reagan administration's use of the White House Office of Public Liaison to spread disinformation about Nicaragua and the propaganda efforts of the Office of Public Diplomacy in the State Department. Bipartisan backing has also been given to the overseas efforts of quasi-private institutes like the National Endowment for Democracy (NED) and the American Institute for Free Labor Development (AIFLD) to bolster U.S. political allies and spread pro-U.S. ideology. (See Chapter Nine.)

HUMANITARIAN ASSISTANCE ON THE LIC BATTLEFIELD

The coordinated use of nonlethal resources to control targeted population groups is one of the main principles of LIC doctrine. The concept of "total war" calls for the close coordination between all military and economic aid programs and the expanded use of humanitarian aid in low-level conflict situations. In Central America, the drive to integrate nonlethal resources into U.S. counterrevolutionary strategy is occurring in three ways: 1) closer coordination among the military, CIA, and AID in LIC situations, 2) increased involvement of the Department of Defense (DOD) in nonmilitary assistance, and 3) enlistment of private resources.

AID as a LIC Partner

In the opinion of most LIC proponents, during the 1970s AID was too caught up in the Vietnam Syndrome. To remedy this weakness it was recommended that the agency should now begin to put more of its resources at the disposal of counterinsurgency campaigns and U.S.-backed military initiatives. After the Vietnam War, AID had become more circumspect about using economic aid for military purposes such as civic action and pacification programs. Previously AID had directly funded about 30 percent of the Pentagon's military civic action programs in Latin America.[15] During the Vietnam War, AID worked closely with the military in pacification and counterterrorism campaigns and openly teamed up with the CIA to support anticommunist tribal mercenaries. "All of this was done," pointed out Douglas Blaufarb, a former CIA station chief, "under the formal rubric of refugee emergency assistance, resettlement, and rural development in order to conform to AID categories of approved activity." AID's programs, he said, "constituted the civilian front of an unconventional war which could not have been prosecuted without the aid program."[16]

According to LIC precepts, AID and DOD should be closer partners. Dr. Michael Ryan of the Defense Security Agency (DSA) suggests that "a synergism exists between economic and military aid."[17] He contends that AID should not stand off to the side in low intensity conflicts as it has frequently done since the end of the Vietnam War. Instead, in an insurgency or pre-insurgency situation, AID-administered ESF and development assistance "should be directed at the proximate causes of discontentment among disaffected citizens." Ryan noted that this integrated approach is now occurring in El Salvador, which he categorizes as a "high priority case."

The push to involve AID more closely in military operations has shown several signs of success in countries besides El Salvador. In Guatemala, AID provided the supplies, technical assistance, and funding for the army's "security and development" campaign in the conflictive Altiplano. Its projects along the Nicaraguan borders in Honduras and Costa Rica are also examples of the agency's increasing willingness to participate in military-related operations.

Armed Humanitarians

The release of the Kissinger Commission's report in January 1984 advanced the cause of those in the Pentagon who advocated tighter coordination between economic and military aid in the region. The report stressed both the development and security needs of Central American nations. Two days after the release of the Kissinger Commission report, Secretary of Defense Caspar Weinberger dispatched an interdepartment memorandum that noted that "legislative constraints, inadequate budgetary authority, and organizational impediments" severely limited DOD's role in addressing the development problems in Central America.[18] To remedy some of those problems, the Weinberger memorandum announced the formation of the DOD Task Force on Humanitarian Assistance.

Faced with congressional opposition to increased military aid to Central America, the Reagan administration sought to further its essentially military goals through the delivery of nonlethal aid. Increasing quantities of ESF and Title I assistance were used to pad government budgets drained by militarization and the costs of war. The administration also seized upon the concept of "humanitarian assistance" as a way to justify expanded U.S. intervention in the region. One of the first official uses of the term "humanitarian assistance" to describe nonlethal aid to the contras and to counterinsurgency campaigns in Central America came in December 1983 when an NSC directive allowed the Pentagon to transport privately donated humanitarian assistance to the region on a "space available basis."

Beginning in 1984, references to the need for humanitarian assistance to Central America became more frequent. In June 1984, the DOD task force issued its recommendations, and soon thereafter an Office for Humanitarian Assistance was set up in the Pentagon. In 1985, the president asked for and received $27 million in humanitarian assistance to the contras.

With Reagan's approval, the National Security Council also began organizing a private network to support the Nicaraguan counterrevolutionaries. Within the State Department, the Nicaraguan Humanitarian Assistance Office (NHAO) was established to handle deliveries of congressionally allocated nonlethal aid.

The *DOD Task Force Report on Humanitarian Assistance* broke ground in the Pentagon for the increased use of nonlethal aid in low intensity conflicts in Central America. The introduction to the report noted that pressure was building "both within and outside of DOD," for the Pentagon to take more initiative in the area of humanitarian aid. "Right-wing groups," it stated, "have been pressuring the Pentagon to step up its nonmilitary role in the fight against communism." To respond to this pressure, the task force addressed five possible categories where the Pentagon could increase its involvement in humanitarian assistance: civic action, transportation, international disaster assistance, surplus property disposal, and medical programs.[19] To follow through in each of these categories, the DOD task force felt that there was a need for more interagency cooperation; that congressional action should be encouraged to expand resources and eliminate existing restraints on the use of humanitarian assistance by DOD; and Title 10 (the law that establishes DOD's functions) should be revised to make humanitarian assistance/civic action part of DOD's mission.[20]

Following the release of the task force report, an array of new DOD initiatives appeared in the area of humanitarian assistance and civic action, including:

- Creation of an Office of Humanitarian Assistance within the Pentagon.
- Lowering of DOD transportation tariffs for all humanitarian supplies.
- Allowance under the provisions of the Denton Amendment, for DOD to provide transport on a free and space-available basis for supplies donated by private relief organizations.

- Allowance under the provisions of the 1986 Stevens Amendment for DOD to use its operation and maintenance funds for projects considered incidental to authorized actions.
- An acceleration of SOUTHCOM's civic action training and operations.
- Use of Economic Support Funds (ESF) and other AID money in El Salvador and Guatemala to finance civic action projects administered by the national armies and coordinated by U.S. military advisers.
- Permission under the provisions of the 1986 McCollum Amendment for DOD to transfer nonlethal excess property to organizations in foreign countries as part of civic action programs.
- Closer coordination between the Pentagon, AID, and the State Department in disaster assistance operations.
- A revamping of U.S. Army Civilian Affairs doctrine FM 41–10 by the U.S. Army Special Warfare Center to make it the focus for institutionalizing humanitarian assistance in military planning.

Dr. Robert Wolthius, DOD's Coordinator for Humanitarian Assistance, acknowledged that "all of the Humanitarian Task Force's recommendations for changes in the Pentagon operations are being implemented," including increased AID-State Department-DOD cooperation. "The cooperation has been accomplished on a working basis. I now have almost daily contact with State/AID and the Refugee Programs Office."[21] Two additional initiatives being advocated by Wolthius' office are the modification of ESF authorizations to allow AID to work directly with DOD on developmental civic action training and implementation, and a broader interpretation of Title 10 to allow the expanded use of DOD assets for humanitarian assistance. Wolthius sees a crucial role for this expansion in Central America, adding: "I think we learned from Vietnam that contests like this are not only about military tactics but also about winning the hearts and minds of the people."

Enlisting the New Right Humanitarians

Private aid and mercenary involvement form an essential part of the LIC effort in Central America. In his keynote address to a 1983 conference on Special Operations, Secretary of the Army John Marsh noted the special role of civilians in low-level war:

> The twilight battlefield of low intensity conflict . . . is an enormous area in which private sector resources can be used. We must find a way to incorporate into a grand strategy the total resources of our society. We live in a nation that has been the global pioneer in industrial development, marketing, advertising, and communications. Now we must harness these resources in a common security endeavor.[22]

In response to the call, the main U.S. government institutions encouraging stepped-up private involvement in the conflict in Central America were the National Security Council, the Pentagon, and AID. Private groups have always been used by AID to distribute food, provide technical assistance, and manage development projects. But because of the Reagan administration's emphasis on private-sector involvement, AID turned over more of its programs to private voluntary organizations (PVOs) and to U.S. businesses, and worked to bolster the Central American business community. The aid flowing through private groups was used for more overtly political activities as well, such as supporting the agrarian reform in El Salvador, working with the Guatemalan army's pacification plan, and providing supplies to the contras. While many private groups working in Central America rely primarily on nongovernment sources of funds and supplies without direct support from the U.S. government, several of the larger ones still work hand in hand with the U.S. embassy and the Pentagon.

The private network to support counterrevolution in Central America began forming in 1983—a time when the contra war was picking up steam with the help of the CIA and when military civic action programs were getting underway in

Guatemala and El Salvador. The White House and the National Security Council called for private-sector help to enforce the Reagan Doctrine of anticommunism in Central America. A diverse group of right-wing organizations, retired military and intelligence officials, mercenaries, TV preachers, and plutocrats took up the challenge.[23] General Harry Aderholt, head of the Air Commandos Association, said, "Maybe we in the private sector can take over and win down there." Tom Reisinger, the director of Refugee Relief International (a branch of *Soldier of Fortune* magazine), said, "We believe in President Reagan's challenge for the private sector to parallel government efforts in supplying needed assistance to those suffering in the midst of armed conflicts."

The phenomenon of private groups aiding counterinsurgency and counterrevolutionary campaigns supported by the U.S. government is not a new one. Many of the leading figures and organizations currently involved in Central America played a similar role during the Vietnam War. Groups active in Central America like World Medical Relief, Air Commandos Association, and Project Hope were also active in Southeast Asia.

A large percentage of the groups and individuals who jumped on the bandwagon to aid counterrevolution in Central America were part of the New Right movement that arose in the late 1970s. They proclaimed that their aid to the contras was an example of a "private-sector solution." "Conservatives have decided to do for the freedom fighters what the American left of the 30s did for the communists in Spain," asserted Richard Viguerie, publisher of the *Conservative Digest*. But the private nature of this counterrevolutionary support was mostly a matter of appearances. Unlike the private backers of the contras, the Lincoln Brigade and other supporters of the Spanish Republicans were not organized and coordinated by the CIA, White House, or National Security Council. Their support was not shipped on military aircraft and distributed in conjunction with the U.S. government's own civic action and humanitarian assistance programs. And their contributions were not tax deductible. Moreover, the Spanish aid went to a democratically elected government challenged by monarchists and fascists.

The Reagan administration, needing a figure outside government to coordinate the private fund-raising efforts, chose retired General John Singlaub, the head of the United Council for World Freedom and the World Anti-Communist League. The administration advised him on how to structure the campaign within the confines of the laws that bar U.S. citizens from supporting foreign wars. Singlaub, a veteran of covert operations in Southeast Asia, was selected as the "authorized" contact for private fund-raising because of his military background and intelligence connections. While Singlaub was the main private coordinator of the campaign, Lieutenant Colonel Oliver North was the government's in-house coordinator. North served as a company commander in both conventional and unconventional operations in Vietnam. Following the congressional cutoff of covert aid to the contras, the NSC assigned North to manage a joint public-private drive to assist the contras. He provided the contras with direct military advice, met frequently with FDN (Nicaraguan Democratic Forces) leaders both in Washington and in Central America, and advised private donors on how they might contribute to the contras. North also set up logistical supply lines for the contras. As part of his job, North worked closely with such groups as the Air Commandos Association, United States Council for World Freedom, and the Citizens for America.

In the eyes of the contra supporters, the Nicaraguan counterrevolutionaries were not only fighting for freedom and democracy but also for capitalism and free enterprise. Seeing their own interests threatened by revolution in Central America, many corporations and business owners put their money behind the contras. As Malcolm Forbes, editor of *Forbes* business magazine, remarked: "For moral and strategic reasons, Congress had better vote for a healthy flow of support for the contras. Their fight is our fight, too."[24]

The FDN's Mario Calero admitted that well-known U.S.

corporations provide funds, sometimes laundering the money through paper organizations in Panama and other countries. General Singlaub explained that he frequently approached companies that had done business in Nicaragua or hope to invest there in the future.[25] Another fund-raiser for the contras noted that "fund-raising efforts have paid off best with people who used to work in the government who are now in corporations with defense contracts."[26]

Humanitarian Assistance and International Law

The expanding use of officially coordinated nonlethal aid not only stretches the definition of humanitarian assistance but also undermines its legal framework. The Geneva Conventions of 1949, the Geneva Protocols of 1977, and the United Nations Charter establish legal parameters for the distribution of humanitarian assistance. All accords have been flagrantly violated and ignored by the U.S. government's efforts to disguise its counterrevolutionary operations.

According to international custom, humanitarian assistance is to be indiscriminately provided to needy noncombatants. It is not to be used to accomplish political or military objectives. Under the terms of the Geneva Conventions, humanitarian relief workers, meaning those who assist the victims of any conflict, are protected parties in the rules of war. Such workers must observe strict neutrality and refrain from any direct or indirect interference in the war operations. Generally, these workers belong to "an impartial international humanitarian organization" like the International Committee of the Red Cross or to an organization associated with a "state which is not a party to that conflict."[27] The impartiality and nonpolitical standards for humanitarian assistance are not met by U.S. government programs or by those private operations that are backed directly or indirectly by Washington.

The most blatant usurpation of the meaning of humanitarian assistance was the congressional approval in 1985 and 1986 of over \$50 million in humanitarian assistance to the contras. Other similar aid has been provided to the contras and their families by AID and right-wing private groups. But the use of nonlethal aid for military purposes has extended beyond the contra war. In El Salvador, AID is the main source of assistance to the displaced victims of the war. Since the United States is a party to the conflict, this aid can not be considered strictly humanitarian. In fact, AID, the U.S. MilGroup (DOD mission stationed within a country), the Salvadoran Army, and the Salvadoran government ministries have collaborated in using this assistance as a tool in the counterinsurgency war.

Aid to the contras and supplies given to military civic action programs is not humanitarian. Whether the assistance is in the form of food, army boots, or Christmas gift packages, it constitutes paramilitary aid because it either directly supports combatants or is discriminately provided to civilians on only one side of the conflict. Commenting on the paramilitary nature of humanitarian aid to the contras, Joseph Mitchell, former director of the AID Office of Foreign Disaster Assistance, said, "Congressional advocates evidently believe that humanitarian aid to combatants engaged in civil war is somehow different from aiding them militarily as if food, clothing, and shelter are not rations, uniforms, and tents."[28]

As the LIC doctrine developed, the Pentagon and defense planners placed an increasingly higher military value on humanitarian assistance. While some improvement in the conditions of Central Americans does result from official U.S. humanitarian assistance, its main purpose, according to the DOD, is to "serve . . . overall foreign policy objectives."[29] The increasing use of humanitarian assistance in Central America distorts the true meaning of the term, but it may also have more serious implications. It may presage an upsurge of what is known in international law as "humanitarian intervention." This could take the form of a military assault whose stated purpose is to safeguard U.S. nationals living abroad who are not being adequately protected by the host country. The main justification for the U.S. invasion of Grenada, for example, was the alleged need to save U.S. lives. In Central America, the influx of U.S. relief workers could help justify a similar action. Another concern is that the position and credibility of international and U.S. relief workers who are impartial are imperiled by the proliferation of ideologically and politically tied humanitarian assistance programs.

CIVIC ACTION AND NATION BUILDING

The term "military civic action" (or civic action) covers a wide range of military operations designed to influence the civilian population. The basic objectives of civic action are to polish the public image of the military, to improve rural socioeconomic conditions and thereby reduce leftist insurgency, and to encourage the formation of strong national institutions capable of withstanding internal revolutionary challenges. Civic action programs range from public relations efforts like the sponsoring of Boy Scout troops to pacification programs that aim to reduce the popular base for guerrilla insurgency. It was not until the mid-1950s that military civic action was accepted by State Department and Pentagon officials as a legitimate part of the U.S. defense mission. With the rising threat of revolutionary wars in the third world, there arose greater recognition of the need for programs that would improve what the Pentagon now calls "internal defense and development."

The British experience with civic action in Malaya also provided the Pentagon with a model for its campaigns in the third world.[30] In their decadelong effort to crush guerrillas in Malaya (now part of the independent nation of Malaysia), the British relied on such tactics as rural development programs, counterterror, resettlement of potential guerrilla supporters to protected villages, civilian defense, psychological warfare, food distribution and control programs, and paramilitary squads. Appointed as the High Commissioner of the British-occupied Federation of Malaya in 1952, General Sir Gerald Templar is credited with the first use of what would become the enduring buzz phrase known as civic action. Upset about the failure of the counterinsurgency campaign to stop the guerrillas by strictly military means, Templar said that "the answer lies not in pouring more soldiers into the jungle, but rests in the hearts and minds of the Malayan people."[31]

During the 1950s, General Edward Lansdale emerged as the major practitioner and theoretician of this strategy. Lansdale coined the term "civic action" to describe the work of a psychological warfare unit in the Philippines. Called the Civil Affairs Office (CAO) and developed with Lansdale's help, this unit was created "not only [to] perform combat psywar [aimed at Huk guerrillas] but also [to] improve the attitude and behavior of troops towards civilians."[32] After his Philippines assignment, Lansdale went to South Vietnam in the late 1950s to establish the first civic action of the incipient counterinsurgency war. Still a leading advocate of political warfare, Lansdale was appointed in 1982 to a special Pentagon task force on low intensity conflict.

Civic Action in Central America

In the Western Hemisphere, military civic action became an integral part of the Alliance for Progress. President Kennedy and many prominent U.S. scholars thought that the military could play a key role in the modernization of Latin America. "The new generation of military leaders," noted Kennedy, "has shown an increasing awareness that armies cannot only defend their countries—they can, as we have learned through our own Corps of Engineers, help to build them."[33] Civic action programs sponsored by the Pentagon encouraged armies to become "nation builders" by training them in administration, infrastructure construction, and the economics of development.

The Central American armed forces immediately warmed to the idea of military civic action. They regarded it as a way to improve their public image, to expand their power, and to fight insurgency.[34] In Guatemala, the military began staging Christmas parties for children, while in El Salvador, the army's "Operación Niño" dropped candy and gifts on rural villages by parachute to demonstrate the military's Christmas spirit.[35] While some civic action programs may bring immediate relief to the poor, they do not begin to solve the region's fundamental problems. Military civic action is a way to preserve and extend military power. The blurring of normally distinct lines between social services and coercive manipulation confuses people and thus lessens active resistance to government schemes. In his 1975 book *The United States and Militarism in Central America,* Don Etchinson described civic action as a process of militarization:

> Essentially civil action training has promoted militarism by aiding the military as an encompassing government establishment. Because the Central American countries have historically been plagued with political militarism the training of soldiers to assume civilian jobs eliminated the development of civilian government employees. If civilian governments are ever to develop in the five militarized Central American states, the armed forces must not be taught to be more ubiquitous and powerful than they already are.[36]

Civic Action in Guatemala

The first experiment in military civic action in Latin America occurred in November 1960 in Guatemala where U.S. Army teams arrived and established a civic action branch of the Guatemalan army. Guatemala was the pilot project for the Civil Affairs Mobile Training Teams (CAMTT) that the U.S. Army later sent throughout the third world. In his book *Counterinsurgency Warfare,* Major John Pustay of the U.S. Air Force Academy wrote that this first CAMTT "conducted civic action training programs in fourteen major Army commands, indoctrinating four hundred officers in the process, and prepared a comprehensive plan for such nation-building operations."[37]

In late 1960, Guatemalan President Ydigoras created a civic

action section of the Ministry of Defense and requested the U.S. Army Mission in Guatemala to assign a permanent, full-time officer to direct it. In addition, the U.S. military mission in Guatemala trained the program's civic action officers. The U.S. military also regularly visited each area of the country and selected projects for the Guatemalan armed forces to undertake. Guatemalan troops wore emblems emblazoned with the words: "Acción Civica Militar—Seguridad y Progreso." As in other Central American countries, AID and various U.S. PVOs worked in unison with the military civic action programs. The AID Mission in Guatemala had a civic action coordinator who was previously the civic action officer for SOUTHCOM.[38] CARE distributed food through the army's civic action programs, and groups like the Amigos of the Americas sent volunteers to Guatemala to contribute to the military civic action efforts.[39]

Civic Action in Somoza's Nicaragua

The inauguration of civic action in Nicaragua in the early 1960s was intended to improve the public image of the *Guardia Nacional,* the army of dictator Anastasio Somoza. According to SOUTHCOM, all civic action projects were "initiated, planned, and executed by the Government of Nicaragua"—not by the U.S. military. While that might technically be true, the impetus for the projects came from U.S. military missions and training courses. During the Somoza years, more members of Nicaragua's National Guard were trained by the United States than were any other armed forces in Latin America.

One result of this training was the Guard's reputation of technical efficiency. The Somoza regime put great emphasis on the development of the country's own *Academia Militar* as well as additional officer training by the U.S. military. The senior year of the *Academia Militar* was held at Fort Gulick in the Panama Canal Zone, with the expense of this training borne by the United States. Nicaraguan police officers also spent the last two months of their training in the Canal Zone. Richard Millett, the author of *Guardians of the Dynasty,* wrote that the in-country role of U.S. military included counterinsurgency training, cooperation with the Guard's civic action program, monitoring the use of equipment provided by the United States and the performance of personnel trained at U.S. expense.[40] Part of U.S. civic action training was actually instruction in police and political intelligence work. Using funds allocated for civic action, teams of Green Berets trained members of the National Guard in "interrogation, raids, confessions, and search" techniques.[41]

The National Guard claimed that its civic action programs were "being developed and carried out in conformance with the plans of the Alliance for Progress." According to Millett, the *Guardia*'s "functions extend well beyond those usually encompassed by a military or even a constabulary force." It ran the postal service, supervised water supplies, and controlled internal transportation and communication. "The great diversification of *Guardia* functions . . . put thousands of civilians as well as its force of enlisted men under the officers' control. . . ."[42] In the 1970s, the National Guard's civic action program worked in close cooperation with the AID-funded Operation Well-Being, a rural development project that focused on areas of insurgency. The Sandinista guerrillas charged that civic action and Operation Well-Being were being used to increase military control and intelligence-gathering capabilities.

Civic Action in El Salvador

Before civil war broke out in 1979, El Salvador boasted a highly organized military civic action program. Each year, the Ministry of Defense published a Civic Action Plan that outlined the annual schedule of operations, which emphasized construction work by the army's engineer corps but also included literacy, health, and public welfare programs.

El Salvador's military and elite regarded civic action as a vital part of the general drive for economic development and improved public relations.[43] Technical assistance for civic action came from both the U.S. military mission and AID. According to U.S. officials, a highly favorable attitude toward this strategy prevailed among military officers. One U.S. officer said that the results of civic action training were "a high degree of expertness and a strengthening of corporate loyalty, though officers still showed little inclination to accept the principle of civil supremacy."[44]

Civic Action Back in Style

Military civic action is experiencing a strong comeback in Central America. After a period of indifference during the 1970s, the Pentagon has taken renewed interest in civic action as part of the counterinsurgency response to rising popular resistance in the region. The recent interest also results from the growing acceptance of LIC doctrine, which calls for economic and psychological measures to support military objectives.

Captain Robert S. Perry of SOUTHCOM's Political/Military Affairs Division called the new emphasis on civic action "one of the integral parts of the U.S. Southern Command's security development program."[45] It is a "cost effective and important component of any corrective or deterrent effort, as has been demonstrated in Guatemala in its recent successes against an active insurgency." Captain Perry described civic action as "an economy of forced investment that gets to the heart of some of the main causes of low intensity conflict and paves the way for a durable partnership between civilian and military counterparts in those nations wise enough to exploit the opportunity."[46]

For successful nation building and counterinsurgency, SOUTHCOM is pushing for better integration of U.S. military and economic programs in Central America through a concept it calls "security development." As Lieutenant Colonel David Caldon, the Chief of the Policy and Strategy Division of Political/Military Affairs at SOUTHCOM, summarized: "Security development encompasses such supplemental tools as combined exercises, small unit exchanges, intelligence exchanges, civic action initiatives, personnel exchanges, representational visits, public affairs activities, special orientation teams, and ship/aircraft visits to name but a few—along with security assistance."[47]

Going beyond strictly military initiatives, security development means tighter coordination with economic aid programs outside the traditional purview of the Pentagon. What Caldon and other LIC strategists want is the coordination of development, humanitarian, and security assistance so that all facets of U.S. aid form "a cohesive whole in support of a national commitment to protect our vital interests."

Civic action programs, especially when they are part of U.S. military maneuvers, often have direct strategic objectives. They are used to gain intelligence about isolated rural areas and to construct roads that might later be used to transport combatants. Calling for more civic action programs in Central America, Captain John Athanson, in a report entitled "Aiding Our Neighbors," said that increased civic action programs "would provide an excellent opportunity to refine forward deployment and embarkation planning and to test U.S. forces' ability to live, operate, and maintain equipment under adverse tropical conditions in remote areas." In addition, civic action projects would allow the military "to maintain a low-cost, active military presence in the region while ostensibly carrying out a humanitarian, nonmilitary mission."[48] Athanson and others advocate using the delivery of humanitarian assistance as a way to plan and train for military intervention in Central America. Rather than pulling into a local port with the medical supplies, "amphibious ships could deliver the material, personnel, and support equipment over-the-beach in remote regions, via tank landing ship and utility landing craft operations."[49]

The civic action campaigns underway in Central America fit into three overlapping categories: 1) programs separately carried out by U.S. military personnel, 2) programs jointly implemented during combined exercises with other nations, and 3) programs managed by the local government and army. The U.S. military hosts its own civic action efforts in Honduras and Panama (countries where it has a large permanent presence) and sponsors joint programs with local armed forces in Honduras, Costa Rica, and Panama. Civic action in the third category is carried out by local forces but often relies heavily on U.S. funds, supplies, training, and planning. In El Salvador and Guatemala, today's civic action programs are not just attempts to spiff up the army's public image but are part of larger pacification campaigns that aim to increase military control over the rural population.

In Costa Rica, various Civil Guard units received regular training by U.S. Special Forces. Green Berets instructed the guardsmen in the techniques of "counterinsurgency and development,"[50] while Seabees and Army Engineers participated in construction projects. The Pentagon proposed sending "combat engineers" to build roads and airstrips along the northern border with Nicaragua, but (due to Costa Rican popular opposition) the United States may settle for civic action exercises with the country's National Guard units.[51] At any rate, U.S. Army Engineers escalated militarization of Costa Rica's northern border zone by building barracks for Civil Guard units there.

In Honduras civic action occurred both in conjunction with military exercises and as part of the operations of the Palmerola Air Base, the main U.S. installation in Honduras. Captain Brian Mahoney, chief of civic action at the Palmerola Air Base outside Comayagua, conceded, "Our programs are for enhancing U.S. security. There is no humanitarian thrust. We just want people to have a higher opinion of us." Another officer at Palmerola added that the United States wants "to win hearts and minds" so as to "preempt support for some future guerrillas."[52]

Civic action sponsored by Palmerola took the form of public relations projects. "We focus on the town of Comayagua," explained Mahoney, "because that is where the troops go on their leisure time." On Thanksgiving and July 4th, the base sponsors festivities for the children in the area. Plans were underway for U.S. soldiers to rebuild the town's church and central plaza, and each of the units at the base was assigned to assist local schools and community centers. One of the major problems faced by Mahoney was the red-light nightlife that sprung up in this small town as a result of all the GIs. Prostitution and venereal disease were rampant. The army doctors at the base gave regular checkups to the prostitutes and the Palmerola soldiers to prevent more cases of disease.

In outreach to other Honduran villages, U.S. soldiers traveled around the country handing out clothing, toys, and medicine provided by U.S. private organizations. Palmerola regularly supplied air transport to AID and the Ministry of Health for medical service and development throughout Honduras. The civic action projects that occurred simultaneously with military exercises in Honduras were funded out of DOD's operation and maintenance budget on the grounds that some army personnel receive training by their participation. Oscar Seara, the military liaison officer for the United States Information Service (USIS) in Honduras, claimed that road-building civic action projects in rural Honduras offered a good opportunity for military and National Guard engineers to learn construction skills. "It's against the law to build roads in the United States because of competition with private enterprise, but here the military can do it," Seara explained.

In 1985, SOUTHCOM launched a program designed to encourage longer term and more coordinated operations in Central America as an alternative to "sporadic, quick-fix civic action programs." The ultimate objective was "to reduce the effect of Soviet block (Communist) movements in Central America." SOUTHCOM civic action seminars show the region's armies how to: "build popular support for government, reduce the effect of communist movements," and "raise the capital outlay needed to develop a communist movement." In SOUTHCOM's view, military civic action programs are competitive with communist efforts to win popular support by serving the people. An increase in government or military expenditures in these endeavors would lead, SOUTHCOM argues, to a "reduced threat of insurgency because of the need for a greater outlay of funds required [by the guerrillas] to counter the government programs."[53]

Through a series of civic action seminars, SOUTHCOM is helping countries to develop National Civic Action Plans that outline the ways different government and international agencies can assist in meeting the goals of nation building. One of the major achievements of the Panama seminar program, according to SOUTHCOM, was the way it taught the military how to coordinate its "nation building" with nonmilitary organizations and international humanitarian assistance. The Panamanian army's Civic Action division found out, for example, "how the U.S. Agency for International Development could assist their country" in its National Civic Action Plan.

Immunization Against Revolution

A long-standing civic action program managed by the U.S. Navy is Project Handclasp. Based in San Diego, California, Project Handclasp gathers supplies from U.S. private corporations and organizations for distribution at Navy ports of call. U.S. sailors personally hand out everything from beans and rice to stuffed dolls and treadle sewing machines. Commander Charles Tevelson, the director of Handclasp, said that "all military exercises have a community relations component," and that Project Handclasp has been more active lately in Central America.[54] During the Big Pine II maneuvers in 1983, the U.S. MilGroup in Honduras and SOUTHCOM requested that Project Handclasp supply them with medical supplies.

Commander Tevelson tries to push the materials that he has in surplus. "We have lots of mouthwash, so if they are planning to have a DenCap [dental civic action] operation, I make sure they have more mouthwash." Because of surpluses in other goods, Project Handclasp distributes Wham-O Squirtin' Sticks and chewable vitamins to Guatemalan orphans while villagers living near U.S.-Honduran maneuvers receive boxes of disposable diapers.[55]

Pentagon strategists have proposed the expanded use of military medicine in low intensity conflict. Major General William P. Winkler, commander of the Academy of Health Sciences, concluded that, "Military medicine is the least controversial, most cost-effective means of employing military forces in support of U.S. national interest in low intensity conflict situations."[56] Lieutenant Colonel James Taylor, chief of SOUTHCOM's Humanitarian Services Division, suggested that military medicine has "a new, exciting role" to play "in supporting U.S. national interest" to see that the region does not "slip completely into Cuban and Soviet spheres of influence."[57] This role calls for military doctors to enter "preselected target population areas in conjunction with engineer signal, civil affairs, psychological operations, and intelligence personnel before the tactical situation can deteriorate to open conflict." Advocates of an expanded role for military medicine readily acknowledge that AID has primary responsibility for humanitarian aid and development projects. But they feel that the military can complement AID operations by sponsoring massive immunization programs, providing transportation for AID humanitarian assistance, digging wells, and airlifting supplies.

Medcaps or Medretes (Medical Readiness Training Exercises) teams became very active, especially in Honduras, where they participated in the frequent military maneuvers. The Medretes team in Honduras boasted that the medical program is "our biggest card, showing them our best face." Captain Carol Corn, supervisor of Medretes at the Palmerola Air Base in Honduras, said that medical teams go out to rural villages three times a week, treating as many as 5,000 people in one day. The money for such ventures comes from training funds, stated Corn, explaining that, "We can't reproduce this medical experience in the United States." But as Corn and other Medretes personnel readily admitted, most of what these medical teams do is pass out aspirin and pull teeth. "It's mostly public relations," she conceded. "We really can't do much. We treat them for parasites, but we can only treat them once and then they go back to eating the same stuff."

A report issued by Aesculapius International Medicine after a trip to Honduras by two public health specialists, Doctors Steven Gloyd and Paul Epstein, leveled harsh criticism at Medretes. The report concluded that Medretes were "insensitive to the particular health care needs of Hondurans. Most of the treatment they gave out was inappropriate and the good they did was probably offset by the side effects." The two doctors who conducted the investigation found that the Medretes teams had no real knowledge of the best treatment of infant diarrhea, one of the most common problems they encountered. Instead of treating these cases with oral rehydration (recommended by the World Health Organization and the Honduran Ministry of Health), the Medretes doctors had distributed Kaopectate, which doctors Gloyd and Epstein explained has little effect on infant diarrhea and can be harmful in many cases. The Medretes teams also gave out an antiparasitic drug that kills parasites that affect North America children but is useless against hookworm, the primary parasite affecting Honduran children. The physicians also questioned the Medretes' dental work, which consisted of pulling teeth and no restorative work. One military dentist admitted that as many as 30 percent of the tooth extractions performed were unnecessary. Honduras is in dire need of basic health programs like preventive care, sanitation, and clean water, noted Gloyd and Epstein, but the foreign medical programs "undermine the fragile progress made by the Hondurans by encouraging the myth that the best medical care comes from high technology and North Americans."[58]

Despite these criticisms, the Medretes program has expanded in Central America. National Guard medical teams jet in and out of the region, joining the army's own Medretes teams and Navy doctors from the Tropical Medicine Program in Panama. Summing up the place of medical civic action in Central America, Colonel Joan Zatchuk, medical unit commander at Palmerola Air Base in Honduras, said, "It is hoped that health care gives the local population hope for the future, a stake in their government, and immunization against becoming revolutionaries."[59]

Calling Up the Guard

The military buildup in Central America included an unprecedented use of national guard and reserve units in military maneuvers and civic action. Between 1981 and the end of 1986 guard units from over 35 states received training in the region. Participation by the Army Reserve in training exercises in Central America was virtually unheard of before 1983, but in recent years the isthmus has become a favorite training spot for weekend warriors. The Department of Army acknowledged that Central America locations are now regularly used to train reservists and that "Army Reserve participation in Overseas Deployment Training exercises in Central America is projected to grow."[60] The U.S. military relies on the guard and reserve units for most of its civic action and Psyops capability. The U.S. Army has 98 percent of its Civil Affairs, 68 percent of its engineers, and 61 percent of its Psyops personnel in reserve components.[61]

The mobilization of the reserve units is in part the result of recent studies by the U.S. Army Training and Doctrine Command that call for an enhanced and significantly more important role for the civil affairs (CA) forces of the reserve units. This new role falls within an emerging concept called civil-military cooperation. Colonel James R. Compton of the U.S. Army Reserve predicted, "The role portends early mobilization and deployment for CA elements, utilization in the forward combat zone as well as in the communications zone, and a linking of civil-military experts. . . ."[62]

Besides their expanded role in maneuvers and exercises,

SOUTHCOM plans to involve the reserves and guard units in what it calls "militia-to-militia contacts" that will bring U.S. civilian-soldiers together with various militia units in Central America.[63] The Pentagon said that Central American exercises present an excellent opportunity for training the civilian-soldiers. Speaking for the National Guard, Joseph G. Hanley said that maneuvers abroad offer the most realistic training for those in the Guard part-time. He added that, unlike the United States, the region has no environmental restrictions that hamper training. "If you're building a road, you don't have to worry about the width of the culverts, about the Environmental Protection Agency. . . . Those are not concerns down there."

THE PENTAGON'S OTHER FACE

Economic aid and humanitarian assistance programs are important tools of LIC strategy. Coordinated closely with military assistance, such programs strengthen repressive military structures. They are used as vehicles for intelligence, psychological, and covert operations. Through its aid to the contras, Washington has contorted the meaning of humanitarian assistance to cover nonlethal military aid and even defensive weapons like anti-aircraft missiles.

Within the DOD, State Department, and armed forces, there has been a deeper appreciation of the political side of third-world conflicts. To fight on that political front, nonlethal programs are being used as LIC weapons in Central America. They may seem to be the friendly face of the Pentagon, but are in fact a mask for intervention and counterrevolution.

6 Terror and Development in Guatemala

Our economic aid "is directed at the rural poor, especially the Indians" and "addresses the underlying social/economic conditions which fan insurgency."
—AID Administrator
Peter McPherson, 1983.

In 1986, the Guatemalan military vacated the National Palace and turned over the blue-and-white presidential sash to Christian Democrat Vinicio Cerezo. The transfer of power to a civilian government followed three decades of almost uninterrupted military rule.[1] The inauguration of Cerezo occurred in the wake of a seven-year period of state terror that left over 75,000 dead, 100,000 orphaned, and nearly one million displaced. It was not popular pressure that caused the switch from military dictatorship to democratic rule. Rather it was the result of an elaborate pacification and stabilization plan drawn up by the military itself. The military recognized the need to improve the country's international image and attract more international aid; and it saw the value of channeling economic and political challenges into a democratic political system which it controlled.

The Reagan administration pointed to the democratization of Guatemala as a prized result of its foreign policy. Many counterinsurgency experts in and out of the Pentagon saw Guatemala as a country that demonstrated the validity of the LIC principle of total war in which security campaigns are combined with development initiatives. Of all the Central

107

American countries, Guatemala has the longest history of mixing security and development.

A TRADITION OF ASSISTANCE

From 1944 to 1954 Guatemala experimented with democracy and social reform. Two popularly elected presidents, Juan José Arévalo (1944–50) and Jacobo Arbenz (1951–54), launched a series of populist reforms, including a land redistribution program and laws safeguarding the right to organize. President Arbenz in 1952 announced a modest agrarian reform program that caused serious repercussions in Washington. Among the landholdings expropriated and turned over to landless peasants were uncultivated estates owned by United Fruit. This action angered several officials in the Eisenhower administration who had business connections with United Fruit. Corporate and government cold-war aficionados saw little difference between the nationalism of the Arbenz government and the policies of the Soviet Union. With the help of the administration, United Fruit mounted a national propaganda campaign against the Arbenz government that culminated in 1954 when President Eisenhower authorized the CIA to plan and finance a military coup to overthrow the democratically elected government.[2]

The post–1954 period in Guatemala provided Washington its first practical experience in using economic aid to stabilize and guide the development of a Latin American nation. On a visit to Guatemala to express official U.S. support for the new regime, Vice President Richard Nixon declared that the 1954 coup was "the first instance where a Communist government has been replaced by a free one. . . . The whole world is watching to see which does the better job."

With large sums of U.S. economic assistance and "know-how," the Eisenhower administration planned to turn Guatemala into a model for capitalist development throughout the hemisphere. While total foreign financial aid to Guatemala amounted to only $2.5 million in the 1951–54 period, it zoomed to $101.2 million (including $18 million from the U.S.-controlled World Bank) from 1955 through 1958.[3] President Carlos Castillo Armas, who had led the CIA-backed coup, told a U.S. reporter that if it had not been "for the technical and financial aid of the United States, it wouldn't have been possible to carry our program out."[4]

Soon after the 1954 coup, the U.S. International Cooperation Agency (ICA)—AID's predecessor—set up an office in Guatemala City. The mission grew from 28 employees in 1954 to 165 employees in 1959, including 94 U.S. citizens,[5] and eventually constituted what amounted to a parallel government. Each ministry and department of the Guatemalan government had a corresponding office in the ICA. The agency also tried to reshape Guatemala's economy in ways that complemented the interests of the United States by promoting increased U.S. investment and encouraging more agroexport production. In the case of agrarian reform, ICA staff supervised the dismantling of Arbenz's progressive land distribution program. Estates were returned to the oligarchy, and 100,000 Guatemalans lost the plots of land they had gained under the civilian government.

Despite U.S. economic and technical assistance, Guatemala did not become a shining model of democracy. By the time Kennedy became president, Guatemala had become an embarrassment rather than a showcase. The 1954 coup put the country back into the hands of the military and oligarchy and paved the way for the national security state in Guatemala. Gordon L. Bowen in his 1984 study in *Armed Forces and Society* called the U.S. involvement in the post–1954 period a case of "penetration politics." Caught up in Cold War paranoia and its allegiance to U.S. corporate interests, the U.S. government altered the balance of Guatemalan political forces. Rather than lobbying for a return to civilian rule, the United States stressed "the expansion of the military's role in Guatemalan social and political life."[6]

As guerrilla operations increased in the 1960s, U.S. participation in the country's counterinsurgency project also expanded. More U.S. advisers arrived, and in 1963 AID created its own civic action office to coordinate development programs with the military civic action efforts underway in areas of rebel activity. Appointed to direct this office was the former head of the U.S. Southern Command's civic action division.

Lincoln Gordon, the U.S. Coordinator for the Alliance for Progress, told Congress in 1967 that AID was requesting more money for Guatemala because "the government's anti-guerrilla campaign has included stepped-up social and economic measures" in the guerrilla zone. "Guerrilla activity," he explained, "tends to generate a need for increased U.S. development assistance."[7] In line with the military's goals, AID projects were meant "to calm the people down" by instituting economic development projects that would reduce popular support for the rebels.[8] One Guatemalan *campesino,* commenting on pacification programs, told Eduardo Galeano, author of *Guatemala: Occupied Country,* that "for us to get drinking water, it seems necessary to have guerrillas nearby."[9]

The combination of civic action programs, terrorism, and repression managed to end the guerrilla rebellion by 1970. Colonel Carlos Arana Osorio, who served as chief Guatemalan officer in charge of the counterinsurgency campaign in the northeast, estimated that 70 percent of his success in pacifying the province of Zacapa was due to the social work of the army, and only 30 percent was due to the power of weapons.[10]

Just as its involvement in Guatemala in the 1950s had given the United States its first experience in stabilization in Latin America, its support of Guatemala's military regime in the 1960s gave the United States its first taste of pacification and counterinsurgency in the region. The counterinsurgency war of the 1960s and almost two decades of U.S. military training prepared the Guatemalan military for the next outbreak of insurgency. To pacify communities linked to the rebels, the army in the 1980s is again using civic action programs, international economic aid, and psychological operations.

A PACIFICATION PLAN FOR THE 1980S

Military and death-squad terror succeeded in keeping the country relatively free of organized popular resistance until the mid-1970s, when peasant leagues, labor unions, Christian associations, and students regrouped to demand change. After the 1976 earthquake, an upsurge of community organizing was encouraged by progressive Catholic clergy and financially supported by foreign development organizations, both private and governmental. During the same period, two new rebel armies—Guerrilla Army of the Poor (EGP) and Organization of People in Arms (ORPA)—were patiently and quietly organizing the populations of the northwestern and western provinces. In sharp contrast to the earlier guerrilla armies, EGP and ORPA worked closely with the country's Indian communities and counted many Indians among their leaders.

The rise in popular organizing and the new eruption of insurgency were met with state terror. The bloodbath began in the province of Quiché soon after the earthquake, seriously escalated in 1979, and by 1981 expanded to cover the entire highlands or Altiplano. From 1978 to 1982, President Romeo Lucas García and his brother Defense Minister Benedicto Lucas García directed the campaign of terror. The military hoped to crush all signs of resistance in the highlands—from church groups concerned with social justice to peasant unions. While the army claimed to be fighting communists, most of the actual targets of military violence were Indian communities suspected of sympathizing with the guerrilla cause.

During the four years of the Lucas García government, the Altiplano was put under military siege and death-squad activity was rampant throughout the country. In March 1982, General Efraín Ríos Montt took power in a coup d'etat. Montt, who had been the presidential candidate for the Christian Democratic Party (PDC) in 1974, promised to end the corruption and repression that characterized the Lucas García regime. While death-squad violence in the cities markedly declined, Ríos Montt stepped up the rural counterinsurgency campaign. Trained at U.S. counterinsurgency schools and a former director of the Inter-American Defense College in Washington, Ríos Montt was well prepared to oversee the military's offensive against the guerrilla rebellion. Ríos Montt approached counterinsurgency with a biblical vengeance, relying on his defense minister, General Oscar Mejía Víctores, to coordinate military operations. A member of the Gospel Outreach church based in Eureka, California, Ríos Montt believed he was chosen by God to eradicate the subversion.

The scorched-earth tactics used by Lucas García were intensified, causing entire Indian communities in the Altiplano to flee to Mexico. Along with the killing came military-style development; burning down Indian villages and murdering suspected supporters of the guerrillas was not considered enough to eradicate the roots of rebellion. Adopting the language of counterinsurgency theory, the military called for the simultaneous implementation of both security and development campaigns. The new approach was outlined in the National Plan of Security and Development, which was approved by the military regime a month after Ríos Montt took over the National Palace. The army proclaimed that "Development is the new name for peace."

The "security" half of the new counterinsurgency plan, called *Victoria 82,* dominated military operations during the first year of the Ríos Montt regime. The three objectives of *Victoria 82* were to deny the subversives access to the population that constituted their political and social base; rescue possible individual guerrillas, neutralizing or eliminating any who do not wish to be integrated into normal life; and destroy the enemy's Permanent Military Units.[11]

The massacres and assassinations did not eliminate the guerrillas, but the counterinsurgency operations spread terror throughout rural Guatemala and helped to break the links between the population and the rebel armies. Ríos Montt then introduced the terrorized residents of the highlands to his now famous "Beans and Guns" ("Frijoles y Fusiles") counterinsurgency campaign. The "guns" or security part of this campaign referred to a military initiative to place all teenage boys and men in civil defense patrols or PACs (Patrullas de Autodefensa Civil). Obligated to guard the entrances and patrol the streets of the villages, the PACs were developed by the military not to defend Indian communities, as the army claimed, but to maintain control over the Indian population. The development component of the counterinsurgency effort involved the distribution of food allotments in the conflict areas to women and men in exchange for labor performed on public works projects approved by the military. These food-for-work programs served to increase Indian dependency on the military while at the same time providing labor for its development projects.

In August 1983, General Mejía Víctores, also a product of U.S. counterinsurgency training, led a military coup that named him the new chief-of-state. During his regime (August 1983–January 1986), the military expanded the pacification campaign initiated under the Ríos Montt government, giving increased attention to the nonmilitary aspects of counterinsurgency. Calling his new plan *Firmeza 83,* Mejía Víctores, like his predecessor, recognized the need to broaden military control over the countryside to prevent another peasant rebellion. In addition to setting up military outposts in all but the smallest towns, the new regime gave great attention to the soft side of the counterinsurgency war through refugee resettlement, rural development, psychological operations, model villages, and development poles.

Firmeza 83 proposed the integration of public, religious, and private sectors into the campaign; the grouping of civil responsibilities in conflict areas under military command, and the changing of the term conflict areas to "areas of harmony." To formalize *Firmeza 83,* Víctores upgraded the old Civilian Affairs Division (created in 1961) by giving the new Section of

Civilian Affairs and Community Development (S-5) vast powers. The S-5 became one of the five major military command sections and had authority over 12 newly created Civilian Affairs companies that directed civil defense patrols, model villages, development poles, and psychological operations.[12] Members of the S-5 teams, many of whom did not wear uniforms, portrayed themselves as social workers interested in the welfare of the people. While the S-5, not the government, supervised what passed for development activity, the main objectives of the Civilian Affairs companies were intelligence, Psyops, and control of the population in the conflict areas.

The other military organization given new authority was the Committee for National Reconstruction (CRN), which originally was established in 1976 to manage earthquake relief programs. While most of its workers are civilians, five of CRN's ten directors are high military officers. In 1986, President Cerezo appointed Federico Fuentes Corado, a former Minister of Defense, as president of CRN. CRN serves as the channel for all international aid to the conflict zones and has authority over the activities of all voluntary organizations in those areas. The CRN directorate calls its activities "military humanism," and boasts that its relief and development activities have begun to rectify the socioeconomic problems in the Guatemalan countryside. "These are no longer times," said CRN in 1985, "of impoverished committees, honorable ladies' charity associations, or groups of dreamers." In Guatemala, charity and humanism became military missions.

Both the pacification programs initiated by Ríos Montt and Mejía Víctores and the expanded operations of the CRN after 1982 were products of the "developmentalist" faction in the Guatemalan armed forces. This internal faction had grown over the years as a result of foreign training programs (from Taiwan and Israel as well as from the United States). When the CRN was formed in 1976, it received enthusiastic backing by the developmentalist officers who saw the value of strengthening the military presence in rural areas through civic action. Because the Lucas García regime sharply reduced the funding and power of CRN, it was by 1982 merely a skeleton of what it had been in the 1976–78 period. Ríos Montt revived the CRN with the support of the developmentalists and with the help of international financial and food assistance from AID, the IDB, and the UN World Food Program (WFP).[13] As the CRN's public relations officer said, "Before the CRN was responding to a natural disaster, but we are now responding to a social and political one."

Operation Ixil: Testing Ground for Pacification

In the early 1980s, the first military planning for pacification focused on the Ixil Triangle—the part of northern Quiché where backing for the guerrillas had been the strongest. Because of this support, the Ixil Triangle had been the scene of some of the worst military massacres; the countryside is still scarred by 49 burnt and abandoned villages. A 1981 military document called *Operation Ixil: Plan for Civilian Affairs* described the pacification options as seen by the military developmentalists. Most of the strategies proposed in this document were later put into practice in the Altiplano.[14]

Operation Ixil recommended a two-phase campaign. The first comprised the military measures required to secure the area. The goals of phase one included: "finishing off the subversives," "finishing the implementation of the ideological campaign," and "completing the organization of the civil defense patrols." The second phase introduced pacification programs that would return the Ixil Triangle "to law and order by convincing the local population to be more patriotic." According to the analysis in the Operation Ixil document, the government had lost control of the Indian people because of their geographic and cultural isolation from national social and political life.

A multifaceted pacification plan, Operation Ixil was designed to gain control of the population through education, development assistance, work programs, and model villages for refugees and suspected guerrilla sympathizers. It recommended a "Campaign of Psychological Action," which was an "intense, profound, and well-planned psychological campaign to capture the mentality of the Ixils in order to make them feel part of the Guatemalan nation." The Operation Ixil plan recommended establishing a committee that would coordinate the work of all government agencies and ministries concerned with development. According to this proposal, the coordinating body would be headed by the local military commander and would include representatives from 13 different government agencies (all of which receive AID funding). The employees of these government agencies, like the agricultural and education ministries, would continue to be paid by the government but would be subject to military control. This concept was later used as a model for the Inter-Institutional Coordination Committees (IICCs), which were established by Mejía Víctores in late 1983. The IICCs formed a network used by the military to coordinate operations of all government ministries and PVOs responsible for some aspect of rural development.

Development Poles: Vision of Pacification

In two years, pacification in Guatemala had evolved from the rudimentary "Beans and Guns" approach initiated by Ríos Montt to a sophisticated strategy that integrated all the main elements of a textbook pacification campaign. Borrowing from the terminology of development assistance, the military called this new, improved approach "integrated rural development."

The Ixil Triangle and the Ixcan/Playa Grande area in the Northern Transverse Strip (*Franja Transversal del Norte,* lowlands covering the northern reaches of three provinces) were designated by the military in 1984 as the first of the country's seven Development Poles (*"polos de desarrollo"*). Each geographical pole was to become a center of economic, political, and social growth. The original seven poles covered predominantly Indian-populated areas where support for the guerrillas had been the strongest and the violence most intense. Over 440 Indian settlements that were razed by the army's scorched-earth campaign were located within these development poles.[15]

A 1984 government decree established the development poles of the highlands as the "maximum priority" for all public ministries.[16] Working under the supervision of the IICCs and the CRN, all the agencies counted on international funds, particularly from AID and the Inter-American Development Bank (IDB), for their work in the highlands. Model villages were constructed within the poles as resettlement camps for Indians displaced by counterinsurgency violence. They were similar to the strategic hamlets used for pacification purposes by the United States and the South Vietnamese Army during the Vietnam War. With the help of civil defense patrols, the Guatemalan army rounded up refugees, most of whom were severely malnourished and disease ridden. Once under military control, the refugees were often obligated to build the model villages and to reconstruct roads, schools and bridges destroyed during the height of the violence. For their work, the Indians received food provisions supplied by the United Nations and the United States but distributed by the army, government agencies, and PVOs.

By early 1986, approximately 50,000 Indians were living in the so-called model villages. The army called them "small paradises," but the militarized nature of these new communities prompted the Archbishop of Guatemala City to label them "antimodel villages."[17]

Located in the center of the Ixil Triangle is the model village of Acul, the first of its kind completed by the army. Displayed prominently in many plazas throughout Quiché, S-5 posters exalted the accomplishments of Acul. Acul lies over a mountain from Nebaj, the major commercial center of the Ixil Triangle. The military finished an all-weather road to Acul in 1984, but only the military and government employees use the road. The Ixil Indians climb the mountain over an old dirt path. Visible from the mountaintop are the many homes in the valley and on the slopes that were destroyed by the army. In Acul, the Indians live in two-room wooden houses laid out in a grid, each house with its own number on streets with names like "Liberty" and "Army."

The development pole of Playa Grande, located in the Northern Transverse Strip, was built at the center of an AID-funded colonization settlement that began in the late 1970s. The outbreak of war disrupted the AID project, and most of the settlers in this isolated region fled into the bush to escape the violence. Colonel Isaac Rodriguez, the army commander at Playa Grande, blamed the guerrillas for the many civilian deaths in the area. In contrast to refugee accounts of the wave of army terror, Rodriguez claimed that "the guerrillas burnt everything: houses, churches, health centers, everything." He clarified that the army's presence, with a military base that borders the new model village, was "to create a sense of security so the people would come back to their homes. We give the people security, and we give them food."

In Playa Grande, the army worked with CARE and AID in what Rodriguez called a "community development program" in which the Indians built homes, schools, and other community infrastructure as well as cultivated the agroexport crop cardamom in return for a daily food allowance. In the overall development scheme for Playa Grande, Rodriguez emphasized that "the first step, the most important step was to build roads to these communities. Then 'techo minimo' (simple housing), electricity, and water." As in the other model villages, psychological operations have played a prominent role in the army's pacification efforts at Playa Grande. Explaining the need for the army's re-education program, Colonel Rodriguez said that when people returned to their communities, they needed "ideological orientation to make them more responsible and to have a more patriotic, nationalist consciousness and to make them more resistant to the subversion." At Playa Grande, the army scheduled weekly meetings "to talk about their problems. We call this re-education and development process the pacification plan of the country."

The switch to civilian rule in 1986 did little to alter the politics of counterinsurgency. Army control remained paramount in the countryside, and the military high command remained the final arbiter of government policies. Disappearances and political murders continued to be an almost everyday affair in Guatemala. Meanwhile, the guerrillas were regaining strength and organizational capability. The infrastructure of pacification—development poles, model villages, coordinating committees, S-5 teams, and civil patrols—carried over unaltered to the Cerezo government.

PACIFICATION: A JOINT EFFORT

The smiling face of counterinsurgency in Guatemala could not have pressed forward without international development funds and food donations. While the army oversaw the campaign, it depended on foreign assistance to implement its programs. Foreign aid provided the food for the "Beans and Guns" campaign, the aluminum roofing for the model villages, the materials for road building, and the medicine and other supplies for the army's civilian affairs teams. The budget for the CRN came almost entirely from foreign aid organizations and primarily from AID.

"Democratization" money from AID paid for the 1985–86 elections that put a civilian administration in the National Palace but left the military with the real political authority. Funds from USIA underwrote a psychological operations campaign designed to convince Guatemalans that they were indeed living in a democracy. Stabilization assistance from Washington went to prop up the new government, and U.S. aid created a series of business, labor, and research organizations that played an important role in formulating the economic and social policies of the new civilian government. The official aid to pacify and stabilize Guatemala was complemented by humanitarian assistance and pacification operations of U.S. private organizations like the Air Commandos Association, Gospel Outreach, and Friends of the Americas.

Since 1954 AID has been a major figure in Guatemala. Almost every Guatemalan ministry has received AID money. The rural roads department, the planning department, and the agricultural extension service actually owe their existence to AID. During Jimmy Carter's presidency, new AID funds for the government of Guatemala were cut off as a result of his displeasure with the country's continuing violation of human rights. However, AID dollars continued to flow into Guatemala through previously authorized assistance packages and indirectly through the programs of PVOs. After 1983, economic aid from the United States to Guatemala steadily increased, rising from $13 million in 1980 to over $160 million in 1987.

Unlike neighboring El Salvador where AID works closely with the army, AID in Guatemala has taken care to keep a public distance from the military. Instead pacification funds have gone to government agencies and PVOs whose activities are coordinated by the military. AID also supports the CRN, which poses as a civilian institution, but is under the direct supervision of the military. Like in El Salvador, much of AID's contribution to pacification comes from local currency generated from ESF and Title I programs. In 1985, the United States renewed military aid to Guatemala. Congress approved the Pentagon's request for nonlethal military aid, including nonarmament spare parts, construction equipment, and "items of a humanitarian nature, such as medicine, medical evacuation helicopters, and ambulances."[18] In a previous request, the Pentagon acknowledged the country's civic action efforts in the Altiplano were "tied to a counterinsurgency program."

While AID might not have assisted in the planning of the pacification campaign, as it did in the 1960s and as it is doing currently in El Salvador, AID assistance provided many of the building blocks on which that campaign was based. Without U.S. economic assistance, the military could never have mounted such an extensive pacification campaign. "The predominant thinking in Guatemala," explained Gary Adams, AID's Guatemala desk officer, "is that you can get more done with honey than with bullets. You provide people with honey and that takes them away from the guerrillas." AID is a main supplier of that "honey" to the Guatemalan government.

The United States has acknowledged the connection between Guatemala's development programs and its counterinsurgency campaign. The embassy noted in 1983 that the "food, shelter, and work" programs of the Guatemalan government were initiated as part of a "counterinsurgency social-action program."[19] But both the AID Mission and the U.S. Embassy in Guatemala denied any joint planning or significant support of pacification programs in the highlands. The almost one-to-one correspondence between AID's rural development programs—involving food assistance, rural electrification, refugee relief, road construction, housing, and nontraditional agriculture—and the military's own development plan makes this denial less than credible.

In its 1984 budget request, AID noted that its development program coincided with that of the military government. The AID Mission told Congress that it believed it important "to improve the current economic situation and address the political unrest in the Altiplano." It could implement all of its goals, the agency claimed, and at the same time "support the government of Guatemala's commitment to provide for the previously disadvantaged population in the Altiplano." According to AID: "The government views AID as the best source of assistance in the development of the Altiplano, and consequently AID can have a major impact in shaping programs undertaken there."[20] Supporting the request for additional funds to Guatemala, AID Administrator Peter McPherson said that the program of the AID Mission in Guatemala "is directed at the rural poor, especially the Indians" and "addresses the underlying social/economic conditions which fan insurgency."[21]

In 1984, CRN director Colonel German Grotewald said that his organization "depends on AID for our programs in the highlands." His executive secretary, Oscar Gallegos, boasted that CRN "doesn't spend a penny of its own funds" for the programs and services it oversees in the development poles. The International Cooperation Division (ACNI) of CRN manages the foreign grants and the work of international PVOs. But as CRN made explicit in its principles, the "programs and geographic destination of such international cooperation will be decided by CRN"—not by the international donor.[22]

Similarly, Colonel Mario Paiz Bolaños, director of the army's Civilian Affairs division, explained that the army spends very little of its own money in the highlands. Because of its role as coordinator of development, the Civilian Affairs office can make certain that AID-funded schools, housing, and roads are placed in locations that the army regards as strategic. Another S-5 official, Dr. Luis Sieckavizza, noted that even though the United States may publicly disassociate itself from the military's civic action program, "there are a lot of ways to do it under the table."

Arthur Dewey, assistant secretary of the State Department's refugee program, told the Guatemalan army in late 1984 that he approved of the return of refugees from Mexico to the model villages being constructed by the army along the border. Dewey also expressed support for the system of Inter-Institutional Coordination Committees. He called the resettlement work within Guatemala impressive. "My government looks favorably upon the poles of development," crooned Dewey, "because they show the goodwill of the government to grant Guatemalan refugees a better form of life since land, potable water, electricity, and other necessary services are being made available to them."[23]

AID also applauded the military for the development poles. In March 1985, it stated that "the principal beneficiaries of the program are the inhabitants of the villages that are being rebuilt." AID reported that the government was "encouraged by the rapid acceptance of this plan by the Highland Indians— judging by their return to their lands and their provision of manual labor to rebuild their communities." And "the sooner these areas are reconstructed, the sooner the affected population can once again become productive members of society." Like CRN and the army, AID insisted that Indians themselves are guiding the course of development in the highlands. According to AID, the "beneficiaries" of the model villages

> help the CRN select the location and assist in the general design of their rebuilt town and its infrastructure. They also participate directly in the construction of their houses, water systems, roads, and other infrastructure. The strong desire to re-establish their lives has led these participants to work voluntarily under difficult physical conditions.[24]

On several occasions during the formation of the development poles, AID specified that its funds be sent directly to model villages in Huehuetenango and Alta Verapaz. By 1985, AID publicly acknowledged that its programs might have been used within the development poles and actually suggested funding the local IICCs. In a March 6, 1985, letter to Senator Patrick Leahy, AID's Jay Morris said:

> Our programs have been conceived, designed, and executed independently, and there has been no plan or attempt to coordinate these programs with the model villages program. Since our regular programs operate all over the western highlands, however, it is conceivable that some activity in agriculture, health, education, or family planning may have provided services in an area designated as a Pole of Development or model village area. . . . The formerly displaced persons who settle in the model villages, however, have at least the same degree of need as other low-income persons in the highlands, and so in the future, we would not seek to exclude them from services and benefits provided by civilian ministry programs of broad region-wide scope which we support.[25]

Since 1983 the Altiplano and the Northern Transverse Strip have been what AID called its "target area" in Guatemala. AID directed its funds to the very parts of Guatemala designated as unsafe by State Department Travel Advisories. By mid-1984, 80–90 percent of all AID dollars were going to the regions where army violence was most severe. According to

AID in Washington, the focus on this part of the country had nothing to do with the Guatemalan government's own programs in the region but reflected AID's concern for the welfare of the resident Indian population.[26]

Justifying the fact that nine out of every ten AID projects in Guatemala involve the Altiplano population, Robert Queener, AID regional officer for Central America, stated:

> The highlands became more of a single-minded focus in the 80s because the people there have been left out. The Indians haven't received the benefits of development. Getting the government of Guatemala to develop the highlands is a policy change. The aid also helps social and political stability. We want to see that the government meets the needs of the Indians.

AID-Style Reform and Democratization

AID is using its increased assistance as leverage for reform in Guatemala, but not the kind advocated by peasant and worker organizations. The reforms suggested by AID benefit mostly the private sector, particularly the agroexporters. In recent years, AID has attempted to mold the economy in line with the recommendations of the Kissinger Commission. Since the elections, higher levels of economic assistance to Guatemala have increased AID's ability to dictate policy decisions in the country.

In its Policy Dialogue Plan for 1986–87, AID stated that in the past several years it carried out a dialogue about economic and political structures with officials of the military government from "authorities at the highest central government level" to those "at regional government levels through formal briefings and program discussions with departmental governors [who were appointed by the military], military commanders, and members of the departmental coordinating committees." AID promised that in coming years it would use its leverage to demand reforms such as cutbacks in public spending, currency devaluation, higher gasoline prices, higher taxes, more concentration on rural development, increased incentives for the private sector, and support for IMF austerity measures.

AID is taking care not to alienate the Guatemalan oligarchy. In fact, it has designed its projects to coincide with the interests of the oligarchy. The AID mission noted that agrarian reform is "an unacceptable concept in present-day Guatemala." Instead, it recommended that discussions and negotiations be pursued with the private sector before embarking on the Commercial Land Markets Project in which private sector credit institutions would be used by AID as the channel for land-sales financing. Similarly, its Agribusiness Development program is designed to seek joint ventures between U.S. investors and the local private sector, and (like its other agricultural development activities) to increase nontraditional export production in the highlands. AID set aside $10 million for a Private Sector Project to increase credit and opportunities for the business community. In 1986, the agency began placing most of its agricultural credit money in private banks rather than working through the state agricultural bank Bandesa.[27]

The Economic and Social Reordering stabilization plan announced by Cerezo soon after taking office reflected the monetarist priorities of both AID and the Guatemalan private sector. The plan was formulated in close consultation with the major business associations and with U.S. government officials in the course of several trips to Washington. To further solidify the position of the private sector in new democratic Guatemala, AID backed the creation of several business associations to better represent private-sector interests and to help carry out AID's vision of economic progress.[28] According to AID, the job of the business associations is to keep the government in line with economic principles that call for unrestrained private-sector activity. Pleased with the power of the Guatemalan business community, one senior AID official in Guatemala said, "In this country, the private sector truly challenges the government and is a real force for development."

Starting in 1985, Guatemala began receiving special attention from President Reagan's "Project Democracy" initiative spearheaded by the National Endowment for Democracy (See Chapter Nine). Working through new private-sector organizations funded by AID, NED paid for a series of seminars about democracy, communism, and private enterprise. One such seminar hosted by the Camara de Libre Empresa brought Guatemalan and Salvadoran business leaders together to discuss more active private-sector participation in politics. NED also funds two political think tanks to assist the democratization process. The Center for Political Studies (CEDEP), which also received AID funds to assist the election process, acts as a forum between government and the private sector. The other political think tank funded by NED is the Association for Social Studies (ASIES), an organization close to the Christian Democrats. Another NED-funded group working in Guatemala during the elections was the National Republican Institute for International Affairs which conducted a national political survey designed to "reinforce the democratic aspirations of the Guatemalan people."[29] NED also pumps money into a Study Center in Guatemala sponsored by the American Institute for Free Labor Development.

Guatemala is the main focus of a new Central America Peace Scholarships project, which was recommended by the Kissinger Commission. The principal purpose of this program is to "promote democratic processes and counter a high level of Soviet Bloc [educational] efforts." By 1990, the $29 million scholarship program plans to bring over 5,000 Guatemalan Indians to the United States to learn about the "American way" through AID-funded instruction and educational tours in Washington. A related AID initiative aimed at the highlands is the agency's support of a Highland Indian Institute to establish a group of Indian leaders allied to AID and the Guatemalan government. In yet another typically surface-level move, AID, rather than dealing directly with the major causes of poverty in the highlands, kicked off a population control campaign in Guatemala "with increasing special attention to the indigenous population."

Using its considerable influence, the U.S. government augmented its money spigot by encouraging international financial institutions to support Guatemala. In the last several years, the World Bank and the Inter-American Development Bank (IDB) both initiated larger lending programs for Guatemala. Washington also authorized loans for rural development in the country through the Central American Bank of Economic Integration. Since 1982, these multilaterals have funded a number of projects in coordination with AID and the military government including rural roads construction, the promotion of nontraditional agriculture, and rural communications.

FOOD FOR WORK AND CONTROL

From the beginning of the "Beans and Guns" program of Ríos Montt, food distribution by the army was the foundation of pacification in Guatemala. Food donations came primarily from AID's PL480 program and the UN's World Food Program (WFP) but also from private groups like the Christian Broadcasting Network (CBN). Throughout, the CRN has served as the coordinator of food distribution for the army.

WFP distributed its food through the CRN, which used the donations for food-for-work projects. These projects mostly involved road construction but also entailed work on new housing, electrification, telegraph lines, schools, health centers, irrigation for vegetable production, and latrines in rural communities, mostly in conflict areas. A 1983 WFP agreement with CRN called for the construction of 1,200 kilometers of roads, 120 bridges, and 15,000 low-cost homes through food-for-work projects.[30] WFP's food distribution program was valued at about $1 million a month.[31]

Explaining the pacification logic of the food-for-work program, Saul Figueroa, chief of the military's civilian affairs office in Huehuetenango, said, "If the subversives had invited these people to go with them and had given them a means of subsistence these people [the guerrillas] would be winning." Conversely, Figueroa would argue, the army is winning because it has the beans to hand out to hungry *campesinos.* [32]

According to AID, most of the food being distributed by the military in the model villages comes from WFP, not from the United States. Technically this is true, but virtually all WFP's supplies in Guatemala are originally provided to the United Nations by the United States. The familiar U.S. red-white-and-blue shield and the Alliance for Progress handshake are emblazoned across the bags of corn and cans of vegetable oil that the WFP hands out to the inhabitants of the development poles.

AID's 1986 Country Development Strategy Statement recommended the expansion of the PL480 program "to provide for displaced persons who are temporarily located in safe-haven locations and to enhance the effectiveness of self-help labor in labor-intensive development programs in the target areas." The report noted that expanded food-for-work projects in the highlands could address the lack of services and infrastructure, which "has been identified as a major constraint to the development of the country, both politically and economically."*

In 1984, for the first time in history, Guatemala received $7.5 million in Title I food. The 1984 Title I agreement required the Guatemalan government to use the funds generated by the sales of Title I food aid for government-operated "community development projects" in the highlands. The revenues generated by Title I sales covered a large part of CRN's budget. AID claimed

---

*AID's food assistance flows through two PL480 programs: Title I and Title II. Title II covers the distribution of U.S. food to poor people through relief and food-for-work programs. Title I and other food aid programs like Section 416 go directly to the host government as a way to assist the country financially. Section 416 food aid is a particular boon to Guatemala's struggling economy since this assistance comes as a grant and doesn't have to be paid back. Title I food is purchased by the recipient government, but at very low interest rates usually with a 5-year grace period and 30-year repayment schedule. Both Title II and Section 416 programs increased substantially in Guatemala during the 1980s, with Title I jumping from zero in 1980 to over $19 million in 1987 and Section 416 increasing from zero in 1980 to $12.6 million in 1986.

that these funds were not being used in the model villages, but it also admitted that it did not carefully monitor local currency funds.

Malnutrition and hunger are certainly serious problems in Guatemala, especially in the highlands. But the bags of corn and cans of vegetable oil bearing the U.S. emblem distributed to Indian men and women do not help resolve the long-term agrarian problems that are responsible for malnutrition and rural rebellion. In fact, the army has declared its intention to use this international aid as an instrument of pacification and a way to avoid upheaval over issues like agrarian reform. The United Nations and the United States insist that the donated supplies are for humanitarian relief, but they have not taken measures to see that the food is distributed free of political quid pro quos. A report by Americas Watch, a human rights monitoring group, concluded:

> International food aid becomes another instrument of military control. That is, hungry peasants must pledge allegiance to the government, work on government projects, and obey military commands in order to obtain food. . . . The situation provides the military with one more form of coercion, with one more weapon in its campaign to consolidate its control and domination of civilian life in the highlands.[33]

Roads for Barefoot Peasants

For the last 30 years, road building has been a priority for economic aid programs in Guatemala. In the 1950s and 1960s, AID and its predecessor agency paid for the construction of the Atlantic and the Pacific highways. Washington announced that these were necessary infrastructure improvements to attract foreign investment and to promote the modern agroexport economy. An underlying assumption, however, was that a revolution would be less likely to occur if the Guatemalan economy was yet more dependent on the international capitalist market.

By the late 1970s, AID's tactics had changed. Roads remained the first priority, but the emphasis switched from coastal roads to rural access roads. AID felt that an extended transportation network in the Altiplano and the Northern Transverse Strip would help initiate the production of agroexports and integrate these areas into national political and economic life. Road construction in the countryside became part of AID's new commitment to integrated rural development and nontraditional agroexport production. But it also had important implications for what the Pentagon calls "internal security."

Between 1978 and 1986, about 40 percent of AID's development assistance budget (not counting ESF and food assistance) was used for rural roads in the Altiplano and the Northern Transverse Strip. Road-construction funds flow to Caminos Rurales (the rural roads division of the transportation ministry), CRN, and the Institute for Agrarian Transportation (INTA). Before 1978 Caminos Rurales was a skeleton agency with a tiny budget. By 1984 the department had expanded from 7 to over 300 employees with an annual budget of $8 million.[34] According to Pedro Aguerra, the army's public relations officer, most of the money for road building by the country's army corps of engineers comes from Washington.

Road construction and maintenance programs are part of AID's agricultural projects such as Small Farmer Development and the Highlands Agricultural Development. The other underwriters of rural road construction are the Inter-American Development Bank (IDB) and the Central American Bank of Economic Integration (CABEI)—both of which depend on funding from the United States. AID justified its disproportionately large investment in rural roads on the grounds that they spark rural development by: 1) increasing marketing opportunities for small farmers, particularly those growing nontraditional crops, 2) providing construction jobs for the unemployed, 3) facilitating the government's colonization and resettlement projects in frontier regions of the Northern Transverse Strip, and 4) improving farmers' access to agricultural inputs like pesticides and fertilizer that are imported from the United States.

Among the positive effects of road building in the highlands, according to AID, is the increased integration of Indians into the dominant society and through more frequent contact with government representatives. This "should provide the incentive and the opportunity for Indians to learn Spanish, which in turn will assist Indian participation in the economic, social, and political mainstream."[35] In its Highlands Agricultural Development Project—with a budget dominated by road construction and maintenance—AID noted that "Indians have traditionally isolated themselves and have been fearful of government and other official contacts. Their new appreciation of the government of Guatemala [resulting from increased contact] will have considerable significance in the development of a politically stable rural area."

In calling for better "integration" of highlands Indians into national life, AID echoes the sentiments of the Guatemalan military. But this view conveniently overlooks the integral (though highly exploited) role Indian laborers play in the national economy. The country's agroexport sector depends on the seasonal labor of highlands Indians, and the national economy also relies on Indian farmers to produce most of the country's basic grains. Indians, however, have maintained a separate cultural identity and consider the nation's political system oppressive and contrary to their interests. AID and the country's military hope that a better transportation network in the highlands will break down this historical isolation and thereby reduce the susceptibility of the Indian population to guerrilla organizing.[36]

Even though a counterinsurgency war was being waged, AID in 1984 said that labor-intensive road building was "an ideal type of project to implement within the current Guatemalan Highlands environment."[37] Not only would small farmers be able to market their surplus because of the roads, AID said, but the road building would provide thousands of labor-intensive jobs for the unemployed. For their "pick and shovel" work carving roads out of mountain slopes, Indian men were paid

$1.00 a day or were compensated through food-for-work programs.[38]

AID continues to make rural roads projects its top development priority despite its failure to show that new or improved rural roads in the Altiplano have contributed significantly to the welfare of the area's Indian population. In fact, its only evaluation of the program showed little or no correlation between rural roads and the incomes of small farmers. The report noted that "farmers producing only for family consumption before roads were built did little better afterwards, since transport costs had not been their main production constraint." According to the study, farmers in one isolated Indian village "were not able to produce enough surplus for sale to benefit directly from the road." In addition, the report stated that there had been no coordination between the placement of roads and the installation of other projects like irrigation systems that were supposed to help small farmers.[39]

The project evaluation made no mention of the violent political situation in the highlands, but the USDA consultant who submitted the report said privately: "The first thing these roads do is get the military out to where the action is," adding that "if the military wasn't up in these mountains there would be no violence." Most observers expressed similar opinions. A Guatemalan agronomist working on an AID small farmer project in San Marcos said, "You'll see right away that there is always a military outpost at the end of all the roads in the Altiplano. The roads are for the security of the country."

Through its Small Farmer Development Project, AID has financed the construction of new roads into the Northern Transverse Strip as part of an ongoing AID-funded colonization project. The civilian-military elite in Guatemala welcomed AID's initiatives not only as a way to establish a stronghold in this isolated (but strategically important) border region but also as a way of making this rich agricultural area more accessible. Guatemalans commonly refer to the Franja Transversal region as the "Zone of Generals" because, as soon as new roads opened up the region, army officers appropriated the best land.

Referring to new roads built in the Ixil Triangle, the army proudly declared that "the Indians no longer have to carry sacks of corn on their backs over difficult paths."[40] Roads or not, Indians still walk. Many of them do not even own a pair of shoes, let alone a truck to travel the new rural roads criss-crossing the highlands. In isolated areas like the Ixil Triangle, only government and army vehicles can be seen using the new roads. In Nebaj, the commander of the local S-5 Civilian Affairs division acknowledged that the new roads were a major part of the counterinsurgency war. "If we had the money and machinery to make roads all through this area, we'd get rid of the guerrillas quickly."

PVOS PITCH IN

In recent years, Guatemala has experienced two waves of private voluntary organizations. The first influx of PVOs followed the 1976 earthquake, when approximately 75 foreign organizations came to the country to help with relief operations. Seeing the severe socioeconomic conditions in rural Guatemala, many of these PVOs stayed in the country and established development programs that often involved the formation of cooperatives. However, the terror that swept through the Altiplano eventually forced virtually all the PVOs to shut down operations in the highlands. Many Guatemalan development workers on these PVO teams were killed by the military. It was not until 1983 that private organizations began to return to the Altiplano.

The second wave of PVOs included a new breed of right-wing and fundamentalist groups. They arrived first in Nebaj, brought in by army helicopters. Many of these PVOs were attracted by the evangelism of Ríos Montt. Supplies for the early pacification work in Nebaj came from Love Lift International, the relief division of Gospel Outreach. Help also came from such figures as Pat Robertson of the Christian Broadcasting Network

(CBN), Lorin Cunningham of Youth with a Mission, and Representative Jack Kemp (R-NY). Another influential individual in the pilot pacification work in the Ixil Triangle was Harris Whitbeck, a U.S. citizen who served as an adviser to Ríos Montt and who had close connections with several PVOs that worked with the military, including Partners of the Americas, the Carroll Behrhorst Clinic, and the Program to Assist the Residents of the Altiplano (PAVA). Whitbeck arranged for military transport of supplies and PVO personnel to areas chosen by the military for its initial pacification work.

During the Ríos Montt regime, the Summer Institute of Linguistics (SIL), part of the U.S.-based Wycliffe Bible Translators, re-entered the Nebaj area. While the work of the institute involved translation of the Bible into Indian languages, the institute also served to propagate a vigorously anticommunist ideology. According to SIL's Helen Elliot, "Ríos Montt heard that we knew the language and helicoptered us into Nebaj, and then we started distributing blankets, food, and tin roofing as well as setting up schools." She said the institute served as "a bridge between the military and the people." In 1986, SIL signed a contract with AID for its Integrated Rural Development Program for the Mayan People. Among other things, the project translates government and military documents into Indian languages. SIL also trained most of the people for AID's bilingual education program.

While nearly a hundred evangelical groups currently operate programs in Guatemala, other religious organizations have not been allowed such freedom. Among the main victims of the military repression that dominated the country since 1976 were catechists of the Catholic Church. These catechists often worked with PVOs or government ministers as social service and community trainers. Evangelists moved in to fill the void created when Catholic churches were closed, catechists killed, and clerics driven out of the country. Today, in many Indian villages, there is a fundamentalist mission on every other block and many evangelists now fill the training positions formerly held by progressive catechists. Most of the material support for the new evangelist operations comes from believers in the United States, but many also receive food, transportation, and funding from the U.S. government.

Not all Protestant denominations share the conservative philosophy of evangelicals like Jimmy Swaggart, Jerry Falwell, and Pat Robertson—all of whom have missions in Guatemala. According to a Guatemalan minister with a traditional Protestant church, "The main goals of these new religious sects, besides raising money, is to keep Christians divided, implant conservative work-ethic values, and, probably most important, to keep the status quo."⁴¹ Another Protestant who heads a major Guatemalan PVO felt that the military was using the right-wing evangelical groups to pacify people by keeping them divided and dependent. "These U.S. evangelist sects," he said, "don't address the problems of Guatemala but advocate individualistic solutions. They are manipulating people with their faith."⁴²

Along with the right-wing evangelists, two anticommunist Catholic organizations from the United States established operations in Guatemala. Roberto Alejos, a prominent oligarch who allowed his land to be used for training the Bay of Pigs invasion force against Cuba in 1959, directs the activities of the Knights of Malta and Americares in Guatemala. Alejos, who proudly displayed photos of himself with the pope, said that the two U.S. organizations work together in Guatemala, where they distribute medicine and other supplies. Americares solicits donations and contributions from U.S. corporations, and the local Knights branch arranges for the storage, transportation, and delivery of the supplies within Guatemala. Alejos credited the guerrillas for the opening up of the highlands. "Now the government and everybody else is there trying to solve the problems," he announced.

Another set of new-right humanitarians also came to Guatemala at the outset of the military's pacification plan. The Air Commandos Association (ACA), a group of retired U.S.

military officers headed by General Harry Aderholt, boasted that they distributed over $10 million in supplies in 1986, mostly to the development poles. The Air Commandos established a clinic in Nebaj, and set the staff working intimately with the local military outpost, depending on the army for transportation, housing, and food. Jody Duncan, the daughter of an ACA member and director of the group's operation in the Ixil Triangle, explained that most ACA members had worked in Vietnam and Laos in pacification programs and wanted to put their goodwill and experience to work in Central America. Her view of the situation in the Altiplano conflicted with that of most observers and residents, except for the military itself. "There is no fear of the military here," she claimed. "You can see kids playing with the soldiers in the streets. The guerrillas, not the military, are responsible for all the destruction up here." Accounts of military violence were explained, she said, by the practice of the guerrillas stealing, and then wearing military uniforms to deceive the people.

Another flag-waving group, the Washington-based National Defense Council (NDC) organized a medicine distribution network through the Guatemalan military. In 1985, NDC bragged that it handed out $12 million worth of supplies in the conflict areas. "We believe in liberation, private enterprise, and the constitution," crowed Carlos Ramirez, NDC's director in Guatemala.

Several, more "traditional" PVOs have also undertaken projects that contribute to the army's pacification of conflict areas. An official of the Salvation Army said that in 1984 AID pressured his organization to work in the highlands. AID's petitions to the Salvation Army were repeatedly turned down at the lower levels of the organization, but the National Board finally acceded, bowing to the argument that they could not refuse to help Guatemalans simply because of politics. "But they don't see the other side," lamented this Salvation Army representative. "They don't understand that it's just as political to be giving aid."[43]

AID also enlisted Project Hope to assist in caring for displaced persons in the highlands. Under the supervision of the army, Project Hope helped refugees with housing, health care, and other basic needs. In addition to its work among the displaced, the PVO took over an "integrated rural development" project in San Marcos in the western highlands. Project Hope also collaborated with PAVA on a needs assessment for the highlands—a study that assisted AID and the Guatemalan military in targeting pacification projects.

CARE, the largest PVO operating in Guatemala, distributes PL480 Title II food in areas of conflict through its Mother and Infant Care program and various food-for-work projects. Most prominent in the development pole of Playa Grande in the Franja Transversal del Norte, CARE distributed food to about 6,000 families and managed a nontraditional agroexport production project to grow cardamom. CARE has also cooperated closely with AID and the Guatemalan army in Playa Grande. Rejecting criticism of its role in the pacification effort, Christian Nill of the CARE office in Guatemala City protested, "We try to do our own work in Quiché and Huehuetenango because it is where the poorest people are."

Another PVO relying on U.S. government assistance is the Penny Foundation—known in Guatemala as Fundación del Centavo (FUNDACEN). Created in the 1960s with money from the AID-backed Pan American Development Foundation, it is directing AID's Commercial Land Markets Project. This $12 million project was conceived by AID as a way to distribute plots to landless *campesinos* without having to expropriate land. With AID financing, the project functions somewhat like a real estate agency, arranging sales to *campesinos* who could not afford to buy land at commercial interest rates. AID then provides the new landholders with economic assistance to produce nontraditional agroexports. Both the government and AID hope to divert the building pressure among *campesinos* for real land reform by promoting this project.

DEVELOPMENT AND SECURITY UNDER A CIVILIAN GOVERNMENT

When Vinicio Cerezo took over the presidency in 1986, the army's presence in rural Guatemala had never been more comprehensive. It had created a network of outposts throughout the conflict zones; and through the IICC system had given itself an official role in all development work. The Civilian Affairs division supervised the work of over 1,800 promoters (trainers), and the CRN was at its strongest. (In 1987, Cerezo appointed Rolando Paiz Maselli, a businessman who had worked closely with S-5 in designing the development poles, to head the CRN.) The military had not eliminated the leftist insurgents, but the combination of terror and pacification severed the links that had developed between the rural population and the guerrillas.

Democratization was included in the military's counterinsurgency plan as early as 1982. The military regarded the election of a civilian government as a way to reduce the appeal of the guerrillas, improve the country's international image, pacify popular discontent, and attract foreign aid. In addition, the military wanted the burden of a heavily indebted and recessive economy placed on the shoulders of civilian politicians. In 1984, Mejía Víctores proclaimed a "democratic opening" as part of that year's national program of Institutional Renewal 1984. The plan called for elections for a National Constituent Assembly, a campaign to find international aid, and intensified rural development in conflict areas. The following year, the military announced its Stability 1985 plan, which called for presidential elections, further attempts to better international relations, and extension of pacification programs. The army labeled 1986 the year of Consolidation.

The election victory of Vinicio Cerezo did not come as a surprise to most observers. It was a vote of hope for an end to state terrorism, and many regarded Cerezo's candidacy as the last chance for peaceful reform. But Cerezo came to the National Palace with his hands tied. In fact, he helped tie them himself. Sharing power with the military was something for which the Christian Democrats had long prepared themselves. During the 1970s, the party ran developmentalist military candidates in the presidential elections (General Efraín Ríos Montt in 1974 and ex-CRN head General Ricardo Peralta Méndez in 1978). Cerezo explained this concept of joint power in his book *The Army: An Alternative,* in which he said that the military has played an important development role in other third world countries. He proposed "the creation of a new order, the key to which will be the taking of power by the National Army and the Christian Democrats."[44]

Shortly after his inauguration, Cerezo quipped that he had been "given the government but not the power." The power rested in the hands of the military and the oligarchy. In its quest to enter the National Palace, the Christian Democrats during the previous decade had worked to gain allies among both the economic elite and the military. The party dropped much of its ideology of "economic justice" while adopting a pragmatic, opportunistic approach. The way to power was through the powerful, and the Christian Democrats actively integrated oligarchs and officers into their ranks.

Cerezo, a skilled politician, talked like a populist during the election campaign, promising to lead the way to democracy and development. He portrayed himself as a popular leader uncompromised by the bloody past and ready to fight for a new future for Guatemala. All the popular sectors supported Cerezo's candidacy, and even the coalition of guerrilla groups, the Guatemala National Revolutionary Unity, promised to give Cerezo a chance to turn the country around. On the wave of this support, Cerezo and the Christian Democrats finally arrived at the National Palace. But they came deeply compromised not only by their alliances with the military and oligarchy but also by promises made during the campaign.

Besides pledging not to infringe on the considerable power of the military, Cerezo assured the oligarchy that there would be no programs like agrarian reform that challenged their wealth. Before assuming office, he agreed not to tackle the country's two main obstacles to broad-based democracy and development, namely the military and the oligarchy. As added insurance, the Mejía Víctores regime that preceded Cerezo issued a series of decrees to formalize the civil defense patrols and Inter-Institutional Coordinating Committees and to protect military officers from any possible future prosecution for human rights abuses.

During his first year, the new president held firm to his promises to the military and elite despite mounting popular pressure for land reform, an end to the civil patrols, and the prosecution of those responsible for human rights violations. Upon taking office, Cerezo announced a program of "harmonization" *(concertación)* and stabilization. With the military watching and AID giving guidance, the Christian Democrats and the main business organizations formulated the new government's economic program. Excluded from this harmony and victimized by the resulting economic stabilization plan were the popular sectors. The program called for the liberalization of prices, incentives for export production, and a cutback of social services. In appointing members of his administration, Cerezo selected a team of fiscal conservatives who adhered to the monetary theories espoused by U.S. supply-side economists like Milton Friedman. The stabilization program hit workers, peasants, and the middle class hard, with real wages dropping precipitously, prices skyrocketing for basic goods, and social services disappearing. The interests of the majority who had voted for Cerezo were ignored after the election was over. During his first year in office, Cerezo was able to proceed with this austerity plan without causing widespread protests because of the lack of strong popular organizations—something that is likely to change before his term expires.

Despite the new government's obvious efforts to accede to the wishes of the business community, especially the export-oriented sectors, it found itself the target of vicious criticism by the political parties more closely associated with the economic elite. The smallest overture to the popular sectors and the reluctance of the Cerezo government to express support for the Nicaraguan contras were both roundly condemned. The opposing right-wing political parties also criticized the government's inability to move the economy forward. But, as Cerezo was quick to point out, the private sector itself was showing no signs of increasing investments and exports despite all the incentives and monetary measures the government had instituted on its behalf. The oligarchy made no concessions for the sake of national harmony. By demanding everything its way, the economic elite proved to be a politically and economically destabilizing force—in much the same way that the demands of the Salvadoran oligarchy served to destabilize the democratization experiment in that country (See Chapter Seven). Without social reforms and stifled by an unchecked oligarchy, the conditions that bred popular rebellion in the 1970s were not eased, but rather were exacerbated.

Those who hoped that Cerezo would use his election victory to begin chopping away at the military's power were sorely disappointed. During his first year, the new president scrupulously abided by the terms under which the army had agreed to give up the National Palace. To watch over the civilian government in order to insure pliant behavior, the military placed two colonels in the government to accompany the president and vice-president in all their public dealings. As a consequence, little was done to assert civilian control over the apparatus of counterinsurgency. The civil patrols, although reduced in number, continued to be an important part of the military's rural infrastructure, especially in the conflict areas. The IICCs also continued to function, albeit only on a local and regional level, and were renamed development councils. Although the IICCs were no longer headed officially by the military commander, it was still at the discretion of the local army command to authorize all development activity in the conflict zones. In addition to the power exercised by the area commanders, the local military commissioners (civilians delegated to carry out military functions such as recruiting) and the Civilian Affairs teams kept tight military control over even the most isolated hamlets.

At its inception, the Christian Democratic government decided that agricultural development could be directed in a way that extended its political base. Cerezo appointed Rene de León Schlotter, the founder of the party, as head of the newly created Ministry of Urban and Rural Development. The party hoped to develop export-oriented cooperatives and small businesses to spur rural development and build a rural base of support for itself.

At least initially, the military agreed to increased civilian control over rural development activities. It was interested in devoting more of its attention to training, improving its combat capabilities, and restructuring its network of army bases. Its new slogan, "stability for development," indicated this heightened concern for military security and a reduced emphasis on the soft side of the war. In part because of renewed concern about its internal strength and in part because it was losing enthusiasm for development, the military was ready to give the civilian government a role in pacification.

Despite this window of opportunity, the Cerezo government, for its part, did nothing to challenge the military's pacification infrastructure. In fact, both Cerezo and Minister León Schlotter personally inaugurated new development poles. Cerezo told one group of new development pole residents in Alta Verapaz that, "The Army, the civilian government, teachers, *campesinos*, and workers, forgetting their differences, must work together in order to live in peace."[45] According to León Schlotter, the development poles were "a fundamental part of the policy of the government to benefit the people." He said that a "principal objective" of his ministry was "to combat the subversion ideologically, in much the same way as the Army has been doing through the Inter-Institutional Coordination System."[46]

Campaign rhetoric notwithstanding, the Christian Democrats' grand plans for rural development went nowhere. One reason was the refusal to cooperate in government-sponsored development initiatives by the private sector and opposition parties. They objected on the grounds that business, not the public sector, should be given the main role in rural development, further charging that the party's plans were simply a vehicle to extend the power of the Christian Democrats. The party's lack of experience in the countryside, political infighting, and a tight budget also contributed to the government's failure to follow through with its development plans.

Over time, the Cerezo government's inability to implement its plans became a rising concern for the military. In the development poles, military commanders complained that the social services and development programs the army had started were falling apart because of the inefficiency of the civilian government. This concern became manifest in a document prepared by the Civilian Affairs Section entitled, "Analysis of the Failures of the Government's Integral Development Strategy."[47]

The lack of progress in the development poles, or the "integrated development areas" as they started to be called in 1986, was a problem both for the residents of these areas and for the military. Without food, work, and sufficient land, Indians were abandoning the model villages, and the pacification campaign was losing momentum. This disintegrating situation may herald a reassertion of full control over rural development by the military. Even before the end of 1986, local military commanders claimed that Indian peasants were asking the army to regain control from the corrupt and inefficient politicians.

It is certainly true that the military, because of its authority and resources, implemented projects faster than the civilian government. But the failure of rural development programs pointed more to the weaknesses of the actual strategy than to difficulty with implementation. The military was able to promote beans, guns, and model villages. Yet both the military and the civilian government were unable to spur real development.

The pacification program that began with "Beans and Guns" allowed the army to gain initial control over the Indian population but failed to show any long-term results. What passed for development were really tactics to maintain power over the population. Food distribution and work programs—the real drawing cards of pacification—proved to be only temporary solutions to deep-seated problems. Once the roads and model villages were built, there was no more work, and consequently no food. In model villages, Indian families sit in their new electrified *techo minimo* homes with no food, no work, and no plots to farm. Instead of improving, conditions are deteriorating in these target areas.

Not wanting to tackle the economic inequities in Guatemala, the government turned to foreign-designed development strategies (like the promotion of nontraditional agroexport production) which leave historical oligarchic structures intact and offer little hope for the poor. Nontraditional crops are not suitable for most of the mountainous highlands, and the majority of Indian farmers have neither enough land nor resources to risk cultivating crops that do not have a secure market and which they themselves do not eat. Completed model villages like Acúl and Acamál have been unable to produce marketable quantities of nontraditional cash crops, let alone surpluses in staple goods like corn and beans. In the name of development, the Indians have sadly watched while pacification measures designed to increase "security" are substituted for those that would give them economic independence.

In pursuing its strategy of counterinsurgency through terror, pacification, and democratization, the military demonstrated its efficiency and sophistication. But the strategy neither eradicated the roots of rebellion nor eliminated the insurgent forces. It did pacify Guatemala, but probably only temporarily. Unless the government takes bold steps to meet the needs of the popular sectors and reduce the power of the oligarchs and generals, it is likely that the country will once again fall victim to a new cycle of political instability and mass terror.

CHAPTER **7** The Other War
in El Salvador

> *"Military efforts [are] not sufficient to win a*
> *guerrilla war. Such a war is less a fight for*
> *territory than for people."*
> —AID Mission, San Salvador, 1985.

For proponents of LIC doctrine, Central America is a field laboratory for post-Vietnam counterinsurgency strategy—with El Salvador as the main testing ground. From the beginning of the civil war in El Salvador, the U.S. government has been determined to orchestrate a counterinsurgency war that pays close attention to political as well as military considerations. The campaign to win (or at least control) the allegiance of the Salvadoran people has played a crucial role in the U.S. counterinsurgency project. The "other war" of pacification has closely complemented the military campaign.[1] The way the other war has been played out in El Salvador clearly illustrates both the power and the limits of low intensity strategy.

The other war has never been simply a sideshow of the civil war. Since the formation of the military-civilian junta in early 1980, the nonlethal side of the war has been at the forefront of the counterinsurgency conflict. At least three times more foreign aid has been devoted to the other war than to the shooting war.

AID serves as the quartermaster for the other war, coordinating a seemingly bottomless supply of funds, provisions, and consultants that constitute its nonmilitary bailiwick. The agency also works closely with the U.S. Military Group (Mil-

145

Group), CIA, United States Information Agency, National Security Council, and embassy staff in formulating and implementing nonmilitary aspects of counterinsurgency strategy.

The three main thrusts of U.S. economic aid programs—stabilization, pacification, and private-sector support—have all been operative in El Salvador. Without U.S. economic aid, the counterinsurgency war would have quickly lost its forward momentum. It would be difficult to underestimate AID's role in El Salvador since 1980. Between 1980 and 1987, the agency distributed over $1.6 billion in economic aid and over $325 million in food assistance.[2] "This country could not survive one day if AID cut off economic assistance," observed a highly respected Salvadoran scholar—an opinion that is shared by most observers of Salvadoran political affairs.

Through the provision of ESF grants, Title I food assistance, and various other credits, AID tries to stabilize El Salvador's war-torn economy and weak government institutions. Part of this stabilization effort is directed at the business community in the belief that a healthy, export-oriented private sector would revive the economy and provide a strong bulwark against revolution. AID also guides and funds the evolving pacification efforts associated with the U.S. counterinsurgency project. It plays a key role in all major aspects of pacification, including the implementation of social programs, political reforms, and civic action.

With the help of the American Institute for Free Labor Development (AIFLD), the agency spearheaded the agrarian reform program of 1980, which was designed to win over rural support for the new government. Politically, AID helped plan and pay for all elections in the country since 1982; and it provided the funds to organize the popular base of support for the Christian Democratic Party. From the institution of the National Plan of Security and Development in 1983 to the more recent United to Reconstruct pacification plan, AID grants have enabled the military to proceed with its efforts to control the rural population through the distribution of supplies and services.

The enormous sums of economic assistance injected into El Salvador since 1980 reflects U.S. concern with the current leftist threat. But even during the 1960s and 1970s—years of direct military rule and no visible insurgency—El Salvador was also a favored recipient of U.S. aid. In the mid-1960s, AID recommended increased support for El Salvador, telling Congress that the country was continuing on its "course of steady progress" and praising its military government as "a model for other Alliance [for Progress] countries."

During the pre-war period, AID found that it could work well with the Salvadoran military and the country's oligarchy, both of which strongly supported the agency's economic modernization plans. "El Salvador has been pushing social reform and economic development on a broad front," reported AID in 1967. The country "has taken a leading role in the Central American Common Market and has fostered a good climate for foreign investment."

REFORM AS PACIFICATION

In the 1960s, popular organizations of workers, peasants, and students began forming with the support of progressive clerics of the Catholic Church. At the same time, the United States started to pay more attention to El Salvador, particularly in the context of the Alliance for Progress. But instead of supporting poor and progressive sectors, U.S. economic aid bolstered conservative labor organizations and reactionary industrialists while military and police aid strengthened the repressive apparatus.

During the 1970s, popular organizations became increasingly radicalized. After the Salvadoran armed forces prevented an elected civilian government from taking power in 1972, many Salvadorans concluded that there was no hope for change through the electoral process. The popular organizations expanded as students, workers, peasants, and church people joined together in strikes and marches demanding reform and an end to repression. But in the late 1970s, repression intensified under the regime of U.S.-trained General Carlos Humberto Romero. Death squads and rural paramilitary units led the assault against the nonviolent popular opposition.

In October 1979, just months after the Sandinistas overthrew Somoza in Nicaragua, a coup in El Salvador led by young, reform-minded officers ousted General Romero. Washington refused to lend full support to the new junta government, which included Social Democrat Guillermo Ungo, who was closely tied to popular organizations and is currently a leader of the Democratic Revolutionary Front (FDR). Instead, the Carter administration in early 1980 backed the formation of another military-civilian junta that included hardline military officers and the right wing of the Christian Democratic Party. Denied the right to assume his elected post in 1972, José Napoleón Duarte was chosen to head the U.S.-backed junta.

In March 1980, the junta announced a series of reforms designed to create a base of popular and financial support for the government. These changes included nationalization of the banking sector, nationalization of agroexport trading, and a land distribution program. The agrarian reform program was the most prominent part of the package, but the reforms were accompanied by increased repression of dissidents. Only a few days after the announcement of the agrarian reform, the military declared a state of siege, and the counterinsurgency war began in earnest with ever-increasing infusions of U.S. military and economic aid. In April 1980, the mass organizations and two left-of-center political parties (Social Democrats and Popular Social Christian Movement) formed the FDR. Death squads responded by wiping out or driving into exile hundreds of leaders of the popular opposition. The Farabundo Martí National Liberation Front (FMLN) was created later in 1980 to link the four guerrilla armies who were now openly fighting the new junta.

The Promise of Agrarian Reform

Although opposed by the oligarchy, the land redistribution plan enjoyed the support of the military high command. The main objectives of the plan were to create a political base for a "centrist" government and to prevent the further radicalization of the peasantry. From its inception, the agrarian reform was a top-down program controlled and financed by the United States. The decrees instituting the program were hastily drawn up with little discussion or consultation.

The program was divided into three categories of land appropriation and distribution.* Soon after the announcement of the reform, it was hailed by AID and the U.S. embassy as a bold step to change unjust land tenure and improve the lot of the poor. In 1980, AIFLD consultants Roy Prosterman and Mary Temple claimed that the program would become "the most sweeping agrarian reform in the history of Latin America when fully implemented."[3] The amount of land scheduled for expropriation and the number of potential beneficiaries (300,000 *campesino* families) did make the program seem like a major shakeup in the country's land tenure. In the U.S. Congress and in foreign capitals, news of the land reform proposal was taken as strong evidence that the new government was serious about its promises to undermine oligarchic power. A massive public-

---

*Phase I targeted estates with over 1,200 acres and covered 10–15 percent of the country's arable land. The Phase I land was to be redistributed to cooperatives formed among the former full-time employees of the expropriated estates. Phase II was directed at holdings between 220 and 1,200 acres and covered about 20 percent of the nation's farmland. It was called the "heart of the reform" because it was aimed at the economic base of the oligarchy. Due to strong opposition by the landowners, Phase II of the program was quickly dropped. Phase III included all rental lands under 17 acres, accounting for another 10 percent of the farmland. Under the law, peasants cultivating these rental properties were eligible to apply for title to the land. Theoretically, 40–45 percent of the nation's land was to be redistributed.

ity campaign about the reform instilled hope that life was finally improving for the rural poor. With a bottomless budget from AID, AIFLD deployed hundreds of "promoters" to organize rural support for the reform and for the new military-civilian junta.

The Salvadoran agrarian reform was designed by U.S. experts, financed by U.S. economic aid, and carried out by U.S. organizers and technicians. The month the program was announced, El Salvador received a large shipment of military aid, a big inducement for the military to support the land redistribution. Determined U.S. support for the program and a flood of U.S. dollars into the economy smothered most opposition to the program from the oligarchy. The promise of compensation for their holdings in cash (25 percent of value) and bonds (75 percent) somewhat mollified angry landowners.

The AID mission in San Salvador directed the program and considered it primarily as a tool of political stabilization. The Salvadoran land reform, it said, was "a political imperative to help prevent political collapse, strike a blow to the left, and help prevent radicalization of the rural population." To carry out this strategy, the program set out to create a sector of conservative small farmers and a network of cooperatives organized by AIFLD.

Phase III, which gave *campesinos* title to rented plots, was designed not to improve the life of these peasants but to give them a proprietary interest in the country. This phase was tacked onto the program at the last minute for AID and AIFLD by Roy Prosterman, a land reform specialist who had no direct knowledge of Latin America. The basic concept of his Phase III plan was to turn over small parcels of land to 117,000 peasant families, giving them an economic and political stake in the U.S.-backed government. Prosterman had designed an almost identical program for AID as part of the U.S. rural pacification campaign in Vietnam. In fact, he gave the Salvadoran program the same name he used for his Vietnam agrarian reform, "Land to the Tiller." Having failed in Vietnam, Prosterman saw a second chance in El Salvador to "turn the tables" on the guerrillas.[4]

While the underlying goal of the agrarian reform was predominantly political, AID considered the political and economic implications of the reform to be closely interwoven. Discussing the Phase III program, one AID official exclaimed, "There is nothing more conservative than the small farmer. We're going to be breeding capitalists like rabbits."[5] Initially, AID (like Prosterman) was convinced that, with technical assistance from AIFLD and other quasi-private organizations, the Phase III beneficiaries would become an economically important sector of farm owner-operators that would boost the production of basic grains and be tightly integrated into the capitalist agricultural economy. It soon became obvious, though, that most Phase III lands could not support even one family let alone produce large marketable harvests.

Phase I properties were turned over to peasant cooperatives, which were organized by AIFLD representatives. AIFLD attempted to use these cooperatives as its base for a "democratic" peasant movement. Cooperative leaders received technical as well as ideological training from AIFLD, and many of them were put on AIFLD's payroll. The decision to create cooperatives instead of subdividing Phase I lands for individual beneficiaries was made because AIFLD was concerned about the loss of production efficiency that would result.[6]

AIFLD, which had directed rural pacification efforts since the mid-1960s, was given the leading role in coordinating the critical pacification work of the 1980s. Using an organization it funded and created, the Salvadoran Communal Union (UCS), as its organizing base, AIFLD developed a social infrastructure in government-controlled rural areas to build peasant support for the reform process. It also organized land reform beneficiaries to support U.S.-backed "democratization" and counterinsurgency initiatives. Peasant organizations created by AIFLD were especially prominent in the 1980–1984 period when widespread repression obstructed organizing by independent groups. AID recognized that the political objectives of agrarian reform would not be achieved simply by distributing land. Peasants in the reform sector had to be given at least the illusion of power and participation in the reform process. AIFLD did this through a "massive information campaign" that flooded the countryside with radio and written propaganda about the important place that *campesinos* had in what the army called the "new El Salvador."[7]

The Reform Crumbles

To justify its ever-increasing aid requests for El Salvador, the Reagan administration often pointed to the alleged success of the agrarian reform program. Yet behind the administration's wall of favorable propaganda was an ill-conceived, blood-soaked program. AID's own evaluations of the agrarian reform consistently concluded that Phase I cooperatives suffered from massive debt, no working capital, large tracts of unproductive land, labor surpluses, and weak management. According to AID's Inspector General, there was little hope that these cooperatives would ever become financially viable. They had been given poor land, no technical assistance, and were paying high interest rates to compensate former landowners. About 45 percent of the Phase I land was nonproductive and "most of the remaining land was of poor quality."[8]

Phase III beneficiaries face equally dim prospects. Six years after the reform began, only 18,000 of the 117,000 potential beneficiaries had been granted titles. Others had been given provisional titles, but AID in 1986 projected a maximum of 45,000 potential beneficiaries of Phase III. Close observers estimated the final number of beneficiaries much lower. At least one-third of those who received provisional titles were not working the land because they had been "threatened, evicted, or had disappeared."[9] Peasants have become neither food self-sufficient nor economically independent through their participation in Phase III. Most of these parcels cannot sustain continuous food production and need to be left fallow for a year or two before replanting. Yet beneficiaries are tied to the land for as much as 30 years (the time given to compensate the government for the land).[10] Laurence Simon of Oxfam America observed that the planners of the agrarian reform obviously did not consider land use patterns. "To do so would have required a commitment to rural development instead of pacification or counterinsurgency."[11] Both Phase I and III were undermined by the absence of credit, technical assistance, training, and popular participation.

As a result of the 1982 elections, Roberto D'Aubuisson's ARENA party gained a position in the coalition government, dashing *campesino* hopes that the promises of the reform would be honored. By taking control of the Ministry of Agriculture and ISTA (Salvadoran Institute for Agrarian Transformation), ARENA was able to block further redistribution and obstruct technical assistance and credit programs. When the Constituent Assembly passed a new national constitution in 1983, there was no mention of "agrarian reform." Instead, the constitution emphasized that the government "recognizes, promotes, and guarantees the right of private property" and "will promote and protect private initiative." Without specifically dismantling the land reform, the new constitution guaranteed landowners the right to rent out their property—a thinly veiled attack on Phase III. Another provision raised the maximum size for private holdings to 605 acres and gave landowners until January 1987 to sell off property above the 605 acre limit—enough time to rearrange title ownership among family members in the event that the limit is ever enforced.

Requiem for a Reform

The presidential victory of Duarte in 1984 temporarily revived hope among *campesinos* that land reforms would once more gain momentum. But those hopes were soon crushed as Duarte appeared more concerned about building support among the elite than in consolidating worker and peasant backing. Duarte's failure to enforce all phases of the agrarian reform and to increase government assistance to reform beneficiaries caused many peasant leaders to join the popular opposition to his administration. The renewed strength of the oligarchy ruled out any hope of true land reform under the Christian Democratic government. Even Duarte's Deputy Minister of Agriculture felt that the agrarian reform had run its ill-fated course. "This is a future without promise," he demurred. "Land will go back to the owners, and the people will be kicked off."[12]

Evaluated in purely political terms, land reform in El Salvador was partially successful—certainly more so than the program instituted by AID in Vietnam. At the critical stage in El Salvador, when Washington was rapidly escalating its involvement, the agrarian reform convinced congressional representatives and many U.S. citizens that the Salvadoran government was indeed on the path toward democracy and social justice. As a result, massive sums of U.S. military and economic aid flowed into the country and kept the government and the economy afloat. "The agrarian reform has done a lot to take the heat out of the massive drift of the *campesinos* to the violent left," one government official told *Time* magazine.[13] As slim as the benefits of the land reform were, many *campesinos* did feel that things were changing for the better.

Agrarian reform did not seriously weaken the oligarchy. In fact, members of the landed elite grew more determined and united in the face of the perceived threat to their land holdings with the implementation of each phase of the reform. They succeeded in postponing and substantially weakening Phase II, excluding many Phase I estates from expropriation, cutting short Phase III and impeding the flow of government services to reform beneficiaries.[14]

Instead of choosing to extend its base among workers and peasants, the Duarte government offered the oligarchy larger concessions and assurances against further reforms. Right-wing groups, like the ARENA party and the National Association of Private Enterprise, regained the initiative and demanded that Phase I estates be re-privatized. Since 1984, AID has directed an increasing sum of economic aid into agribusiness operations controlled by the very oligarchs who opposed the agrarian reform so vigorously. Moreover, it encouraged former Phase I landholders to use their compensation bonds to set up agro-industries on the lands held by floundering cooperatives. Beginning in 1985, AID also permitted the Salvadoran government to use local currency generated from U.S. food aid and Economic Support Funds to compensate landowners.

AID now dismisses the possibility that there can be any significant improvement of rural social conditions through land reform, even though land concentration in El Salvador remains among the worst in Latin America. "Hope for El Salvador's economic and social problems," says AID, "rests largely on the development of light industry, agroindustry and non-farm sources of employment."[15]

Agrarian reform was all but dead in El Salvador by 1984. AID had initially projected that between one-half and two-thirds of the rural poor would benefit. By late 1986, however, it was clear that at most only a quarter of the rural poor would receive land, with 10–15 percent being a more realistic estimate. Few among those that did "benefit" from the program actually experienced any improvement in their standard of living, and many were worse off than before. Most of the beneficiaries— both individuals and cooperatives—ended up in debt and plowing lands that are among the worst in the country. While peasants who participated must pay for their land, AID used its economic assistance programs to compensate former landowners, many of whom no longer even live in El Salvador.

El Salvador's agrarian reform neither significantly challenged the oligarchy nor improved life for the powerless. It illustrated the superficial nature of the kind of reformism sponsored by U.S. economic aid. The land reform did not go to the heart of the agrarian crisis in El Salvador but was designed only as a palliative to provide short-term political stabilization.

Nonetheless, it proved to be the boldest initiative in the U.S.-directed pacification strategy in El Salvador. After the election of Duarte, the United States veered sharply away from reformism as a pacification tactic and devoted more attention to civic action and psychological operations.

MILITARY PLANS FOR SECURITY AND DEVELOPMENT

During the first few years of the war, the reformist components of the U.S. counterinsurgency project proceeded according to plan. Through the agrarian reform, the government was able to build a rural base of support for democratization; and this popular base was instrumental in catapulting Duarte to the presidency in 1984. While the Reagan administration was philosophically closer to the right-wing parties, a Christian Democrat government with centrist credentials was considered a better vehicle for low intensity conflict than the political parties of the oligarchy.

Although the other war was going well, battlefield reports were not so positive. The reformist phase of the other war did not win enough hearts and minds to stop the continuing advance of the FMLN guerrillas. By mid–1983, the FMLN had extended its control to a third of the country and was seriously disrupting the country's economic base. Poor leadership and low morale plagued the government's armed forces. Upon reevaluating the war, the United States decided that the troops needed more assistance and better training. It was also decided that U.S. military and economic aid programs should be better coordinated.

This reevaluation of the counterinsurgency war led to the June 1983 announcement by the military command of its National Plan of Security and Development. The plan had four stages: 1) ground sweeps through conflict areas to remove guerrillas, 2) securing the area by establishing civilian defense patrols, 3) the initiation of development and reconstruction projects by civilian pacification agencies, and 4) the resettlement of reconstructed villages with internal refugees. The State Department described the National Plan this way:

> The primary objectives in this strategy have been to dislodge the guerrillas from strongholds, disrupt their logistic networks, secure guerrilla-controlled areas, and, in coordination with civilian agencies, initiate a civic action program to rebuild the social and economic infrastructure. This program consists of reopening schools, building roads, establishing public health and vaccination programs, distributing food, conducting outreach and amnesty programs, and training local civil defense forces to protect themselves following the departure of the military.[16]

The National Plan, the first coordinated attempt in El Salvador to combine military operations with civic action, was seen as a critical new stage in the counterinsurgency war by U.S. and Salvadoran military officers. "This strategy is a turning point in the war," said one U.S. military planner, "We will win or lose on this operation."[17] Lieutenant Jorge Alberto Cruz of the Salvadoran army agreed with that assessment, stating that the plan's call for economic assistance was "the key to winning over the population and in that way winning the war." Colonel Joseph Stringham, then chief of U.S. MilGroup in El Salvador asserted: "The success of the National Plan will ultimately determine the outcome of the war."

To carry out the development (pacification) part of the National Plan, the National Commission for Restoration of Areas (CONARA) was formed in 1983. The goal of CONARA was "to strengthen local authorities and to assist them in restoring essential public services and promoting development in the newly secured areas."[18] Its director and chief officers are former military men, whose new jobs entailed coordinating the reconstruction and development work of civilian ministries. A similar organization called the National Commission for Aid to the Displaced (CONADES) was formed to manage refugee programs. Both organizations, as well as all other components of pacification, relied on AID and other foreign aid organizations for funds and planning assistance.[19]

In the FMLN's opinion, the National Plan was "an integrated plan of counterinsurgency strategy, similar to the pacification program that the United States used in Vietnam."[20] Indeed, several of the U.S. advisers for the National Plan acknowledged that the plan was loosely modeled after the Coordinated Rural Development Support (CORDS), managed by AID in Vietnam. The difference, they said, was that this time pacification would be handled in the field mainly by non-U.S. troops.

Two key Salvadoran provinces—San Vicente and Usulután—were chosen as the first targets of the National Plan. Pacification activities in these agricultural areas, considered a "key battlefield" by the State Department, were labeled Operation Well-Being.[21] The plan called for sweeps of the two provinces by elite U.S.-trained battalions to dislodge the guerrillas followed by a securing of the area with civil defense patrols and army outposts.

Operation Well-Being flopped despite the presence of the elite troops and the injection of at least $20 million in U.S. economic aid. The guerrillas avoided combat with the army battalions; and when the counterinsurgency battalions departed, guerrilla units easily moved back into the area. The army was largely unable to form a network of civil defense patrols due to the unwillingness of villagers to join the patrols, either because they knew they would never be able to withstand an FMLN attack or simply because they had no desire to "defend" themselves against the guerrillas, popularly known as the *muchachos*. So tenuous was the army's hold on these zones that the FMLN guerrillas were actually able to direct the course of reconstruction. As a mayor of one town in the province of San Vicente said, "To keep our schools open and our AID projects functional, we have to accept the terms the guerrillas set."[22]

Security was not the only problem. It was obvious by late

1984 that the development component of the National Plan was also failing. Food and other supplies were diverted by local military commanders and government officials. AID grew exasperated at the mismanagement and corruption that accompanied Operation Well-Being. Despite vast sums of U.S. economic aid, the National Plan could not stop the guerrillas from occupying large parts of the country and even maintaining alternative municipal governments in some areas.[23]

In 1984, the National Plan's extensive "development" proposals were scaled down because of the inability of the army to provide security in rural areas. CONARA and CONADES continued to expand their food-for-work and other relief projects but there was less emphasis on "rebuilding" areas of conflict. To avoid the security problems experienced during Operation Well-Being, the army initiated short-term civic action projects that did not require the steady presence of government troops in a community. This variation of the National Plan still required participation from civilian ministries in food distribution and the provision of medical services, but the army was clearly in command.

In mid-1984, the military greatly expanded its psychological operations and civic action departments. Working with the U.S. MilGroup and AID, military units began hosting civic action programs in rural villages in conflict zones. When army troops occupied an area, civic action teams would supervise handouts of clothing and food and conduct psychological operations blaming the FMLN for the social and economic problems created by the war. Also in 1984, the military high command began formulating a pacification program known as Plan Simiente (Seed Plan) that bore close resemblance to the notorious pacification campaign conducted by the Guatemalan army. Plan Simiente even sported the same alliterated pacification slogan used in Guatemala: *"Trabajos, Techos, y Tortillas"* (Jobs, Shelter, Food). A resettlement phase called Project Mil promised to put displaced families to work in new agricultural projects. However, neither Plan Simiente nor the related Project Mil ever went beyond the conceptual stage, as the international donors that the army hoped to attract were put off by the similarities with the Guatemalan army's campaign.

United to Reconstruct

Aid and training from the United States made the Salvadoran military a stronger, more disciplined, and better organized institution. While recognizing the important role that the civilian government played in the overall counterinsurgency project, the military high command grew increasingly critical of the Duarte government. It was frustrated with the government's failure to maintain popular support and its inability to unite the country behind the war.

Infused with the LIC concept of "total war" where all resources are combined, the military began taking steps to assume control of the political as well as the military side of the counterinsurgency war. Soon after Duarte took office, Defense Minister Eugenio Vides Casanova declared: "All the resources of the state must be placed at the service of our final victory. Only by completely defeating the enemies of the fatherland can we recover peace and prosperity."[24] The armed forces were of the opinion that most of the country's political leaders were more concerned with holding office and securing favors than they were in winning the counterinsurgency war. What was needed was the joining together of all anticommunist forces, and the military decided that it was the only institution capable of forging such a patriotic union.[25]

In July 1986, General Adolfo Blandón, chief of the military high command, presented another version of the National Plan called United to Reconstruct. The rejuvenated National Plan resulted from planning sessions with U.S. military advisers stationed in El Salvador and a team of civic action experts from the U.S. Southern Command (SOUTHCOM) in Panama. The plan, which incorporated most elements of the U.S. Internal Defense and Development counterinsurgency strategy, called for a joint effort by all sectors of society, all government ministries, and international donors to defeat the guerrillas and reconstruct the nation. The announcement of the United to Reconstruct campaign represented a major success for the advocates of LIC strategy in El Salvador.

The United to Reconstruct plan covered three phases of counterinsurgency and pacification: 1) "clean up" operations, 2) area consolidation, 3) organization of civil patrols, and 4) reconstruction and development. Blandón said that "psychological operations, the organizing and training of civil defense forces, military civic action, and the active participation of the population of each area" would all play critical roles in the United to Reconstruct campaign. Lieutenant Colonel Agapito Delagarza, the U.S. MilGroup officer in charge of the National Plan, described United to Reconstruct as a campaign "to unite all aspects of society—armed forces, government, political parties, labor unions, churches, the private sector, and peasants."[26]

Like the National Plan, United to Reconstruct received most of its funds from AID by way of government agencies like CONARA and private voluntary organizations. The emphasis of the United to Reconstruct drive was on the coordination by the military of all nonlethal programs in the countryside. The plan was projected to affect not just conflict zones but all 14 provinces. In each province, U.S. and Salvadoran civic action officials chose target areas for the new pacification initiative. According to AID, "All government agencies, including the military forces, have made the United to Reconstruct zones their number one priority." Lieutenant Colonel Delagarza explained, "CONARA, Psyops, civic action programs, civil affairs, and military operations" would all be used to consolidate these targeted geographic zones. Once that was achieved, the pacification campaign was expected to "expand like a drop of oil to cover the whole country."

Prodding by U.S. advisers for the military to adopt an LIC strategy was one reason for the institution of the United to Reconstruct plan. But the campaign was also a direct response to the FMLN's increased dispersion of forces and intensified political organizing. Upon announcing the program, General Blandón explained that the "subversive war to take power is 90 percent political, economic, social, and ideological and only 10 percent military." It is necessary, he said, for the armed forces to devote a corresponding amount of its resources to winning the "civil population." "Obtaining a military victory is not enough," said the military chief. "It is also necessary to win in the economic, political, ideological, social, and international fields."[27]

Pressing Forward with Civic Action

With United to Reconstruct came an increased emphasis on civic action. Improving the military's public image remains a prime justification, but another primary purpose of civic action is neutralizing the influence of the guerrillas. Usually civic action took place in areas where the military had strafed and conducted ground sweeps to dislodge the guerrillas. It is considered the carrot that comes after the stick, dangled in front of the civilians living in contested areas. "Civic action is high impact, not long-term," explained Lieutenant Colonel David Steele of U.S. MilGroup. "It shows the people that the army doesn't just go in and rape."[28] AID's Richard Nelson said that civic action in El Salvador is "all about showing the flag, one day in and out again. Civic action shows the government cares for the people."

A typical civic action show often began with planes dropping propaganda leaflets on the area. The local army commander then gave a speech about the evils of communism and the virtues of the current regime. Food, toys, medicine, and clothing were handed out to villagers gathered in the plaza. Some battalions featured soldiers dressed as clowns to provide entertainment. Frequently it became a multimedia affair when the army team presented an anticommunist film from the United States, Army barbers cut hair, doctors gave vaccinations, and dentists pulled teeth. "Dental civic actions are great," said MilGroup's Ed Morrell, "because they create an instant success. Pull a tooth and the pain is gone."[29]

The army enthusiastically pushed ahead with civic action as part of its commitment to LIC strategy. In 1986, about eight U.S. advisers in El Salvador were assigned to civic action programs, and teams of SOUTHCOM experts occasionally directed planning sessions. Ed Morrell, the U.S. officer coordinating civic action in El Salvador, said that U.S. MilGroup was trying to arrange about three "civic actions" a week, providing the Salvadoran armed forces with planning assistance, training, and help in arranging the necessary supplies.

AID, through its food aid, medical programs, and development projects, is the major supplier of civic action. As MilGroup's Lieutenant Colonel Delagarza stated, "AID is involved in everything here from training mayors to civic action projects." Most AID assistance is distributed through civilian ministries of the government like CONADES and CONARA. The civic action till is also replenished by funds from the U.S. Military Assistance Program (MAP) grants and supplies from U.S. private organizations who want to help fight communism with donations of clothing, medicine, and personal effects.

To make this supply network function efficiently, cooperation between all those involved is a must, noted Lieutenant Colonel Steele. But he stressed that this cooperation works best with military discipline. "There's got to be coordination from the president of the republic right on down to what the military is doing and what is happening with economic assistance programs," he warned. "We have been pushing the coordination of military civic action with the civilian ministries, but the major problem is that the Ministry of Defense is much more organized than the civilian government ministries and doesn't like to wait around," he added.[30]

During civic action programs, the military tried to organize civil patrols from local men and boys to protect the village against "communist" advances. In return for civic action supplies, the army often insisted that villagers "volunteer." Recognizing the importance of these local units, the U.S. MilGroup assigned a team of U.S. Army Special Forces to provide trainers to the Salvadoran army officers in charge of organizing civil patrols. The successful formation of a civil patrol network, similar to the one established by the Guatemalan military, would have represented a major shift in the counterinsurgency war. It would have demonstrated military control in those conflict areas and *campesino* compliance with the government's counterinsurgency project, while at the same time denying the guerrillas their rural base. But, as with other objectives of the pacification plan, the effort to organize civil patrols fell flat. Without this network, the army was often confined in many areas to the main highways and the larger towns and villages, unless it chose to enter contested zones with a full deployment of troops.

Capturing Hearts and Minds with Private Bait

Most of the handouts (other than food) in the army's civic action events come from a steady stream of donations from U.S. private organizations. Among the largest private contributors to military civic action in El Salvador are World Medical Relief, Americares, Knights of Malta, and the Family Foundation of America. Other donors include the Christian Broadcasting Network, International Aid, Tom Dooley Foundation, National Defense Council, Salvadoran-American Foundation, Church of Christianity, Medical Benevolent Foundation, and Project Hope.

Kenneth Wells, the director of the Family Foundation of America, said he considered the military's civic action program and government refugee efforts "military warfare by another means." The Florida-based foundation has sent barrels of clothing, medicine, and toys to the military. Packed in each barrel is a U.S. flag, which Wells says "offers the only thing they [Salvadoran recipients] can pray for."[31] The foundation relies on a web of corporate backers and charity organizations for its donations while counting on the Pentagon and the Salvadoran military to get the supplies to the Salvadoran people. "My goal is to make armies serve the people," beamed Wells. "A new method of war is developing: Number one, we'll have brilliantly trained soldiers, not only in weaponry, but in service to the people. Secondly, we'll have a flooding of civic action by people who have surpluses; and last, we'll have trained people in villages capable of defending their villages."[32]

The Knights of Malta, an elite international Catholic organization, prides itself on its good connections with the Salvadoran armed forces. The group serves as an intermediary between the military and such U.S. donor groups as Americares and the Tom Dooley Foundation. To augment the private supply effort, the Knights established a warehouse for incoming supplies and a distribution network closely coordinated with the military high command. Miguel Salaverria, a leading Knight and major coffee exporter, said that the Pentagon was "very helpful" in shipping its goods to El Salvador. Once donations arrived in the country, the Salvadoran army handled transportation.[33]

The Knights contributed to the pacification efforts by supplying and working with the army on various refugee resettlement projects and operating clinics and an orphanage. Gerald Coughlin, the director of the Salvadoran Knights and a leader of the U.S. business community in El Salvador, said that the Knights of Malta also had its own "private intelligence network" to sort out pro-government from leftist refugees.

Psyops: A Battle for Minds

The U.S. Embassy, an imposing concrete fortress in San Salvador, is the command center for a critical component of the U.S. strategy of low intensity conflict: psychological warfare. Winning minds has been elevated to a political-military science in El Salvador. From their perch in the embassy, USIA and CIA agents and officers in the Special Forces direct the psychological operations aimed to shape public opinion and change the course of events through well-placed information. The full extent of Psyops in El Salvador is not known, but what is known shows that covert and overt mind-bending operations have become a top priority of the Salvadoran armed forces, the government, and the U.S. Embassy.

In El Salvador, USIA directs a daily information war. It distributes a package of news releases to all the newspapers, radio and TV stations, and major decision makers in the country. In addition, all the radio stations receive Voice of America programming; and USIA-produced news and cultural programs are shown in prime-time slots on two TV stations. USIA's objective is "to work with U.S. and third-country journalists to further their understanding of U.S. policy in El Salvador." Towards this end, it operates an Outreach Program that "sends out publications of keen interest to a select audience of key persons in various political parties and government ministries." And it "works closely with the Salvadoran news radio to ensure the accurate description of U.S. policy and U.S. events reach El Salvador's public."[34]

Facilitating the Salvadoran government and military in the use of sophisticated propaganda has been another task of USIA. In 1983, for example, the USIA hired a right-wing public relations agency called the Mid-America Committee for International Business and Government Operation. This U.S. agency was contracted "to provide media-training assistance to [foreign] government officials and their armed forces . . . [and] to strengthen their effectiveness in the 'War of Ideas.' " Attending one of the sessions were representatives from the Salvadoran army, the Defense Ministry, and the extreme right-wing ARENA political party.[35]

The effort to improve the armed forces' public relations office began with a 1984 trip to El Salvador by Otto Reich, director of the State Department's Office of Public Diplomacy. Following Reich's visit, Henry Cato, former chief Pentagon spokesperson and U.S. ambassador to El Salvador, was sent to advise the

Salvadoran government and military officials on public relations. The military high command took advantage of U.S. help to improve skills in public and media relations.[36] Under U.S. direction, General Blandón, an enthusiastic supporter of Psyops, reorganized the Salvadoran Psyops unit in early 1985. The colonel heading the unit said that he worked under a U.S. adviser to adapt techniques the U.S. military learned in Vietnam. "What we want to do is to take the North American propaganda methods and apply them to what we are doing here in El Salvador," he said.[37]

In July 1985, the Duarte government created the Ministry of Culture and Communications to manage its own psychological operations. Before assuming the direction of the new ministry, Julio Rey Prendes, previously Duarte's chief of staff, traveled to Washington on a USIA grant to consult with U.S. officials, including Otto Reich. Properly coached in the tools of the trade, the ministry immediately began waging a propaganda war to build support for the Duarte government and diffuse the popularity of the FDR/FMLN. Leaflets dropped over guerrilla-held zones, frequent radio and TV spots, posters, newspaper ads, and dissemination of alleged guerrilla documents were all part of this war of ideas. Rey Prendes also had an array of government-controlled media at his disposal: two of the country's six television stations, one of its two TV news programs, one radio station, production facilities that distribute canned news programs to private stations, printing presses, and 24 movie theaters.[38] In addition, Prendes could rely on the four privately owned television stations that are obliged to broadcast five-minute government "microprograms" as well as longer propaganda specials.

A regular theme of this Psyops campaign was that guerrillas, union leaders, and human-rights workers were terrorists or terrorist sympathizers. The FMLN/FDR were said to be behind all popular organizing, strikes, and opposition to the government. Demands for higher wages were equated with acts of economic sabotage. Images of guerrilla destruction were counterposed with images of the military's and AID's reconstruction efforts.

An invisible player in the Psyops effort in El Salvador is the CIA, which advised Congressional intelligence committees that it was running a covert "media relations" operation.[39] Congressional aides with access to intelligence information said that the purpose of this campaign was to change the country's image from that of a cauldron of war and death to that of a country moving toward democracy and economic progress as a result of U.S. policies.

Little Security and No Development

The National Plan, in all its variations, served as a test for LIC strategy in Central America. Despite the strong backing of the U.S. government, the results of counterinsurgency and pacification in El Salvador were not promising for Washington or for counterrevolutionary sectors within El Salvador. The National Plan and United to Reconstruct campaigns failed to meet their objectives of providing security and development.

The armed forces thought they had the security problem solved in 1985. It seemed that its increased air attack and transport capability combined with more rapid deployment of ground troops were wearing down the FMLN. The superior firepower and resources of the government forces were thought to be wearing down the guerrillas and undercutting their ability to mount major attacks. To further undermine the rebel army, the armed forces waged an offensive against the guerrilla zones of control in Guazapa, Chalatenango, and Morazan.

However, it became increasingly obvious by mid-1986 that the FMLN was not on the defensive but was responding to the military initiatives with its own offensive. The FMLN had reorganized into smaller units, spread out into every province, reduced its reliance on its zones of control, and mounted a war of attrition against both military and economic targets. This counterstrategy presented the army with new security problems. It could no longer concentrate soldiers in a few areas but was forced to deploy troops all over the country—not only to protect military sites but also to guard economic targets like mills, warehouses, bridges, electrical towers, and government buildings. By early 1987, two-thirds of the government troops were guarding nonmilitary facilities. Plans to supplement military strength with civil patrols never materialized, and desertions and low soldier morale further complicated the security problem.

The absence of sufficient security frustrated the development plans of the military. The economic side of pacification also suffered from the lack of real commitment to bettering the life of rural Salvadorans. While there was talk of embarking on agricultural development projects, in practice the army's development programs went no further than refugee relief and civic action in which supplies were distributed to captive audiences. Charity, especially in the middle of a civil war, does not win hearts and minds. The things that Salvadorans really wanted—more land, better prices for their corn and beans, higher wages, and an end to the war—were demands that neither the government nor the army was interested in meeting.

Pacification plans were beset with internal contradictions. While the purpose was supposedly to "win people not territory," the military felt it necessary to control territory in order to control people. The two axioms of counterinsurgency warfare—that security is a precondition for pacification and that controlling people is more important than controlling territory—work against each other. To provide security, the Salvadoran armed forces, finding it impossible to eliminate the guerrillas, were forced to depopulate areas. Depopulation, even when it was not accompanied by massacres and heavy army strafing, involved massive relocations and increased popular anger and revolutionary determination instead of winning new hearts and minds.

The United to Reconstruct campaign came to be known in El Salvador as "Disunited to Destroy." While the armed forces hailed United to Reconstruct as 90 percent political and only 10 percent military, the plan was both in theory and practice a militarization of politics. The LIC rhetoric about uniting all forces and resources to destroy the communist insurgency could not disguise the fact that the country was committed to an unpopular, unwinnable war. Seeing the civilian government's inability to unite the country around the counterinsurgency war, the military tried to form a coalition of "patriotic" forces. But there was no coalescing with the church, the unions, or the private sector. Only the Duarte administration and the U.S. government were willing to unite with the military. The campaign underlined the fact that the army and the government were incapable of either uniting or rebuilding the nation, let alone winning the battle for hearts and minds.

REFUGEES OF A LOW INTENSITY CONFLICT

The large population of displaced people (internal refugees) also points to the weaknesses and failures of the LIC strategy applied in El Salvador. At least 10 percent of Salvadorans have been displaced within the country, and another 10 percent have fled to other countries. The internal refugees, surviving as squatters on the outskirts of major towns or in government- or church-sponsored camps, offer living evidence that the counterinsurgency war is neither under control nor of a low-intensity nature.[40]

The number of displaced persons has increased steadily since the late 1970s. The first wave of refugees fled the terror of the death squads, and they were joined by families fleeing the brutality of U.S.-trained counterinsurgency troops and the horror of the air war. In the last few years, most refugees have been the result of the military's attempts to depopulate guerrilla strongholds. Adopting and revising an analogy frequently used by Mao Zedong, the army's counterinsurgency experts said they were "draining the sea" to deny the fish (the guerrillas) a base of popular support.

Acting under the instructions of U.S. advisers, the Salvadoran military has tried a number of versions of "draining the sea." Early on in the war, the "hunter" battalions who were supposed to provide the military shield for Operation Well-Being had little success. When the troops left, the FMLN forces returned to these supposedly secured areas, and in many cases took advantage of the "development" projects that were part of Operation Well-Being. Unable to flush out the guerrillas, the military changed tactics. Relying on intelligence provided by U.S. aerial surveillance, the armed forces began bombing and shelling guerrilla-controlled zones in Morazán and Chalatenango. Because the FMLN had virtually no fixed positions, the bombs and shells fell mainly on noncombatants, not guerrillas. The Salvadoran Air Force claimed that heavy bombing "softened up" these zones for the deployment of ground troops. The idea of the air raids was to force civilians to flee guerrilla-controlled zones, thereby isolating the FMLN and depriving it of popular support.[41]

Both the Salvadoran military and the U.S. Embassy justified the expanded air war on the grounds that the noncombatants living in these zones were active FMLN supporters known as *masas guerrilleras.* [42] As Captain Luis Mario Aguilar told the *Christian Science Monitor:* "The masses are the same as the guerrillas. They are not innocent."[43] For its part, the U.S. Embassy said that the victims of the aerial war were "something more than innocent bystanders."[44]

The air war unleashed in 1984 was roundly condemned by human-rights groups, churches, and solidarity groups in the United States. In addition, it came under criticism from a Pentagon task force on Special Warfare headed by General John K. Singlaub (Ret.), who also served as the chairperson of the U.S. Council for World Freedom and as a liaison between the National Security Council and the Nicaraguan contras. The task force stressed that El Salvador's was a political/military war that should be fought using the LIC tactics. The task force argued that heavy and indiscriminate aerial bombardment was counterproductive because it reduced popular support for the government without significantly damaging the insurgents. "Dropping 500-pound bombs on insurgents is not the way to go," asserted Singlaub, "There is the need for very discriminate firepower."[45] It was the task force's opinion that more selective bombing and better coordination with ground troops could be used to drain the sea without killing such large numbers of noncombatants.

With its latest strategy discredited, the army's counterinsurgency plan again altered its course. Indiscriminate bombing decreased, but the air war continued. To depopulate guerrilla zones, the military in 1986 began to deploy a combination of air and ground forces. After strafing surrounding areas, army troops then moved in, rounding up people living in rural settlements and evacuating them in military aircraft. Before such operations began, the army often tried to starve the population out by restricting their access to food and other basic goods. With the help of the increasingly sophisticated air force, the army forcibly removed rural communities to refugee camps in the cities or near military bases, leaving the guerrilla forces without the cover and support of their popular base. Sometimes, the military gave displaced persons documents which said that they had turned themselves in with "a desire to put rebellion aside and submit myself to the laws of the republic." The evacuees, however, often told another story. "We didn't commit any crime, and we didn't turn ourselves in," said one 52-year-old woman. "We were captured."[46]

The October 1986 earthquake that shook San Salvador resulted in yet another dramatic increase in the number of homeless Salvadorans. The quake leveled shantytowns that had grown up on the margins of the city when many hapless residents fled from their rural villages to the capital to escape the terror of the counterinsurgency war.

Managing the Refugee Problem

Little official attention was given to displaced persons during the first two years of the civil war. Church agencies were the first to help the increasing numbers of internal refugees, but their resources were limited. The Salvadoran government and AID gradually recognized that, if not dealt with, the expanding displaced population was a potentially destabilizing force. In 1981, with U.S. help, the government formed the National Commission for Aid to Displaced Persons (CONADES). By providing some of the displaced with food, medical care, shelter, and temporary jobs (mostly from AID), CONADES tried to stabilize the situation, hoping that this assistance would win the allegiance of the displaced population. From its inception, CONADES, which is run by a committee of government representatives from the Ministries of Defense, Interior, Health, and Planning, was designed to maintain control over the refugee population rather than return them to their homes and help them create self-sustaining lives. Neither AID nor the Salvadoran government ever made much progress toward the implementation of development, reintegration, and resettlement programs.

Most of the food distributed to the displaced comes from the PL480 (Title II) food aid program—either directly from AID or through a special emergency agreement between the State Department and the UN's World Food Program (WFP). The food distribution programs reach about half the displaced population, while a smaller number of displaced persons benefit from food-for-work programs sponsored by AID. Most of this assistance benefits displaced persons who are either registered with government pacification agencies or living in areas under government control.

The nature and amount of refugee assistance have been criticized as inappropriate and inadequate. Refugees participating in AID's food-for-work programs are paid about $1 a day (less than half the minimum wage) to grade and place a layer of rocks over roads around rural villages. These make-work projects, while facilitating military access, do little to improve the living conditions in rural areas and do not pay the workers enough to better their own lives. The small allotment of food staples (about 1,200 calories a day) that refugees receive in AID programs keeps them alive but living in a constant state of hunger and malnutrition.

The wholesale diversion of supplies to the military and the private sector is another area of concern. A CBS report found that large quantities of U.S. food aid "is making its way into the hands of the wealthy and well-connected." The news report revealed that two and a half tons of dry milk, donated by the United States for displaced families, was sold to feed farm animals of wealthy ranchers.[47] There were also numerous charges that the military sold food aid for profit and withheld allotments to pressure rural communities to form civil patrols.[48]

The relief programs have also been criticized for their essentially political nature. A priest interviewed by the *Christian Science Monitor* said that the army distributed food "to reinforce local power structures" (meaning the army and the Duarte government). The priest, who worked with the displaced, added that the distribution programs were used to manipulate people, noting that food was sometimes kept from people to force them to follow government plans. The armed forces stopped distribution if they thought some of the food might be smuggled to nearby guerrillas.[49] In a similar vein, government refugee programs typically exclude displaced people not registered with government agencies or not living in government-controlled areas. Military officers sit on the boards of government pacification agencies, giving the army ready access to the registration lists. Displaced persons expose themselves to reprisals not only by identifying themselves by name but also by divulging their places of origin since those from areas of strong guerrilla support are regarded as leftist sympathizers by the military.[50]

In response to the persistent war, corruption within the Salvadoran agencies of CONARA and CONADES, international pressure for nonpartisan distribution of humanitarian assistance, and the increasing numbers of displaced, AID in 1984 began to appeal for more involvement of Private Voluntary Organizations (PVOs) in the pacification effort. AID also decided to triple the amount of money it was spending on refugee assistance. Suddenly, over $120 million was available for PVOs to carry out AID-authorized humanitarian assistance programs.

PVOs, including Project Hope, World Relief, and the Overseas Education Fund, agreed to accept AID funds for work with internal refugees. Project Hope was contracted by AID to provide health services to about 50,000 displaced persons living in some 60 settlements (including agrarian reform cooperatives) judged militarily secure. Project Hope builds health dispensaries in conjunction with the military's civic action programs. The Salvadoran Evangelical Committee for Assistance and Development, one of several Salvadoran PVOs that receive funding from AID, oversees a food program for selected displaced people. World Relief received AID money for a pilot relocation project, and the Overseas Education Fund is working on an AID-backed refugee project in the San Vicente area—an initial target of the National Plan.

Many PVOs repeatedly rejected appeals by AID to participate. Lutheran World Service has maintained independent refugee relief projects, insisting on complete autonomy. According to the top relief official for San Salvador's Catholic Archdiocese, the Reverend Octavio Cruz, "The U.S. aid always comes within the framework of their counterinsurgency policy." His comments were echoed by other PVO staff members. A representative of Catholic Relief Services (CRS) in El Salvador rejected AID advances, saying: "Accepting money from AID is to accept money from one of the belligerents in the war. AID wants to be an octopus. They already manage the economy and the war. Now they want to control humanitarian aid as well."[51]

Monsignor Roland Bordelon, the top Latin American official of CRS, said: "No matter how much U.S. AID denies this, the plan is a highly political pacification program."[52]

Reintegration and Resettlement Plans

"The reintegration of the displaced into the social, economic, and political life of the country" was the stated objective of the Salvadoran government. With the creation of the Vice-Ministry of Social Development in the summer of 1985, the Duarte government pledged to discard the welfare approach to the displaced and to create reintegration and economic development projects. But, in reality, little has been done to accomplish that goal.

Part of President Duarte's concern was caused by AID's growing dissatisfaction with his government's handling of the situation. He also wanted to keep the displaced population, a potential base of support for the Christian Democrats, under the control of his government. Thus Duarte was uneasy about AID's plans to use PVOs to take over the relief projects, though both he and the U.S. government knew that the existence of such a large displaced population was a potential source of social upheaval. The growing number of refugees was also a clear sign that the war was not winding down and that it was the people, not the guerrillas, who were the main victims of the counterinsurgency campaigns.

Neither did the United to Reconstruct plan offer any solutions. In fact, the result of the new "security and development" plan was the creation of more refugees. The first stage of United to Rebuild was the "limpieza" of guerrilla areas, which in practice meant the "cleaning out" of the people, not the guerrillas. Under the plan, these secured areas would later be resettled, although not necessarily with their original inhabitants. The army's talk of "resettlement," "reintegration," and "development" was not based on any real commitment to give refugees the amount of land, technical assistance, and credit they would need to become self-reliant. That kind of commitment would require a deepening of the agrarian reform, economic measures to redistribute income, and an end to the civil war.

With no such commitments to offer refugees, the army was confronted by a countermovement of displaced people demanding to go home. By early 1985, however, just as the labor movement was regaining its strength, refugee committees began organizing and called for an end to the bombings, access to international humanitarian aid, and a negotiated settlement to the war. In 1986, refugee committees like the Christian Committee of the Displaced (CRIPDES) told the Duarte government that they were tired of broken promises. Instead of waiting for the government and the army to fulfill their resettlement pledges, refugee committees organized caravans of displaced families that set out to resettle their original villages. In at least two cases, the army agreed to allow refugee groups to reconstruct their bombed-out villages, even providing some supplies but maintaining a heavy military presence in the repopulated villages. In other cases, the army prevented such resettlement attempts and arrested the returning refugees, fearing that repopulated villages might once again serve as bases of guerrilla support.

As the war drags on, the refugee crisis continues to worsen. The communities of displaced persons leading desperate lives on the margins of Salvadoran towns are a constant reminder that the government has failed to gain the upper hand in the civil war. In its efforts to isolate the FMLN forces, the military has depopulated many areas of the country, and in the process has created a large dependent population that saps government and international financial resources.

THE DEMOCRATIZATION OF EL SALVADOR

AID says that "democratization" is one of its major programs in El Salvador. Its democratization projects aim to "strengthen those basic institutions fundamental to the democratic process." Those institutions, according to AID, are the judicial system, the police, free trade unions, and the electoral system. Democratization assistance is used to create political and governmental institutions that lend credibility to and help implement the U.S. counterinsurgency project in El Salvador.

Assisting the electoral process is the foremost part of U.S.-sponsored democratization. By supporting Salvadoran elections, Washington hoped to give the country the image of a "fragile democracy" in need of international support. Staging and manipulating elections are nothing new for the United States. In Vietnam, the U.S. Embassy promoted elections in the late 1960s and early 1970s as part of a strategy to demonstrate that South Vietnam was a bonafide democracy worthy of U.S. military support. While proclaiming neutrality, U.S. agencies secretly helped certain candidates.

In Latin America, a prominent case of U.S. manipulation of elections occurred in Chile during the 1964 presidential campaign. The CIA bolstered the campaign of Christian Democrat Eduardo Frei with $3 million, helping him to beat socialist Salvador Allende. Six years later the CIA financed a propaganda campaign to discredit and defame Allende, who nevertheless went on to win the 1970 presidential election. A year after its 1965 military intervention in the Dominican Republic, the United States staged national elections as part of its effort to install a U.S.-allied government in that Caribbean country. Involvement in the electoral process has formed an important part of U.S. strategy not only in El Salvador but also in Honduras and Guatemala, where Washington has helped plan, promote, and finance elections.

The U.S. government began staging elections in El Salvador in 1982—through its embassy, AID, USIA, AIFLD, and the CIA. Millions of dollars poured into the country to train election organizers, buy computers to tabulate votes, sponsor international observers, and even pay for the campaigns of favored parties. Elections served U.S. interests by helping forge a center-right government to serve as a vehicle for the U.S. counterinsurgency project. In addition, elections made the guerrillas appear antidemocratic and legitimized the Salvadoran government, thereby facilitating approval of continued U.S. military and economic aid.

The United States spent $6–8 million to organize the 1982 assembly elections and at least $10.4 million for the 1984 presidential elections, making them the most expensive in Central American history. AID used generous portions of its development assistance money for El Salvador to organize and train the Central Election Council. During the 1984 elections, the political section of the embassy swelled to include ten staff members to monitor the process, making it the largest political section of any U.S. embassy in the world.[53] U.S. government aid for the electoral process was supplemented by such right-wing private funders as the Smith-Richardson, Olin, Scaife, and Grace Foundations.[54]

Besides special funding for the elections themselves, AID used PL480-generated local currency to plan upcoming elections, including the projected presidential election in 1988. By financing electoral registry maintenance, civic awareness programs, and a national voter registration card project, AID said it was "building confidence in the integrity of the electoral process."

More than just paying for the process, the U.S. took an active role in the Salvadoran elections. AID, through AIFLD, paid organizers to encourage workers and peasants to vote for Duarte. And the CIA channeled funds to the Christian Democrats and the National Conciliation Party in 1984 to prevent the victory of ARENA's Roberto D'Aubuisson, a right-wing extremist whose election would have made it difficult for Washington to justify continued U.S. support of the government.[55]

While a great deal of money was spent to guarantee fairness on election day by avoiding double balloting and other fraud, no *bona fide* attempts were made to secure the participation of the political left as represented by the FDR and the FMLN guerrillas. Only two political sectors—the center-right and the extreme right—participated in the electoral process. The elections supported by the United States were not technically fraudulent; but by leaving out the country's main political opposition the results were not representative of popular sentiment.

From the beginning, the U.S.-backed democratization of El Salvador has been severely circumscribed. Excluded were the mass organizations formed in the 1970s, all parties and political factions to the left of center in the Christian Democratic Party (PDC), and the guerrillas. As mentioned earlier, Washington initially selected the Christian Democrats as the more suitable vehicle for its counterinsurgency project in El Salvador. Since 1984, however, the embassy has moved increasingly away from the PDC and toward a newly formed alliance of industrialists, agroexporters, and right-wing politicians. The declining popularity of Duarte is one reason for this shift, but it can also be explained by the Reagan administration's visceral sympathy with the right wing's ideology of unfettered capitalism and extreme anticommunism.

Guardians of Democratization

The training and equipping of Salvadoran police is a major component of Washington's democratization program. The three national police or security forces in El Salvador—National Guard, National Police, and Treasury Police—received considerable assistance from the United States from 1962 to 1974 through AID's now-defunct Office of Public Safety (OPS). Before the OPS program began in 1962, the Salvadoran security forces were loosely organized units beholden to individual oligarchs and political strongmen. The job of the OPS advisers was to shape these poorly trained and uncoordinated forces into a centrally controlled police network capable of combating urban and rural dissidence. AID regularly referred to its program in El Salvador as a model for other Latin American countries. In a 1967 review of the OPS program in El Salvador, AID said that authorities were "successful in handling any politically motivated demonstrations" and noted that, "With the potential danger that exists in a densely populated country where the rich are very rich and the poor extremely poor, El Salvador is fortunate that the Guard and Police are well-trained and disciplined."[56]

OPS and CIA advisers encouraged the Salvadoran security forces to focus their attention on the "political criminals." During the OPS program, U.S. advisers organized and trained the paramilitary force ORDEN (National Democratic Organization), which terrorized the countryside during the 1960s and 1970s and established the presidential intelligence center that guided the operations of the death squads.[57] In the 12 years of the OPS program, the Salvadoran security forces received over $2.1 million in revolvers, grenades, radios, carbines, and mobile units. Two OPS advisers trained police within El Salvador, and some 200 Salvadoran police were given advance training at the International Police Academy (IPA) in Washington.

Democratization by Counterterrorism

Beginning in 1983, numerous U.S. agencies and institutions became involved in a new wave of police training programs. The Reagan administration circumvented the 1974 congressional prohibition against further police training through special exemptions. The actions were justified by the claim that the police were being trained in antiterrorism and to protect the judicial system. AID and the State Department were the main sponsoring agencies, but the actual training was provided by the FBI, the Bureau of Alcohol, Tobacco and Firearms, and various city police departments and educational institutes in the United States. Members of the Salvadoran security forces reported that the CIA also provided training.[58] Over 4,000 Salvadoran police were trained by these programs between 1983 and 1987.

In early 1984, AID, as part of its Judicial Reform program, funded a project in which 60 Salvadoran prison guards received training in the United States. They were organized into a Judicial Protection Unit formed to improve the country's judicial system by keeping witnesses and jurors safe from retaliatory violence. In 1984, AID also provided the funds to create a Special Investigative Unit to probe prominent crimes, especially ones involving U.S. citizens.

Since 1983, Salvadoran security forces have received training as part of the State Department's Anti-Terrorism Assistance (ATA) program. The ATA program, which was formed mainly to beef up security for U.S. diplomats overseas, has been used in Central America for urban counterinsurgency as well. Lionel Gomez, the former deputy director of the Agrarian Reform Institute (ISTA), told Senator Tom Harkin that at least 6 of the 18 Salvadoran police officers being trained through the ATA program in the United States were linked to death squads. Three from the National Guard general staff—including Lieutenant Colonel José Adolfo Medrano (son of the late General José Alberto Medrano)—"are known figures in the political killings, perhaps 3,000 or more," said Gomez.[59]

Mike Kraft, spokesperson for the State Department's Bureau of Diplomatic Security, denied that the ATA program was training death-squad members. "We're not the OPS program, we're politically aware," said Kraft. "We don't advise people who aren't showing signs of change. We're working to get the police to change. They are not perfect in El Salvador but . . . if we pull out, who comes in?" he challenged.[60]

After the deaths of four U.S. Marines in a June 1985 guerrilla raid in San Salvador, the Reagan administration asked Congress to provide $22 million to train Salvadoran police through the proposed Central America Counterterrorism Program. Congress balked at this extensive police assistance package but did allow the administration to reallocate $4.5 million in military assistance funding to be used for police training and equipment in El Salvador. Three counterterrorist police units were formed with U.S. assistance: the Special Antiterrorist Force (CEAT), the Liberator, and the Lightning Battalion. Washington argued that the training of such units did not violate the

1974 restriction of foreign police training. However, a blurred distinction exists between the armed forces and the security forces in El Salvador. For example, army officers command all police units, and the police forces have battalions that take part in the military's counterinsurgency sweeps in rural areas.

Just as political dissidents were the main victims of earlier police training programs, popular opposition groups became the victims of recent police assistance programs. In targeting urban terrorism, U.S.-trained police focused on the growing popular opposition movement. One of the first forays by a U.S.-trained counterterrorist security force was a May 1985 police raid to break up a hospital strike. In an attempt to break the momentum of the nonviolent popular opposition, Salvadoran security forces in 1985 began to arrest key human rights activists, refugee organizers, and labor leaders. One such case of police repression was the May 1986 arrest and imprisonment of the entire nongovernmental Human Rights Commission of El Salvador (CDHES). The human rights activists were forced to sign a confession of "subversive association" by the Treasury Police. About the same time, security forces also arrested three members of the Committee of Mothers of the Disappeared (COMADRES) for their alleged links to the guerrillas.

Despite President Duarte's promise to bring the perpetrators of death-squad killings to justice and the existence of substantial evidence, no officers have been convicted. Moreover, according to the Committee of Political Prisoners of El Salvador (COPPES), the great majority of the country's 900 or more political prisoners have never stood trial or been sentenced. President Duarte has been unable to account for the more than 4,000 disappearances before he took office and unable to stop further disappearances during his own presidency.

Killings and disappearances by the security forces dropped dramatically after 1984, but torture is still common in El Salvador. According to a September 1985 report by Americas Watch, U.S.-trained Treasury Police and National Guard members continue to use electric shock, hangings, suffocation, rape, mock executions, beatings, and other methods of torture on prisoners.

Police training has shown no signs of democratizing El Salvador. Any reduction in death-squad violence and police executions has been due not to U.S. training programs but to international pressure. In 1986, as popular discontent and organizing increased and the stability of the Duarte government weakened, repression against popular leaders steadily mounted. It is likely that as popular forces grow and the U.S. counterinsurgency project continues to lose strength, the antiterrorism training and U.S.-provided police equipment will be used in the same way that U.S. police assistance in previous decades was used—to clamp down on the rising nonmilitary popular opposition.

AID FOR THE WAR ECONOMY

More than a million dollars a day in various types of U.S. economic aid has been pumped into El Salvador in recent years. This aid is used mainly for stabilization and pacification—not to change the conditions of underdevelopment. Most U.S. economic aid works double time in the sense that it not only eases the acute shortage of foreign exchange but also creates equivalent sums of local currency that are used to patch up the government's budget, support the National Plan, and provide matching funds required by many foreign aid projects.

These massive injections of U.S. funds have floated the war economy—keeping the government solvent, allowing the military expenses to increase to a third of the national budget, and paying for war-related expenses like civic action programs and infrastructure repair. Members of Congress have justified their approval of requests for increased economic aid on the grounds that the aid would be used for projects ostensibly designed to ease poverty and halt political repression. But congressional approval did not constitute a middle ground between expanded military intervention and a U.S. pullout. Most of the aid to El Salvador served to fuel the counterinsurgency war.

A 1985 study by three members of the Arms Control and Foreign Policy Caucus of the Congress took exception to the Reagan administration's claim that aid, particularly ESF cash transfer assistance, would bring about "economic and social development."[61] The study stated that "it is crucial to distinguish between U.S. aid programs intended to reform and develop El Salvador's economic and political system (and thereby remove the underlying causes of the war), and those programs intended simply to maintain the status quo prior to the economic collapse brought on by the war." It found that the overwhelming amount of U.S. aid fell into the latter category.

Part of maintaining the war economy meant the imposition of a stabilization plan of the kind commonly recommended by the IMF and the World Bank. With pressure from AID, the Duarte government announced his Stabilization and Reactivation Program in January 1986. Like similar stabilization plans, this was a program of austerity that primarily hurt peasants and workers. In contrast to price increases, cuts in social services, and cutbacks in government employment, included in Duarte's program were measures recommended by AID that gave tax breaks and other incentives to investors who increased their investment and exported more. The program, which was formulated in consultation with AID and sectors of the business community, elicited widespread popular anger. While members of the business community complained about certain aspects of the program, it was mostly in keeping with their own stabilization philosophy, which called for devaluation, export and investment incentives, lower tariffs, and government austerity.

Although the Stabilization and Reactivation Program was imposed in the interests of stabilizing the war economy, it led to increased economic and political instability. Its implementation resulted in decreased consumption but did not spark increased investment. The *paquetazo,* as it was disparagingly labeled by unions, students, and small business owners, galvanized unions and rural associations into mounting antigovernment protests. Another reaction to the *paquetazo,* which was widely regarded as a plan to finance the war economy, was growing popular sentiment in favor of a negotiated peace.

AID's Alliance with the Oligarchy

Part of the popular disaffection with Duarte was his post-election attempts to meet the demands of the business elite, after winning the presidency in 1984 mainly because of his support among workers, peasants, and the middle class. The Duarte administration's failure to pursue reformism and his fear of alienating the private sector were the result of AID's heightened emphasis on economic stabilization and private-sector growth. With democracy in place, albeit without the participation of the political left, AID and the embassy put greater stress on reviving the economy and spurring private-sector investment.

This was a marked change from the first years of U.S. intervention under President Jimmy Carter when the emphasis was on winning popular support for the Christian Democrats and creating a government that would gain international recognition as a democracy. Three reforms encouraged at that time— nationalization of agroexport commerce, nationalization of banking institutions, and agrarian reform—were designed to gain popular approval and at the same time lessened the country's traditional subservience to the right-wing oligarchy. Both the reforms and the Christian Democrat's favored status with Washington greatly angered the oligarchy, but short of opposing U.S. military and economic aid, there was little they could do. The 1981 inauguration of fellow rightist Ronald Reagan, however, and the formation in 1982 of a coalition government that included the rightist parties prevented the full implementation of the reform program. The weak land distribution plan was further debilitated, and the representatives of the oligarchy retained their power in the national banking sector. Only in the area of agroexport commercialization did the oligarchy suffer a significant setback.[62]

While the U.S. government was trying to weaken the oligarchy's hold over the central government, thereby broadening popular backing for the U.S.-sponsored counterinsurgency, it also regarded the private sector as the main source of economic growth. Beginning in 1981, AID directed most of its economic development funds to "private-sector support" projects. While some funds were given to small farmers and entrepreneurs, most of the money flowed to the oligarchy. So substantial was this assistance that an AID official noted in an internal memorandum that U.S. economic aid was the "crucial factor in maintaining the Salvadoran private sector."[63]

The emphasis on private-sector support and the corresponding neglect of disadvantaged economic sectors intensified after the 1984 presidential elections. With a so-called "moderate" as president and a new level of political stability in El Salvador, AID felt satisfied with the success of its program of political reformism, and turned its attention to questions of economic growth. AID set out to institute a program of Reaganomics uncomplicated by concerns about concentration of land and wealth in El Salvador.

While Duarte's Christian Democratic government was a convenient vehicle for counterinsurgency, the Reagan administration placed its hopes for economic recovery on the country's elite private sector. AID has injected hundreds of millions of dollars into the private sector, mainly through an organization of its own creation called the Salvadoran Foundation for Economic and Social Development (FUSADES). FUSADES was established to act as a conduit for private-sector support funds and to lobby for AID's agenda for economic growth. Like AID, FUSADES called for increased foreign investment in export-oriented assembly plants, a heightened emphasis on nontraditional agroexport production, privatization of government corporations, and increased government incentives for private-sector investment in export operations. As AID's standard-bearer in the private sector, FUSADES serves as a think tank for private-sector policies, a wholesaler of AID-supplied credit and foreign exchange, and a promoter of new export-oriented investment in El Salvador. AID also supported a network of other business organizations through a FUSADES branch organization called the Program to Strengthen Associations (FORTAS), which backs a variety of business organizations.[64]

AID argued that it was trying to build new business organizations to strengthen "apolitical" representatives of the private sector. AID and the U.S. embassy consider a modernized private sector an important U.S. ally in the country. AID, in fact, has encouraged the business elite to take an active role in politics, paying for seminars in "Understanding Politics" for FUSADES directors. One political party that received at least tacit U.S. backing was the Liberation Party (formerly Patria Libre), a spin-off of the extreme right-wing ARENA party.

In late 1986, President Duarte announced a new series of taxes that, in turn, reinvigorated oligarchic opposition to the government. In fact, the tax package—called the Tax for the Defense of National Sovereignty—was met with universal derision and opposition. The organized popular sectors (workers, peasants, students, and small business owners) called it a "war tax," and denounced it as a way to continue an unpopular, economically devastating war. For the oligarchy, the tax package, which included direct taxes on business and income, was regarded as an attack on the sanctity of private property and the right to do business. The leading business associations called for Duarte's resignation and showed their power by effectively stopping business activity for an entire day in early 1987. This business shutdown demonstrated the renewed strength and unity of the oligarchy. The crisis also showed the elite's unwillingness to compromise its own class interests to satisfy the political and economic requirements of the war.

While the oligarchy was committed to counterinsurgency, it was not willing to pay for the war out of its own coffers. Nor were the Salvadoran oligarchs willing to send their own sons off to fight the war. Along with the popular sectors, the oligarchy opposed the Duarte government's repeated attempts to institute a national draft.

At this point, the oligarchy felt that the time was right to regain control over the economy, secure political power, and roll back the reforms. Business associations like ANEP (National Private Enterprise Association) and FUSADES recognized that the war needed to be financed, but they advocated measures that did not infringe on their hallowed right to pursue profits. In line with AID's "trickle down" philosophy, the private sector said that revenue-generating measures that bit into its profits meant less money for employment and investment. The elite demanded free commercialization of agroexports, increased privatization of the economy, and more government assistance for agroexporters. While the sentiment for a negotiated peace was expanding among most sectors, the oligarchy called for the government to pursue the war more aggressively. It felt that the adoption of LIC doctrine by the Duarte government and the military high command had handicapped the counterinsurgency efforts. According to the oligarchy, the iron fist of repression and state terror—not food aid or civic action— was the only way to end the war.

The crisis for the Duarte government was also a crisis for Washington. Halfway into his administration, Duarte, the personification of U.S. counterinsurgency strategy in El Salvador, was isolated and ineffective. For support, he could no longer count on either the popular sector or the private sector. He continued to occupy the presidential palace only because of the unenthusiastic backing of Washington, and the military high command and the lack of viable alternatives. The U.S. counterinsurgency project had reached a dead end; "democratization" had produced a government with little support that ruled only at the favor of the military. The counterrevolutionary coalition of government, oligarchy, and military that had existed prior to U.S. intervention was in pieces.

A new economic and political model was needed to continue

the counterinsurgency, but the only ones available were not attractive to Washington. The solution supported by the majority of Salvadorans—a negotiated peace and the formation of a new coalition government—was ruled out by the Reagan administration, the oligarchy, and the military. A military coup that would result in a new military/civilian junta or a right-wing coalition would receive the backing of the oligarchy but would increase popular opposition and endanger U.S. congressional support. Waiting it out until the 1988 elections, when a new government could be formed with some degree of popular approval, would mean continuing economic and political chaos, a situation ripe for organizing by the FMLN/FDR. Massive U.S. military intervention might be an option but only in the advent of an imminent FMLN/FDR victory.

A Lost War

The other war, like the military contest, was from the start a losing proposition in El Salvador. The U.S. government tried to stabilize the country economically by pouring dollars into the central bank and paying for the repair of infrastructure. But the dollars were draining out of the country faster than they were coming in, and the guerrillas were able to destroy economic targets faster than AID was able to rebuild bridges and re-erect electricity towers. Although it was contributing more than a third of the country's budget, AID proved unable to stabilize El Salvador. Aside from the conditions of war, the economy suffered internationally because of lower export prices, shrunken markets, and an increasing debt burden.

By keeping the war economy alive, Washington has destabilized the country while attempting to stabilize it. With each new year of war, the country lost more of its productive capability and national income levels dropped to new depths. The infusion of such large amounts of economic aid distorted El Salvador's economy, making it ever more dependent on U.S. dollars and hiding the seriousness of the country's bankrupt state. Dollars did not provide stability. They did, however, finance the war and maintain the income levels of the elite. In the midst of war, the shopping centers, travel agencies, and luxury restaurants of San Salvador's posh Zona Rosa were doing a booming business as a result of the influx of stabilization funds. Hopes that U.S. aid would stimulate economic recovery were frustrated by the refusal of both local and foreign capitalists to invest in the war-torn country.

The commitment of AID to a strategy of private-sector support highlighted the agency's fundamental lack of understanding of the dynamics of third-world development and underdevelopment. This strategy of development did not produce economic growth. Rather than strengthening the country's political stability, AID's fixation on the private sector worked to undermine its own carefully designed counterinsurgency project. So too, the oligarchy's aggressive pursuit of its own class interests, spirited by AID's promotion of unfettered capitalism, worked to destabilize rather than fortify the counterrevolution. As AID's plan of private-sector support was played out in El Salvador, the contradictions of its overall strategy of counterrevolution became increasingly obvious. While the agency recognized the cause-and-effect relationship between underdevelopment and popular rebellion, it refused to acknowledge the class nature of the economic and political crisis in El Salvador. The U.S. government's own interests and its identification with the interests of the elite outweighed any rhetorical commitment to the poor. This essential class solidarity with the oligarchy prevented the United States from fully implementing reformism and from truly committing itself to justice for the majority of El Salvador's people.

The LIC war in El Salvador has been characterized by a strategy of reform and repression. By 1987, this strategy showed unmistakeable signs of breaking down. The reformist orientation imposed by Washington and carried out by the Christian Democratic government initially succeeded in winning wide public support. But the shallow nature of the reforms and the failure of the government to break with the army and oligarchy resulted in increasing dissatisfaction with both Duarte and the U.S. role in El Salvador.

While the politics of reform failed to gain firm popular support for the counterinsurgency war, neither did the superficial reforms break the power of the oligarchy. By 1986, a reorganized oligarchic sector emerged as a destabilizing element in the U.S. plans for the other war. The "security" or repressive side of U.S. LIC strategy also proved unsuccessful. Eight years after President Carter began pouring military aid into El Salvador, the guerrilla forces had developed into the most powerful army in Latin American history. Not only was there no military victory in sight for the Salvadoran military, but the political support for the FMLN/FDR was growing among all the popular sectors. If El Salvador is a test case for LIC strategy, it has shown itself to be a flawed strategy for dealing with reform and revolution in Central America.

8 The Destabilization of Nicaragua

> *"The form of destabilization [in Chile] was less brutal and less sophisticated than in Nicaragua. . . . Afterwards, there were lots of condolences for Allende and the Chilean people. But we'd rather not have postmortem solidarity."*
> —President Daniel Ortega, 1985

Economic power can be used to topple governments as well as prop them up. President Nixon and Henry Kissinger used U.S. financial power "to make the economy scream" in Chile.[1] "Not a nut or a bolt shall reach Chile," was the U.S. slogan of the economic war against the progressive government of Salvador Allende.[2] The weapons in that destabilization campaign—cutoff of aid and credits, measures to reduce trade, support of private-sector opposition, and the blocking of multilateral loans—have all been wielded against Nicaragua.

Since its inception in 1981, the destabilization campaign steadily acquired momentum. At a 1985 press conference, President Reagan described the real nature of this campaign, saying that he hoped to see the Nicaraguan government "removed in the sense of its present structure" unless it would "say uncle" to U.S. demands.[3] In search of this goal, Washington violated the most basic tenets of free trade and international law.

The campaign has hit Nicaragua hard. The government's advances in literacy, agrarian reform, and health care stalled; and the encouraging growth rates of the first few years faltered.

Rationing of gas, food shortages, a foreign exchange crunch, scarcity of imported goods, and an inability to buy spare parts have been among the hardships Nicaraguans have had to face every day because of U.S. economic destabilization. While not all Nicaragua's internal problems can be attributed to Uncle Sam, most of its political and economic difficulties are at least partially the work of the small nation's powerful northern neighbor.

Destabilization is essentially a political/military tactic that is part of the overall U.S. strategy of low intensity conflict in Central America. The aim is to undermine the Sandinista government while bolstering opposition forces—without having to commit U.S. troops to combat. Washington's drive to destabilize Nicaragua is a campaign with many fronts. The military offensive—the contras, the CIA's covert war, and U.S. military maneuvers in Honduras—has received the most public attention. But at least as threatening to the Sandinista revolution is the campaign to destabilize the Nicaraguan government through nonlethal or economic means. These include:

1. Terminating U.S. bilateral economic assistance and food aid.
2. Setting up obstacles to U.S. trade and investment.
3. Blocking multilateral loans from international financial institutions (IFIs) like the Inter-American Development Bank, World Bank, and International Monetary Fund.
4. Using U.S. economic and humanitarian aid to support the internal and external counterrevolutionary organizations.
5. Orchestrating a psychological-operations campaign against Nicaragua.

AID DURING SOMOZA REGIME: CORRUPTION AND PACIFICATION

U.S. assistance and trade formed the backbone of the dictatorship of Anastasio Somoza. Between 1960 and 1979, the Somoza regime ranked as one of the highest per capita recipients of U.S. economic aid in Latin America. The United States was also the country's top trading partner, accounting for more than one-quarter of its total trade. Economic assistance did little to improve the lot of impoverished Nicaraguans, but it did serve as a generous payoff to the Somoza family for its constant support of U.S. policy. Despite frequent revelations about government corruption and human rights abuses, economic assistance continued to flow to Nicaragua until the last days of the Somoza regime. In 1977, the AID Mission in Managua explained that economic aid should continue to flow to the Somoza regime because "U.S. investment is welcomed in Nicaragua's developing free enterprise economy" and because the country's "foreign policy stresses maintenance of the closest possible ties with the United States."[4]

Aid for the Family

For members of the Somoza family, Nicaragua was a private fiefdom. Virtually all economic aid flowed into family coffers. In the year following the devastating 1972 earthquake, Nicaragua was the largest recipient of U.S. economic aid in the hemisphere. But as any visitor to Managua could attest, the many millions of dollars in aid were not used to reconstruct the devastated capital city.[5] Among Nicaraguans, it was common knowledge that Somoza and his cronies were pocketing these funds, but the State Department refused to turn off the spigot. During the 1970s, AID funds equalled about 15 percent of the national government's expenditures. Father Ernesto Cardenal, a well-known Nicaraguan poet and the current Minister of Culture, suggested to Congress that "the U.S. government should put Somoza on trial for the misuse of U.S. taxpayers' money."

Richard Millett, author of *Guardians of the Dynasty*, told a 1977 congressional hearing that this aid constituted "an important asset to the system" not only because it covered government expenses but also because it kept Somoza and his associates content. "Virtually every project in Nicaragua eventually contributes to Somoza family fortunes," noted Millett. "Projects involving school construction or municipal improvements usually require cement . . . such cement comes from a Somoza-owned plant and is purchased at inflated, government-controlled prices. . . . When funds are appropriated for rural feeder roads first priority is given to building roads to Somoza family properties or those owned by their supporters, especially those associated with the Guardia," explained Millett. AID projects allowed the family to build its political power base by extending favors to members of the nation's oligarchy. Economic aid from the United States also kept members of the National Guard, which was created by the U.S. occupying force in the 1920s, satisfied with the Somoza dictatorship. AID funding "increases its ability to reward supporters, notably retired Guardia officers, with well-paying and often graft-ridden posts either within family-owned enterprises or in the expanded government bureaucracy financed through AID."[6]

Anastasio Somoza never showed much concern for the deep-rooted poverty of most Nicaraguans, but in the 1970s he began to worry about the growing rural unrest. Landless *campesinos* were demanding land, agricultural laborers wanted better wages, and the FSLN guerrillas or Sandinistas were conducting a hit-and-run war against the National Guard in several rural provinces. Somoza struck back with a blend of repression and pacification; both responses depended on AID funds. The National Guard served as Somoza's police and army; its dual status made it the beneficiary of both U.S. police and military training programs. From 1950 to 1979, the United States (through the Pentagon's International Military Education and Training program and AID's Office of Public Safety program) trained almost 6,000 National Guardsmen—making Nicaragua the highest per capita recipient of that form of foreign assistance.[7]

To expand the regime's reach into the countryside, Somoza relied on AID rural development funds. In 1972, the dictator used an AID grant to establish the National Agrarian Committee, which concluded that a serious land crisis was brewing and that without some government response, "a polarization of forces could lead to a social disruption." In 1974, the year Somoza declared a state of siege, AID used the conclusions of the two-year-old National Agrarian Committee report to indicate that Somoza finally was showing some concern for the rural poor. Congress approved funding of a new agency called the Institute for Peasant Welfare (INVIERNO). As with all other government services in Somoza's Nicaragua, international aid, mostly from AID, paid INVIERNO's entire bill.

The new agency emphasized work in three of the country's poorest areas: the Central Highlands, the Central Pacific, and the western part of Zelaya, a large province on the Atlantic coast. In the first two areas, INVIERNO's program established farm cooperatives, information sharing among small farmers, rural credit services, and an agricultural extension service. INVIERNO attempted to give a select group of small farmers a vested interest in the Somoza government. By dishing out credit and technology to farmers, AID hoped to integrate them more fully into the capitalist market and thereby make them less likely to support the more collectivist goals of the Sandinistas. In Zelaya, INVIERNO managed a colonization project that settled landless *campesinos* from the Pacific coast in isolated "agricultural frontier" settlements. As one Latin American scholar observed: "Somoza's agrarian reform essentially amounted to a colonization plan in order to contain and pacify the peasantry by reducing the pressure on land [used] for export production."[8]

Jaime Wheelock, the country's current Minister of Agriculture and at that time a guerrilla commander, described INVIERNO as "a program of counterinsurgency . . . created by AID." He said, "Despite all the official propaganda about this organization, it will soon become clear that it isn't concerned about bettering the welfare of *campesinos*. It is principally a police-like organization, and as such will generate greater opposition to the regime."[9] Wheelock accurately predicted that IN-

VIERNO would "begin organizing in the zones most exposed to the political work of the revolutionary movement. . . . The 'cooperative' programs are designed to ensure effective control of productive units of the population. In this manner, they will become variants of the strategic hamlets of Vietnam." According to Wheelock, no other motive but counterinsurgency could "explain the inclusion of 'information banks' on the target areas, IDs, and the choosing of 'explosive' zones as the first priority."[10]

Reporting from Nicaragua in 1977, journalist Penny Lernoux also concluded that the National Guard was using INVIERNO as a front for its own counterinsurgency and civic action programs. Peasants told her that many of INVIERNO's schools were established by the National Guard and run by military informers.[11] AID's funding of INVIERNO, Lernoux concluded, was "questionable since the project includes a data bank on the local population which can provide valuable information to the National Guard in its campaign against the peasants."

Although Washington continued its support of the dictatorship because the Somoza family was such a dependable U.S. ally, it was obvious that the hated regime could not last indefinitely. To prepare for a future without Somoza, AID took the precaution to forge close ties with the business elite of Nicaragua. It did this by creating and financially supporting several private-sector organizations. In the early 1960s, AID backed the formation of the Superior Council of Private Enterprise (COSEP) and two associated groups. One, the Nicaraguan Development Institute (INDE) promoted "via democratic means and the free enterprise system: community development, cooperatives, education, and government-community cooperation." The other, the Nicaraguan Development Foundation (FUNDE), funneled foreign aid to the private sector through financing and credits. AID considered all three organizations potential power bases in Nicaragua to be tapped in case the Somoza dynasty weakened.

Neither press reports of the Somoza family pocketing economic aid nor strong condemnations by international human rights groups like Amnesty International decreased U.S. economic assistance. In the last years of Somoza's rule, AID acknowledged in its annual reports the existence of corruption and human rights violations in Nicaragua, but it recommended that aid be continued, asserting that the Somoza regime was improving its human rights record.

In 1978, AID representatives beseeched Congress to continue aid to Nicaragua, pointing to "a marked decline in human rights abuses." AID claimed that the assistance was bettering the lives of Nicaraguans and provided an inducement to Somoza for constructive change. By 1979, Carter had cut back most military aid but economic assistance continued. In its last two years—1978 and 1979—the embattled regime received $32.5 million in U.S. economic aid, with another $19 million approved for 1980.[12] More U.S. aid went to Nicaragua from 1976 to 1980 than to any other Central American nation. IFIs like the World Bank also came to Somoza's assistance with multilateral loans. Multilateral assistance to the Somoza government given by IFIs from 1974 to 1979 totaled a whopping $271 million.

AID AND THE REVOLUTION

The assassination of newspaper publisher Pedro Joaquin Chamorro in January 1978 marked the beginning of the Carter administration's attempt to prevent a victory by the revolutionary forces. The State Department unsuccessfully tried to use U.S. aid as leverage to persuade Somoza to lift the state of martial law and to negotiate a settlement of the civil war with the centrist opposition. At the same time, U.S. diplomats began working with certain factions of anti-Somoza groups, including business and labor groups that had received AID funds. To strengthen U.S. links with forces outside the Somoza regime, President Carter authorized covert CIA support for labor unions, the press, and other elements within Nicaragua that could be controlled by the United States.[13] In 1979, the State Department arranged "mediation" talks between Somoza and a centrist coalition called the Broad Opposition Front. When mediation failed, the United States proposed the formation of an interim government composed of all political sectors including Somoza representatives and the deployment of a "peacekeeping" force that would in effect stop a Sandinista victory. All these efforts to manipulate the crisis failed in the face of the growing strength of the guerrillas.[14]

After the Sandinistas toppled the Somoza regime on July 19, 1979, the Carter administration regarded economic aid as a way to give the United States some leverage in the new government. It wanted to increase the power of the "moderate elements," those who had not participated in the armed struggle, and at the same time decrease the power of the Sandinistas. The purpose was to keep the revolutionaries at bay, to foster pluralism, and to keep the private sector strong. With economic assistance, AID could maintain close ties with the business and labor organizations it had previously supported.

Congress eventually approved a $75 million aid package proposed by the Carter administration, but only after extensive debate and the imposition of several unusual conditions. The $75 million economic aid package consisted of $70 million in long-term, low-interest loans, and a $5 million grant. About 60 percent or $45 million of the loan money was to be "made available to private sector enterprises" for imports from the United States. The $5 million grant went not to the government but was directly transferred to the Nicaraguan private sector and other groups close to the United States. Agricultural assistance was targeted for farmers affiliated with private-sector organizations rather than the Sandinista cooperatives. An important part of the AID package was an extensive "publicity campaign" to identify the United States as the benefactor of the projects.

During the debate on the aid package, the House of Representatives—for the first time in 149 years—went into secret session. The topic of the clandestine discussions was the Cuban presence in Nicaragua. Congress attached numerous conditions to the package. No aid could be used to fund projects with Cuban participation, thereby prohibiting support for many educational and health programs. Every six months, the president of the United States had to certify that Nicaragua was not exporting revolution or harboring terrorists. The restrictions imposed on aid to the new Nicaraguan government contrasted sharply with the previous lack of restrictions on support to the Somoza dictatorship. The Nicaraguan government bridled at the politically motivated conditions attached to the aid package. But the Sandinistas agreed, knowing that other donors, particularly the IFIs, would be more apt to approve loans if the country were receiving U.S. aid.

When AID's proposal for the next fiscal year (November 1981 through October 1982) came before Congress, the focus on the private sector was even sharper. AID said that its strategy was "to assist in establishing the economic framework within which Nicaragua's forces of moderation can operate and prosper. . . . The program supports the private sector, which is the strongest force of democratic pluralism in Nicaragua, activities of other private and voluntary organizations (PVOs), and people-to-people projects which strengthen contacts between the United States and Nicaragua."[15]

In 1980, a $7.5 million grant was approved to strengthen private-sector organizations by funding technical assistance to the confederation of business associations [COSEP] and its member organizations, lending capital to the independent cooperative associations [through FUNDE], assisting Red Cross and church community development projects, supporting independent labor unions through the American Institute for Free Labor Development, reinforcing the Central American Business School [INCAE], and funding U.S. professional exchange committees . . . and a U.S. scholarship program administered by a Nicaraguan private sector group.

For the first time, AID gave special attention to the Miskito Indians of the Atlantic Coast. Part of the $7.5 million grant was earmarked for the Social Action Committee of the Moravian Church, which works primarily with Miskitos. Partners of the Americas was also given a grant to cover new projects with the Miskitos and an exchange program with *La Prensa,* the anti-Sandinista newspaper.[16]

Reagan's Response to the Counterrevolution

Like the Carter administration, the Reagan administration stressed the need to support pluralism and private enterprise in Nicaragua. But the new policy toward Nicaragua was more explicitly counterrevolutionary. The objective was not just to control the course of the revolution, but to overturn it. This sentiment was expressed by a plank in the Republican Party platform, which condemned President Carter's offer of aid to Nicaragua and deplored "the Marxist Sandinista takeover of Nicaragua and the Marxist attempts to destabilize El Salvador, Guatemala, and Honduras." The platform plank issued the following oblique warning of future U.S. support for counterrevolution: "We will support the efforts of the Nicaraguan people to establish a free and independent government."

The counterrevolutionary thrust of the party's platform was translated by the Heritage Foundation into concrete suggestions for destabilization. The report, prepared by CIA veteran Cleto Di Giovanni, recommended "a well-orchestrated program targeted against the Marxist Sandinista government." The author suggested, "We [U.S.] should use our limited resources to support the free labor unions, the Church, the private sector, the independent political parties, the free press, and those who truly defend human rights."[17] He encouraged the Reagan administration to embark on a campaign of economic war against Nicaragua. The report, widely regarded to be the blueprint of the administration's early destabilization campaign, noted that "Nicaraguan workers continue to have an emotional attachment to the revolutionary movement," but that "this attachment can be expected to weaken as the economy deteriorates." It went on to conclude, "There are some indications of growing broadly based support to take to arms to overthrow the Sandinista government, and this support could increase as further economic problems develop. . . . Economic shortcomings might provoke at least limited civil unrest by the end of the current harvest season."

Claiming that the Sandinistas supported terrorism, President Reagan in March 1981 cancelled $9.8 million in previously authorized food credits for Nicaragua. The cutoff of food aid hit Nicaragua hard because of the dependence on wheat-flour products that the country's citizens had developed. Over the previous 25 years, U.S. wheat shipments to Nicaragua had jumped tenfold as a result of the U.S. food aid program and pressure from private U.S. grain traders. Ironically, the same day as the grain cutoff, the State Department, unable to produce any evidence to support its previous claims, announced that Nicaragua had "virtually halted all flow of arms" to the Salvadoran guerrillas.

The following month President Reagan terminated all further economic assistance to the Nicaraguan government, but he permitted aid to continue to selected private sector organizations. This effectively choked off $15 million in undisbursed funds from the $75 million congressional authorization, all of which had been designated for government projects.[18] Private-sector projects, however, including those covered by the $7.5 million approved for fiscal year 1981, continued to receive funds.

In June 1982, the Reagan administration asked Congress to reprogram the remaining $5 million in aid to the private sector to further reduce the foreign exchange benefits accruing to the Nicaraguan government. At that time, Otto Reich, then Assistant Administrator for Latin America and the Caribbean at the State Department, outlined the economic assistance that was destined for the many that have stayed in Nicaragua and "peacefully resisted." Reich said that the Catholic Church provided a "dramatic example" of a private-sector organization peacefully resisting the Sandinistas. AID financed the church's "civic leadership training and community self-help program which serves to counter Sandinista anti-church propaganda." Other recipients of AID dollars included the Union of Nicaraguan Farmers and its associated organizations for coffee growers, rice farmers, and ranchers, all of which were competing with the pro-Sandinista National Union of Farmers and Ranchers.[19]

AID funds also went to the Superior Council of Private Enterprise, which Reich said was "the most important organization in Nicaragua in terms of providing an alternative to the government, offering constructive criticism of the government, and maintaining an overall unity within the private sector."[20] By way of COSEP, AID channeled these new funds to the Chamber of Industry, the Chamber of Construction, and the National Association of Professionals—all of which, according to Reich, were "faced with the serious problem of their memberships' livelihood being threatened by government policies."

All these aid programs were designed to supply "a bit of oxygen to the private sector," but they also were meant to build resistance to the Sandinistas by supporting "freedom-loving Nicaraguans" who represent the "last vestige of pluralism." Said Reich: the economic assistance is "more than just financial support of private-sector activities but also is a symbol of political and moral support that is invaluable." As the State Department's Stephen Bosworth explained: "What we wish to do is to maintain these organizations as viable organizations which provide some counterpoint to the activities . . . and the policies of the government."[21] While AID said that the assistance would promote "democratic pluralism," it soon became evident that many of the AID-funded organizations were serving as bases for counterrevolution. Officials of both COSEP and the Chamber of Industry, which also received AID funds, were implicated in counterrevolutionary plots in 1980.[22]

Though desperate for foreign exchange, the Nicaraguan government said in August 1982 that it would refuse to allow the transfer of the remaining U.S. economic aid. It protested that the funds were designated to help the very elements of the private sector who were intent on removing the Sandinista leadership. In a letter to AID, the Nicaragua government said it was refusing the funds because it felt "that the agreements [with the private sector] have political motivations designed to promote resistance and destabilize the revolutionary government." The Sandinistas added that they would be willing to pursue discussion about other types of economic assistance.[23]

AID's history in Nicaragua illustrates how the agency's priorities change according to U.S. foreign policy concerns. During the Somoza era, AID performed several roles. It functioned as a kind of official bag man, transferring funds to Somoza to reward him for his loyalty to Washington. Economic assistance was also used to strengthen the Somoza government through police training and counterinsurgency programs. Finally, AID tried to create a "third force" of private-sector organizations and labor unions that would present an alternative to revolution in the event that the Somoza regime weakened.

After the Sandinistas came to power, Washington tried to use economic assistance to keep the government aligned with the United States and within the world capitalist community. As the new government began to establish its political and economic independence, AID programs were used to shore up the anti-Sandinista private sector and to build an internal counterrevolutionary force.

IDEOLOGICAL AND PSYCHOLOGICAL WARFARE

From the beginning of the U.S.-sponsored counterrevolution against Nicaragua, overt operations have run parallel to covert ones. Information management and psychological operations have played an important role in building support for the contras both inside and outside Nicaragua. The National Security Council and the United States Information Agency have directed this psychological war, with assistance from the CIA, the State Department, the Pentagon, and the White House.

As part of the Reagan administration's public diplomacy efforts, the White House Office of Public Liaison and the State Department's Office of Public Diplomacy began a concerted campaign soon after Reagan's election to manage the public's perception of the Nicaraguan revolution. A key figure in this campaign was Lt. Colonel Oliver North, who was the NSC officer responsible for the council's "psychological warfare operation" and "public perception" efforts against Nicaragua. While at the NSC, North also worked through 1985 with the Office of Public Liaison. From 1983 to 1985, the office engaged in an intense propaganda campaign about Central America that involved 96 seminars and 225 speeches in 75 cities.[24] "The idea is to slowly demonize the Sandinista government in order to turn it into a real enemy in the minds of the American people, thereby eroding their resistance to U.S. support for the contras and, perhaps, to a future military intervention in the region," said an administration official who opposed the Psyops campaign coordinated by North.[25]

The government's involvement in public diplomacy was also manifested through USIA's funding of the National Endowment for Democracy. NED made grants to two "private" organizations that directly support the internal opposition to the Sandinistas. They are Friends of the Democratic Center in Central America (PRODEMCA) and the Free Trade Union Institute (FTUI) (See Chapter Nine). Another major recipient of NED funds is the National Chamber Foundation of the U.S. Chamber of Commerce, which has also played a role in the destabilization of Nicaragua.

In 1985, PRODEMCA received a $200,000 grant from NED to support two organizations of Nicaragua's internal opposition. Part of these funds were used to form the U.S. office of the National Democratic Coordinating Committee, the anti-Sandinista political coalition headed by Arturo Cruz (a member of the United Nicaraguan Opposition or UNO) and founded by COSEP. The office was called the Nicaraguan Center for Democratic Studies. The other part of the grant went to the Permanent Commission on Human Rights in Nicaragua, which is the main source of charges of human rights abuses by the Sandinista government. While other human rights groups like Americas Watch question the objectivity of a U.S.-funded commission, NED contends that the Permanent Commission on Human Rights "provides aid to the victims of Sandinista repression" and that its work is "vital to the survival of democratic forces in Nicaragua."

La Prensa, the anti-Sandinista newspaper in Managua, also received NED funds through grants from PRODEMCA. Explaining its support of the stridently counterrevolutionary paper, NED said: "Endowment assistance has enabled *La Prensa* to obtain the essential supplies it needs to continue publishing. . . . The Endowment is also proud of the vital role that PRODEMCA has played in helping to administer this assistance."[26] In March 1986, two weeks prior to the Senate's approval of aid to the contras, *La Prensa* asked NED to cease its support out of fear that the Nicaraguan government would justify the closure of the paper on the funding links between it and a pro-contra group like PRODEMCA.

PRODEMCA spearheaded the disinformation campaign about anti-Semitism in Nicaragua when it commissioned a report entitled *Nicaragua's Jews: Their Story,* which charged that "Sandinista anti-Semitism" was responsible for a persecution of the country's Jewish community. These charges were refuted by editorials in the *New York Times* and in news analyses in the *Washington Post.* Anti-Sandinista lobbying was another way PRODEMCA used U.S. funds to back the contra war of destabilization. During the 1986 congressional debate on funding the contras, PRODEMCA sponsored a four-day visit to Washington by contra commanders.

Immediately after the Sandinista victory, the budget of the

American Institute for Free Labor Development's Nicaraguan office tripled, with most of it flowing to a small labor federation called CUS (Confederación de Unificación Sindical). Although AIFLD was forced out of the country in 1982, the institute has continued to support CUS—which also receives money from USIA—by covering the foreign travel expenses of CUS leaders. Since 1985, CUS has also been supported by FTUI, which is funded by NED and is a division of the AFL-CIO that works closely with AIFLD. NED said that FTUI would use its grants to give "organizational support to regional trade union groups and to international labor organizations. . . ." It would also provide funds "for emergency organizational support, to assist trade union exiles, and to help counter efforts by anti-democratic groups to subvert the union movement."[27]

According to NED, FTUI's assistance enabled CUS to play "a critical role in defending the rights of workers and in mobilizing and organizing the democratic forces committed to peaceful change in Nicaragua." Through FTUI, NED funded (until 1985) the publication of CUS's monthly magazine *Solidaridad* and another anti-Sandinista magazine published in Costa Rica called *Unidad.*

Besides backing "pro-democratic" labor organizations, NED also supports a branch of the U.S. Chamber of Commerce called the Center for International Private Enterprise (CIPE). In 1985 CIPE used NED funds to finance a study of small businesses and vendors in Nicaragua. The study was sponsored by the Pan American Development Foundation, which has supported the Nicaraguan business organizations FUNDE and INDE with AID money. The study concluded that "microentrepreneurs need to be made more aware of their own identity as part of the private sector" and that "representative business organizations and foundations must be built to promote their full participation in economic and public policy affairs." CIPE noted that the study "underscored the existence of a highly adaptable, often extralegal sector within the economy that ably resists state collectivization, often better than traditional sectors." The study called for the small business sector to become "a political as well as an economic force" in Nicaragua.[28]

Besides its funding of NED, the USIA produces and disseminates information to the media and "decision makers" in each Central American nation, including Nicaragua. In the case of Costa Rica, the USIA post in San José sends an information packet to "some 80 top-level Costa Rican decision-makers" in addition to most of the media. USIA distributes package programs to 20 radio stations. Seven stations, including the top-ranked Radio Reloj and Radio Monumental, transmit USIA's Voice of America (VOA) programs, and 20 correspondent reports are placed every day on Costa Rican radio.[29] The USIA also proudly boasts that it "maintains regular working contact with the five TV stations in Costa Rica" and that "almost all TV material [USIA] provides is readily placed."[30]

The U.S. government, according to some observers, has gone far beyond passing out anti-Sandinista reports to the media. In a deposition submitted to the World Court, Edgar Chamorro, a former top spokesperson for the FDN contras, said, "Approximately 15 Honduras journalists and broadcasters were on the CIA's payroll, and our influence was thereby extended to every major Honduran newspaper and radio and television station." Similar claims came from Costa Rica, where the major media have ardently supported the contras. Carlos Morales, a University of Costa Rica journalism professor who runs the *Seminario Universidad* newspaper, confided that he knew journalists who worked for the CIA because they needed extra money.[31] CIA funds probably finance the four-page newspaper supplement called *Nicaragua Hoy* (Nicaragua Today) produced in Costa Rica and said to be distributed to over 600,000 readers through major newspapers in seven Latin American countries. Additionally, Radio Impacto, one of Costa Rica's most powerful stations, is backed by the CIA, according to Chamorro.

Electronic Psyops

Transborder broadcasting by Nicaragua's neighbors and enemies has become an integral part of a war in which psychological operations share equal billing with military aggression. A recent study by Howard H. Frederick of the School of Communications at Ohio University found that 75 foreign AM and FM radio stations were heard in various parts of Nicaragua. Nine foreign television stations also reached the country. Costa Rica dominated the field with 26 radio stations and seven of the TV channels. The broadcasts were picked up by Nicaragua's estimated 500,000 radio receivers and 200,000 television sets. In contrast, the Nicaraguan government operated 17 radio stations of uneven signal qualities and one television station.[32]

According to international telecommunications expert Frederick, "Electronic penetration must be seen as an integral part of the strategy by Nicaragua's enemies carried out under the rubric of low intensity conflict. Especially important in [LIC]," said Frederick, "are the channels of electronic communication, used so easily to disinform and destabilize." The media war against Nicaragua has several distinct orientations, not the least of which are economic messages in the form of commercial advertising and market-dominated news. The constant barrage of advertisements for appliances and automotive parts, nail polish and headache remedies cannot help but create the impression in Nicaraguan minds that life is more affluent in other countries.

Other uses of electronic penetration are less subtle. The pro-contra/anti-Sandinista content of news broadcasts beamed in from Honduras and Costa Rica is not even thinly disguised. For example, any apparent violation of Costa Rican territory by the Sandinista People's Army is quickly reported, while Costa Rica's acquiescence to contras operating from Costa Rican bases is never mentioned.

Nicaragua's efforts at counteracting the flood of destabilizing propaganda have been hampered by equipment shortages and weak signals that can only reach 60 percent of the country and rarely extend beyond the nation's borders. Additionally, when Sandinista TV airs its 8 o'clock news, the foreign television stations usually put their best entertainment programs up against it. Often, the powerful Voice of America is able to obliterate Nicaraguan air waves on an adjacent frequency.[33]

With CIA assistance, the contras broadcast their own propaganda through three clandestine radio stations operating in Honduras and Costa Rica. Radio 15 de Septiembre, established in 1981, was the first station to launch the contras' psychological operations campaign over the air waves. The CIA set up Radio 15—"the voice of the Christian freedom commandos"— as the official radio of the Nicaraguan Democratic Forces (FDN). Thought to be located about 20 miles from Tegucigalpa, the capital of Honduras, Radio 15 has played a key role in implanting a fear of the Sandinistas among the Miskito Indians of the Atlantic Coast. Also broadcasting from Honduras is Radio Miskut, which is run by KISAN (formerly MISURA), the Miskito contra organization. Radio Miskut broadcasts in the Miskito language from the border town of Rus Rus. Plans were underway in 1986 to establish a contra AM radio station to be called Radio Liberación under the direction of Pedro Joaquin Chamorro, Jr., who edited *La Prensa* until the Nicaraguan government closed the paper down in 1986.[34]

In 1984, USIA began a $1 billion expansion of Voice of America, which included two new transmitters in Central America. The transmitters in Belize and Costa Rica are among the eleven that are planned for the Caribbean Basin. In an unusual and highly secretive agreement, USIA provided $3.2 million for the 1984 construction of a radio station in Costa Rica's northern zone. With a 50,000 watt signal, Radio Costa Rica can be heard throughout Nicaragua. Radio Costa Rica is operated by the Costa Rican Association for Information and Culture, a group of conservative media owners and politicians that was formed by the U.S. Embassy to circumvent a Costa Rican law that prohibits foreigners from owning broadcasting facilities.[35] Besides financing the construction of the highly fortified station, USIA pays an annual $168,000 fee to the Costa Rican association. The official purpose of the station is to "serve the interests of Costa Rica's democracy," but it devotes over half of its air time to VOA programming.[36]

AN ECONOMIC BLOCKADE

The trade war against Nicaragua began several years before President Reagan imposed a total embargo in 1985. An early sign of what was coming was the 1981 cutoff of the trade credits and investment insurance offered by Eximbank and OPIC. While the Reagan administration was encouraging these agencies to increase their operations in other parts of Central America, their activities in Nicaragua were brought to a standstill. The Caribbean Basin Initiative (CBI) also pointedly excluded Nicaragua from aid and trade benefits. Without access to the financial guarantees of Eximbank and OPIC, many U.S. businesses became reluctant to trade with or invest in Nicaragua. Nicaragua suffered from this exclusion, but the government became more determined to diversify their trade and foreign investment.[37]

In a clear breach of international trade law, President Reagan in 1983 slashed Nicaragua's sugar quota by 90 percent—a measure that hurt both the state farms and several large private producers. In June 1983, Reagan ordered all Nicaraguan consular and commercial offices closed down, an action that further obstructed trade and investment by U.S. business in Nicaragua. In spring 1985, Reagan ordered a complete embargo, using the International Emergency Economic Powers Act to justify the measure. When announcing the embargo, Reagan said, "I . . . find that the policies and actions of the Government of Nicaragua constitute an unusual and extraordinary threat to the national security and foreign policy of the

United States, and hereby declare a national emergency to deal with that threat."

The embargo prohibited the imports of Nicaraguan goods and services; blocked direct sea and air transport; and ended the export of U.S. goods to Nicaragua "except those for the organized democratic resistance," that is, the contras. After the embargo, Nicaragua was successful in finding new buyers for most of its exports and new sources for most of its imports. Many Western European nations stepped in to buy Nicaragua's agroexports as an expression of their disagreement with the U.S. embargo. Canada bought 80 percent of Nicaragua's beef exports, and Libya purchased the balance. Socialist countries became the market for 30 percent of Nicaragua's banana exports. Despite the help, the embargo did harm the Nicaraguan economy. Estimates of the first year's cost of the embargo to Nicaragua range from $50 to $90 million.[38] The government, charging that the embargo violated international trading agreements, presented demands for "economic retribution for damages" before the GATT general council.

The trade embargo was another step in the overall U.S. strategy of debilitating Nicaragua, but it probably did little to advance U.S. policy interests in the region. None of Nicaragua's neighbors joined in the embargo, and it resulted in stronger Nicaraguan trade links with Western Europe and socialist countries. Ironically, despite the U.S. government's preoccupation with the welfare of the private sector, it was this sector in Nicaragua that was hit the hardest by the embargo. While the government had already found other sources for capital and intermediate imports, the private sector was almost completely dependent on imports of U.S. machinery, pesticides, and spare parts.[39]

Leaning on the International Banks

During the last year and a half of the Carter administration, relations between Nicaragua and the IFIs were relatively good. The World Bank and the Inter-American Development Bank

(IDB) approved $175 million to help in the reconstruction process, and prospects looked hopeful for another $150 million. Projects receiving assistance included agricultural efforts, reconstruction of war damage, water supply and sewerage projects, rural health services, forestry development, and support for 4-H clubs.[40]

In the summer of 1981, however, the United States began opposing all loans for Nicaraguan development projects from the IFIs—institutions in which the United States plays a highly influential role. "We had an overall political problem with the direction" of the Nicaraguan government, remarked a Treasury Department official in regard to a U.S. veto of an IDB loan for a fisheries project. The United States blocked proposals in formal votes and by delaying techniques. As a result, new World Bank and IDB lending to Nicaragua was halted. To use the administration's own terminology, Nicaragua was put on its "hit list." In June 1983, this practice of blocking all multilateral loans to Nicaragua became official U.S. policy.

When a Nicaraguan agricultural loan came up for approval by the IDB in 1984, Secretary of State George Shultz wrote a letter to the IDB directors, telling them that the approval "would make it even more difficult for the United States to approve new contributions to the bank." In 1984, Nicaragua was the only Latin American member country not to receive an IDB loan. The $60 million proposed agricultural loan, designed primarily to assist the private agricultural sector, would have expanded the production of food for internal consumption and increased the export of commodities. Among other things, the loan would have allowed Nicaraguan farmers to renovate coffee plantations, open up land for cotton cultivation, add 25,000 acres for basic foods, increase the cattle herd by 63,000, and establish 28 chicken farms to increase poultry consumption. Over 15,000 small- and medium-sized farmers would have been the main beneficiaries. The IDB team called the project "technically viable and economically justifiable," and an independent consulting firm gave the project an extremely positive recommendation.[41]

"We read [Shultz's letter] as a threat," said one IDB member. "Even during the time of Allende, there was never such a communication."[42] The Reagan administration's efforts to block loans to Nicaragua went beyond applying pressure on IDB's executive board to interference with the bank's internal process of preparing reports. In December 1985, the IDB's top management, caving in to the wishes of the U.S. government, produced a new technical report on the agricultural loan that Nicaragua had requested; this time they reached negative conclusions. Jim Morrell, research director at the Center for International Policy, said that "by doctoring the report-writing process, U.S. pressure has corrupted the very heart of a major international financial institution." He called the intrusion of U.S. political considerations into the preparation of the technical report on Nicaragua "the most flagrant violation of the charter in the bank's history."[43] The IDB representative from Central America, Alexi De Synegub, remarked: "The U.S. is only one of the 43 countries that make up the IDB, and the rest of the countries agreed to the government of Nicaragua's request for support to the private [agricultural] sector. The more I think about it, the less I understand it because the United States, the self-labelled champion of support of private enterprise, is assuming a position contrary to their own philosophy."[44]

Because the IFI charters call for independent and politically free decision making, Washington often tries to disguise its political opposition to Nicaragua by officially stating that its objections are based on that country's "ineffective macroeconomic policies." This tactic recalls an identical stance against loans to Chile under Salvador Allende. A 1984 study by the Center for International Policy concluded that the "U.S. government violates the spirit of these institutions' charters by supporting or opposing lending to certain countries because of our political relations with them. It technically avoids violating the charter of the IFIs by constructing economic arguments to use in lobbying for its position."[45]

While the United States does not wield as much voting power in the World Bank as it does in the IDB, U.S. pressure has been the main factor obstructing World Bank loans to Nicaragua since 1982. The last loan that Nicaragua received was one for $16 million to finance storm drainage and low income urban projects. The loan request passed with all members except the United States voting in favor of it. In 1981, before U.S. pressure began in earnest, World Bank reports recommended new loans for Nicaragua, saying that the country's economic policy was "encouraging." With foreign aid and good management, "Nicaragua will indeed be able to reconstruct its economy and to continue to enhance the social situation of its citizens."[46] By the next year, however, the World Bank, under U.S. pressure, had reversed its initial positive assessment of Nicaragua and adopted the U.S. position that Nicaragua had to establish an economic policy more favorable to the private sector before loans would be approved.

Contrary to U.S. claims that development loans to Nicaragua would be misspent, evidence shows that Nicaraguan development programs have been efficient, effective, and well-managed. Since 1983, Nicaragua's first concern has been with defense, but it continues to make efforts to improve the lives of the poor. The World Bank called the country's dedication "remarkable."[47] At least until 1984, Nicaragua received consistent good marks for its management of multilateral projects. Reviewing a 1983 urban reconstruction project, the World Bank called it "probably one of the most effective urban projects supported by the bank." The project, which was completed with "remarkable speed," achieved "twice the quantities of road improvements— paving and drainage" as originally envisaged. "This was due in large part to the commitment of the Government authorities, local municipalities, and *barrio* residents to provide immediate benefits to poor areas."[48] Another World Bank report stated that there is not a "smidgen of corruption" in the urban development projects it supported in Nicaragua.[49] And Jaime Belcazar, director of the United Nations Development Program, wrote of Nicaragua: "In the first several years of their administration, they have made extraordinary advances in health, education, and agriculture."[50]

Nicaragua's relationship with the International Monetary Fund (IMF) was rocky from the start of the revolution. The Sandinistas were angry with the IMF for having approved a $66 million loan to the Somoza regime only nine weeks before Somoza left the country. As the Sandinistas predicted, Anastasio Somoza absconded with the loan, leaving the new government with the bill. To make matters worse, the IMF demanded that the revolutionary government immediately repay the loan. Nicaragua has met its debt obligations with the IMF but has neither received nor requested additional financial support. Every other Central American country has received IMF assistance in the 1980s.

Since the United States began its pressure campaign, no major multilateral bank has granted development loans to Nicaragua—despite its relatively good record at meeting multilateral loan obligations. Between 1980 and 1982, Nicaragua made every interest payment on its foreign debt—a record which distinguished it among other debt-ridden third world nations. As of mid-1986, Nicaragua was in arrears with the World Bank, but was current with both the IDB and the IMF.

The U.S.-orchestrated economic war has cost Nicaragua hundreds of millions of dollars in development loans. In 1979, multilateral development loans constituted 78 percent of the foreign loans received by Nicaragua but it has not received one such loan in the last few years.[51] If Nicaragua had been awarded multilateral funding at the same level as other Central American countries, it would have received $313 million between 1982 and 1985 or about $78 million each year.[52]

The influence of the U.S. government also reduced private lending to Nicaragua. When the Sandinistas came to power in July 1979, they found themselves saddled with a $1.6 billion foreign debt—about half of which was owed to private banks. In return for the government's promise to repay this debt, private banks pledged to keep their loans flowing. During the next three years, Nicaragua complied with the loan agreements by promptly and fully meeting its negotiated debt repayment schedule.[53] But new private loans were not forthcoming. During the last three years of the Somoza dictatorship, private banks authorized credit lines of more than $100 million annually even though Nicaragua was in de facto default on its debt payments. In contrast, only a paltry $12 million in new private bank loans reached Nicaragua between 1979 and 1983—a period during which the government paid over $575 million in debt service.[54]

COSTS OF DESTABILIZATION

Destabilization has dashed the Sandinistas' hopes for an economy that would meet the basic needs of all Nicaraguans in the near future. The campaign has squeezed the national budget, restricted access to trade and external financing, undermined agricultural production, and led to increased capital flight. Besides facing the exigencies caused by the economic war, Nicaragua has endured the debilitating effects of an economic sabotage campaign waged by the contras. Bridges have been dynamited, oil deposits ignited, grain depositories destroyed, and the planting and harvesting of crops disrupted. The coffee industry, the main source of foreign exchange, has been a constant target of the contras. In 1985 and 1986, Nicaraguan coffee pickers required government protection from contra attacks. The production of basic foods has also been hit hard by the U.S.-directed contra war since over half of the country's corn and bean crops normally come from what have turned into war zones since 1983. As the contra war has expanded, Nicaragua has dedicated an ever-increasing portion of its budget to defense. By 1985, the country was devoting 50 percent of its budget and 40 percent of production by Nicaraguan industry and agriculture to the military.[55]

Economic destabilization has disrupted the country's development plans and the daily functioning of many economic sectors. Farmers complain that they cannot fix their tractors, and entrepreneurs gripe that they cannot run their businesses profitably with their office machines in disrepair. The lack of foreign capital has weakened the government's capacity to expand agricultural production, energize the fishing industry, and create new urban industries. The effects of the economic war can also be seen in the scarcity of foreign exchange for imports, reduced social services due to the soaring defense budget, and the flight of professionals seeking better jobs and living conditions abroad. British economist E.V.K. Fitzgerald noted another sad consequence of the war: "The country's best leaders, its best technicians, its most promising young people must devote themselves to killing people rather than to developing the country."[56]

The war of economic stabilization has caused huge production losses, particularly in primary industries (agriculture, fishing, and mining). Nicaragua has suffered an estimated 25 percent loss in its export production capability because of the war. This in turn has caused other problems because of the lack of foreign exchange, resulting in loss of production activity in other industries such as construction. According to figures by the UN's Economic Commission for Latin America, 1984 exports would have been 32 percent greater without external aggression, and the economy would have grown at the rate of 6 percent per annum between 1980 and 1985—a rate that would have placed Nicaragua far ahead of its neighbors.[57]

When the Sandinista guerrillas rolled into Managua in July 1979, they took over a country devastated by war and left bankrupt by the fleeing elite. Infrastructure damage from the war—caused mostly by the artillery and aerial attacks of the National Guard—was estimated at close to $500 million.[58] Somoza had depleted the National Treasury, and fleeing capitalists had drained the country of private capital. During the first few years of the revolution, the government managed to set the country on the path of economic growth and development. But the forward movement of Nicaragua began to slow down in late 1983, in part because of the government's own failed policies, but mainly due to the war of attrition directed by Washington. By early 1986, this war had killed nearly 4,000 Nicaraguans, wounded another 4,500, and resulted in the displacement of over 120,000 people living in the war zones. Numerous health centers, hospitals, schools, and government social service offices were destroyed or damaged. Estimates of the cost in dollars from both military aggression and economic destabilization ranged from one to two billion dollars.[59]

AID ON THE PERIMETER

In sharp contrast to its destabilization campaign against Nicaragua, the United States used its entire economic toolbox to stabilize Nicaragua's three neighbors: Costa Rica, Honduras, and El Salvador. All three countries rank among the world's top ten recipients of U.S. economic aid. After the Sandinista victory, Washington dramatically increased food aid, investment insurance, and trade incentives for Nicaragua's neighbors. It also encouraged multilateral assistance and used its influence to persuade the International Monetary Fund to back off from imposing harsh austerity programs in the three countries. In addition to general purpose funds for these governments, aid was channeled into specific projects that supported a concerted counterrevolutionary strategy.

The U.S. government used economic as well as military aid to foment anti-Sandinista pressure on Nicaragua's two borders. Its generous assistance to Costa Rica and Honduras obligated the two nations to accept U.S. foreign policy as their own. Washington's obsession with Nicaragua proved to be a lifesaver for the tottering economies of Costa Rica and Honduras. Besides economic assistance to stabilize the two countries, a variety of nonlethal aid programs created an infrastructure for the contras and a base for a possible U.S. invasion.

Costa Rica: Development in the Northern Zone

In 1983, AID began its $20 million Northern Zone Infrastructure Development Project, located in the undeveloped area of Costa Rica that lies along the Nicaraguan border. A poor and sparsely populated area, the Northern Zone has seen an increase in social tension and in the number of land occupations by *campesinos.* Its proximity to Nicaragua brought the region a new strategic importance and made it a base for the southern front of the contras. AID said that the area was chosen for the extensive development project because the Costa Rican government had expressed "concern about the feelings of isolation and frustration expressed by the population and its proximity to and the constant destabilizing influence of Nicaragua."[60] The Northern Zone is characterized by "a low level of satisfaction of basic needs," and the Costa Rican government has been concerned about the loyalty of the region's population, many of whom are native Nicaraguans.[61]

AID projects for the zone were divided into three categories: colonization, infrastructure improvement, and agricultural development. Colonization involves the resetting of landless *campesinos* in isolated areas in the border region. Also planned are new roads and agricultural programs aimed to increase agroexports from the region. Project designers hope to better integrate the border population into the Costa Rican economy. As part of the project, AID is purchasing unused land and distributing plots to landless peasants. Many farmers and ranchers are also slated to receive AID loans. The Inter-American Development Bank has complementary development activity in the area, and the Peace Corps, CARE, and the World Food Program are also working in the Northern Zone.

New roads along the Nicaraguan border have obvious military implications. Originally, the U.S. government suggested that the U.S. Army Corps of Engineers build the roads, but instead AID contractors were hired for the job, which covers a large swath of border land that was virtually unpopulated except for the contras. Not only do the roads help contra operations but they would also facilitate any future U.S. military invasion of Nicaragua.

While the Northern Zone extends beyond the border areas, the acute interest in the region is clearly of a political nature. Even AID's project description acknowledged that the Northern Zone was being given priority funding because of "geopolitical reasons."[62] The president of Costa Rica at the time, Luis Alberto Monge, noted in 1982 that the region's "relative isolation from the rest of the country exposes it to foreign influence and infiltration." According to Monge, the Northern Zone projects are part of an effort "to better our system of national security."[63] A 1984 study by the Society of Inter-American Planning (SIAP) concluded that the development and colonization projects underway in the Northern Zone had as their objective "the neutralization of the ideological influence of the Sandinista Revolution."[64] President Monge expressed concern that the *campesinos* of the Northern Zone were overly exposed to "the penetration of the ideas of enemies of the Costa Rican democracy. . . . We don't want our compatriots to be unprotected ideologically in the Northern Zone."[65]

Increased U.S. attention to Costa Rica has also involved a U.S.-sponsored military buildup. In 1985, a team of U.S. Army Special Forces (Green Berets) trained 750 members of the country's Civil Guard. The U.S.-trained guard unit responsible for patrolling the Nicaraguan border is called the Lightning Battalion. The guardsmen were trained at a camp near the border.

Honduras: Building a Contra Base

Washington also used nonlethal assistance to support counterrevolution along the Nicaraguan border in Honduras. AID targeted this region for special development assistance and humanitarian aid projects. These projects assisted Nicaraguan refugees, built an infrastructure for the contras, and mollified some Hondurans upset with the contra occupation. The U.S. government also paved the way for the flow of private economic aid to this strategic region.

In 1981, the U.S. government encouraged World Relief (a leading recipient of AID funds) and the United Nations High Commission for Refugees (UNHCR) to set up refugee camps along the border. The refugee camps soon filled with Miskito Indians fleeing the contra war and the Sandinista resettlement programs, and they served as recruiting bases and sources of supplies for the contra armies. In 1984, AID began its own humanitarian assistance program for Nicaraguan refugees living in the border area known as La Mosquitia.[66]

AID specifically prohibited the $7.8 million in humanitarian assistance to the La Mosquitia region from being channeled through the United Nations and World Relief. It felt that neither organization was sufficiently supportive of the contras to serve as a channel for the aid.[67] While UNHCR and World Relief insist on keeping the refugee camps at least 30 miles from the border, AID's program serves areas directly abutting Nicaragua as well as assisting Miskitos not in refugee camps. Representatives from the United Nations and voluntary organizations active in La Mosquitia condemned AID's $7.8 million project. They said it contributed to the tension along the border by supporting the contras and encouraging refugees to stay in Honduras.

In Rus Rus and Danli (a key contra site), AID supplies Friends of the Americas (FOA), an anticommunist "humanitarian" organization, with seeds and tools for Nicaraguan refugees along the border. AID is also paying for well drilling, malaria eradication, and several health programs in La Mosquitia. Additionally, La Mosquitia has been deluged with U.S. PL480 food assistance, distributed by FOA and other groups. Through its administration of U.S. food aid, AID plays an important role in keeping Nicaraguan Miskitos in Honduras and in supporting the work of Friends of the Americas.

Representative Robert Livingston (R-LA), who proposed the $7.8 million aid program to Congress, said that an emergency existed on the Honduran side of La Mosquitia because Nicaraguan Miskito refugees were suffering from severe malnourishment. Livingston said he heard of the plight of the Miskitos from Louis Jenkins, a state representative from Louisiana. Jenkins, co-director of Friends of the Americas, claimed that "tens of thousands of refugees" had been suffering in La Mosquitia. But a closer look reveals that there are only 25,000 permanent residents of La Mosquitia and that UN-World Relief camps (30 miles from the border) provide adequate care for the refugees.

Reports of severe hunger in the area by AID and Friends of the Americas, moreover, conflicted with recent studies of the inhabitants' nutritional welfare—studies that were sent to the U.S. Embassy. The French medical relief group Medecins Sans Frontiers, which works at UNHCR camps, reported that the rate of malnutrition among the refugee population was lower than malnutrition rates in the United States. A doctor who conducted a survey for the Atlanta-based Center for Disease Control "strongly discouraged the institution of (or continuation of) any large scale food distribution program."[68] Even FOA's doctor in Rus Rus, Oscar Otero, said "nutrition is not a problem here."

In addition to providing surplus food, AID also paid for the construction and maintenance of a 108-mile road including several bridges in strategic locations. The agency claimed that the road would help small farmers market their crops and enhance development of the region. The road, however, leads to Rus Rus and Ahuasbila, the very sites where Miskito contras are based. In the same area, AID spent $900,000 for a radio education project managed by the International Rescue Committee (IRC), a U.S. private voluntary organization. The IRC, a long-time servant of the State Department and the CIA in such diverse locations as West Germany, Bangladesh, and Vietnam, works with displaced persons in El Salvador, Honduras, and Costa Rica.[69]

Besides FOA and IRC, many other private organizations admit to aiding refugees in the Honduras-Nicaragua border area. For example, Refugee Relief International (a branch of the *Soldier of Fortune* magazine) supplied the contras with mercenaries and supplies, and the Nicaragua Refugee Fund (a pro-contra organization founded with the assistance of the CIA) raised funds for the contras.

In addition to groups with paramilitary purposes, a rash of evangelical organizations set up operations along the Nicaraguan border. These include Club 700 of the Christian Broadcasting Network (CBN), Jimmy Swaggart's Missions in Motion, Salt and Light, and the Christian Emergency Relief Teams (CERT). Pat Robertson of CBN called the contras "God's army," and helped raise funds for the counterrevolutionaries and their families. CERT's David Courson raised money in the United States by telling people that the "Sandinistas are determined to eliminate all Christians" and that "thousands of people have been brutally murdered because they neither would deny Christ nor submit to the brutal demands of the Sandinistas." On a 1985 mission to Central America, Jimmy Swaggart flew over Miskito settlements in Honduras, dropping candy from his plane for children with his amplified message about Christ and communism drifting over the area.

In 1985, a staff report by the Arms Control and Foreign Policy Caucus called into question the nature of the aid these groups offer. "Most groups call their aid 'humanitarian,' " concluded the report, "but either privately or publicly acknowledge that some of it ends up at contra camps. These groups also have conceded that their 'humanitarian' aid to refugees (which include families of the contras) may indirectly aid the contras by freeing up the contra accounts to purchase weapons and pay combatants."

Bona fide relief organizations are concerned about the political use of humanitarian assistance in Central America. Organizations like Church World Service feel that the involvement of the Pentagon, the White House, and right-wing anticommunist groups in humanitarian assistance programs with an anti-Sandinista message might undermine nonpolitical relief work by casting suspicion on the motives of all private assistance organizations.[70]

SURVIVAL, NOT DEVELOPMENT

In its headlong rush to keep Central America in its pocket, the U.S. government chose the dual strategy of stabilization and destabilization. With generous amounts of aid, Washington persuaded the governments of Costa Rica and Honduras to cooperate with its campaign to weaken the economy of Nicaragua. Destabilization seriously undermined the course of the Sandinista revolution. Early advances in such areas as education and health came to a standstill. The government was forced to adopt the austerity measures of a wartime footing. And the population's commitment to the revolution was tested constantly by the deepening economic hardships, the tension of war, and the psychological operations directed by Washington. Instead of ensuring that the Sandinista revolution would maintain its promise of democracy and economic pluralism, destabilization forced Nicaragua to limit constitutional freedoms and to militarize certain regions.

The campaign of destabilization also had negative consequences outside Nicaragua. Washington politicized the IFIs in its drive to deprive Nicaragua of desperately needed foreign exchange and development capital. By continually violating international trade law, the United States earned the wrath and disrespect of the world community. In the process of destabilizing Nicaragua, the United States was destabilizing the region as a whole. The campaign squashed most hopes for increased trade among Central American nations and prevented regional solutions to common problems of underdevelopment. The U.S. strategy of using bilateral aid to prop up selected governments had the result of further isolating each country, while strengthening the connections with Washington. While bleeding Nicaragua, Washington used the almighty dollar to pressure other countries, including Mexico, to adopt foreign policy positions and economic programs not in their long-term interest. And by supporting the contra war and counterrevolution inside Nicaragua, Washington minimized the prospects for peace in Central America.

Destabilization smothered the early hopes for peace and prosperity within Nicaragua. It has drained human and economic resources but not the commitment to defend the revolution. Destabilization did not force the Sandinistas to say "uncle." But the campaign made the Sandinistas scale down their ambitions and concentrate on the simple survival of the revolution.

CHAPTER **9** AIFLD: Agents and Organizers

"We don't strike, we're democratic."
—Roberto Cazares,
    AIFLD Central America director, 1984.

At the forefront of Washington's low intensity invasion of Central America is a U.S.-based labor organization called the American Institute for Free Labor Development (AIFLD). The operations of AIFLD, which is a branch of the AFL-CIO funded by the U.S. government, can be found in all seven countries of Central America. As the paradigm of an LIC organization, AIFLD's operations cover such low-intensity conflict activities as pacification, Psyops, public diplomacy, intelligence, and political manipulation. To achieve its LIC objectives, AIFLD conducts programs that organize and educate "free-trade unions" and "democratic" rural associations.

AIFLD and several other branches of the AFL-CIO's International Affairs Department have served as fronts for U.S. ideological and political intervention around the world for several decades. Part of the new surge of "quasi-private" organizations in Central America, AIFLD and groups such as NED, Freedom House, and PRODEMCA claim to be spreading democracy and freedom. In the name of democracy, a far-reaching infrastructure of U.S.-controlled labor, business, political, and antipopular organizations are being established in the region. A closer look at AIFLD reveals just how extensive and destructive this "democratic" network really is.

A Long Record of Government Service

The involvement of organized labor's leadership in foreign policy and operations dates back to the turn of the century when the AFL backed U.S. military intervention in Puerto Rico, Cuba, and the Philippines. Under the leadership of Samuel Gompers, the AFL also supported the U.S. government's efforts to establish economic and ideological hegemony in Latin America. The role played by the AFL and later the AFL-CIO (merged in 1955) in U.S. foreign policy steadily expanded as the century advanced. By World War II, the AFL had its own international affairs department headed by a team of ardent anticommunists including Jay Lovestone and Irving Brown. In 1944, the AFL formed the Free Trade Union Committee (FTUC), which teamed up with U.S. intelligence operations in Europe. The FTUC, which was headquartered in the offices of the avidly anticommunist International Ladies Garment Workers Union (ILGWU) in New York, sought to combat leftist union organizing and establish U.S. control over the European labor movement. The AFL's International Affairs Department working with the FTUC organized the U.S.-controlled International Confederation of Free Trade Unions (ICFTU) in 1949.

World War II brought labor, business, and government into a patriotic coalition. Nelson Rockefeller, who recognized the pivotal role of labor unions in political movements, played a key role in this formation of a tripartite alliance. As the head of the State Department's Office of Inter-American Affairs, Rockefeller called upon labor leaders to work with him in intelligence operations in Latin America. Serafino Romualdi, who later became the first executive director of AIFLD, had close links to ILGWU and worked under Rockefeller as an agent for the Office for Strategic Services (OSS), the intelligence agency that preceded the CIA.

After the war, Romualdi joined the AFL's International Affairs Department and became the organization's "labor ambassador" to Latin America. His task was to undermine the growing strength of nationalist, anti-imperialist unions and to build a regional confederation based on cold war politics. In 1948, Romualdi, working closely with the State Department, succeeded in organizing such a confederation, which since 1951 has been called the Inter-American Regional Organization of Workers (ORIT). Over the years, ORIT has provided strong support for U.S. policy in Latin America. Working in tandem with ORIT are several international associations called international trade secretariats (ITSs), which are groupings of national industrial unions in the same or related industries.

With the help of men like Lovestone, Brown, and Romualdi, the CIA broadened its relationship with the AFL and later the AFL-CIO. CIA funds were channeled to international trade secretariats like the Postal, Telegraph, and Telephone International (PTTI), which was controlled by Joseph Beirne's Communications Workers of America (CWA). Foreign labor organizations also received CIA money laundered through fictitious private organizations and foundations set up by the intelligence agency.

Soon after the Cuban Revolution, the U.S. government decided that a new "free labor" organization was needed to combat the advances of leftist unions and to spread U.S. anticommunist ideology throughout Latin America.[1] Inspiration for the creation of AIFLD came from a training course for conservative Latin American unionists run by the CWA under its president Joseph Beirne. AIFLD was founded in 1961 with commitments of financial support from the AFL-CIO, U.S. corporations, and the U.S. government.

While the U.S. government's backing of AIFLD was not a secret, CIA funding of labor operations abroad did not come into public view until 1976. According to a report by the Senate Select Committee on Intelligence, the CIA by 1967 had budgeted more than $6 million for labor programs—the funds being distributed through "fictitious entities established by the CIA." These revelations about the CIA's involvement in

AIFLD and other AFL-CIO international activities sparked bitter debate within the labor federation, especially after the 1964 military coup in Brazil, in which both the CIA and AIFLD played prominent roles.[2] Subsequently, the CIA was forced to reduce its funding of international labor operations.

As one alternative to direct CIA funding of foreign labor operations, AID in 1968 began the practice, still common today, of channeling grants to the international secretariats. But rather than directly linking the ITSs to the U.S. government, AID furnishes AIFLD with "union-to-union" funds. AIFLD in turn funnels these funds to unions like the Communications Workers of America, which then pass the money on to their international secretariats. Not all ITSs, however, have succumbed to U.S. control; many fulfill the important service of representing workers on an international front against transnational corporations. The halt to the CIA's indirect funding of labor operations through dummy foundations has not stopped the CIA from using AIFLD as part of its network in Central America. In 1975, former CIA agent Philip Agee described AIFLD as a "CIA-controlled labor center financed through AID." According to Agee, "The real purpose of [AIFLD] was to train cadres to organize new trade unions or to take over existing ones, in such a way that the unions would be controlled, directly or indirectly, by the CIA."[3]

The Corporate-Labor Connection

From AIFLD's inception, it has been tied not only to the U.S. government but also to transnational corporations with investments in Latin America. The first director of AIFLD's board of trustees was J. Peter Grace of the WR Grace Company. Grace was joined on the board by representatives of the Rockefeller family and companies like Pan American Airways and Anaconda, while other major investors in Latin America like United Fruit and ITT contributed financially to AIFLD.

The increasing acceptance of a conservative concept of unionism known as "business" or "contract" unionism was a factor that brought labor and capital together. This is a philosophy that stresses cooperation between labor, business, and government. It rejects the concept of class struggle, arguing that both owners and workers have common interests. Through AIFLD, both the U.S. government and U.S. corporations have encouraged business unionism. This conservative approach to organizing in Latin America is an attractive concept to U.S. investors. As J. Peter Grace once explained: "AIFLD urges cooperation between labor and management and an end to class struggle. It teaches workers to help to increase their company's business and to improve productivity so that they can gain more from an expanding business."[4]

The most enduring area of common ground between the labor bureaucracy and corporations is their shared anticommunist ideology. On the home front, union and corporate leaders are often locked in conflict. But beyond U.S. borders, mutual anticommunism brings them together. William Doherty, AIFLD's current director, believes the key question in Latin America is whether the region will move toward communism or democracy. "All other questions remain secondary."[5] By supporting repressive governments and creating its "free" labor unions, AIFLD has helped create the kind of business climate in Latin American countries that attracts runaway U.S. companies looking for a cheap and pliant work force.

The official connection between labor and business was severed in 1980. After George Meany died, the new AFL-CIO leadership under Lane Kirkland decided that the situation was embarrassing and requested that AIFLD's corporate representatives leave the board. Grace stepped down as AIFLD chairperson, 9 of the original 34 board positions were eliminated, and representatives of transnationals no longer were invited to serve. Grace assured AIFLD, however, that he and other business leaders would continue to collaborate with AIFLD "in a friendly and supportive capacity."[6]

Training to Beat the Reds

Training unionists has always been AIFLD's primary activity.* Since its beginning, the institute has trained over 500,000 Latin American unionists. Most of these unionists have attended incountry courses while 4,300 have attended the George Meany Center for Labor Studies outside Washington, D.C. An elite group of graduates from these programs moves on for advanced training at several U.S. colleges, including Georgetown University in Washington, D.C., and Loyola University in New Orleans. Every year some 15 handpicked labor leaders from Central America travel to the United States for training.[7]

While AIFLD offers courses in such topics as labor/management relations and union structure, its main objective is to teach its members how to counter leftist organizing efforts. The ideological nature of AIFLD training can be seen in the titles of some of its course offerings: Totalitarian Ideologies, Workers and Political Education, Comparative Political and Economic Systems, Role of Labor in a Developing Democracy, Recognition and Analysis of Extremist Propaganda, and Recognition and Defense Against Infiltration and Front Organizations. AIFLD students not only leave training sessions ideologically

*Training programs in Latin America are not the exclusive domain of AIFLD; the U.S. Department of Labor, AID, and the USIA all sponsor instruction for unions and government labor ministries as well as meetings between Central American and U.S. union leaders. AID pays for most of the international labor training programs of the Department of Labor. The USIA has three educational programs that involve Central American labor leaders. Under the American Participants program, a handful of U.S. experts travel to Central America each year to speak on labor issues. The International Visitor Program and the Voluntary Visitor Program sponsor visits to the United States of applicants chosen by the U.S. embassy in each country. In both programs, tours for labor leaders are arranged by the Free Trade Union Institute (FTUI) in collaboration with USIA.

strengthened but frequently also come away with stipends that allow them to put into practice what they learned.

When AIFLD arrived in Central America, its organizing focus was urban trade unions. But as the years went by, the institute shifted its concentration to organizing rural associations. Although AIFLD maintains an affiliation with a trade union confederation in each country, it has not been able to move these organizations from their marginal positions in the wider labor movement. AIFLD's interest in rural organizing also has to do with the fact that many small farmers are more apt to accept AIFLD's nonconfrontative, self-help approach and its capitalist ideology. The most compelling reason, however, behind AIFLD's emphasis in the countryside is the political importance of establishing a conservative base in rural Central America to offset militant *campesino* movements.

AIFLD formed its Agrarian Union Development Department (AUDD) in the early 1970s to oversee rural organizing. Five of the nine AUDD country programs in Latin America are in Central America: El Salvador, Guatemala, Costa Rica, Honduras, and Panama. The largest AUDD program is in El Salvador, where its representatives oversee U.S. involvement in the agrarian reform program. AUDD's overall goal is to "strengthen and expand the free and democratic trade union movement among rural workers and small farmers in Latin America and the Caribbean, principally through rural development service projects, education and training programs, and rural institution building."[8] Noticeably absent from these examples are organizations that would challenge traditional rural power structures and improve the wages paid to the workers on agroexport plantations.

Organizing with a Blank Check

AIFLD's operations have never come under close public scrutiny despite the fact that it relies on taxpayer revenues.[9] The institute has promoted "democratic" unions behind a decidedly undemocratic veil of secrecy. Because AIFLD is technically not a government agency, it is not subject to congressional investigation nor is it covered by Freedom of Information laws. Even though its staff is paid with U.S. government funds, they function as private employees in Central America. AIFLD has no publicly available annual report. Even AFL-CIO union presidents do not have access to AIFLD's budget.

As a tripartite alliance of labor, business, and government, AIFLD originally was to be financed by all three partners. Neither labor nor business, however, has ever contributed more than 5 percent of AIFLD's total budget. Though over 60 corporations have donated to AIFLD, these contributions have covered only a small portion of the institute's budget. While AIFLD might be a tripartite alliance in terms of its anticommunist ideology, when it comes to paying the bills it is little more than a branch of the U.S. government.[10]

Congress has paid very little attention to AIFLD. Even the CIA undergoes more congressional oversight than AIFLD—because, unlike AIFLD, the CIA is categorized as a government, not a private, agency. AIFLD also bypasses the standard evaluation procedure of AID. It has been over a decade since the main AIFLD program handled by AID's LAC (Latin American and Caribbean) office has been evaluated. Year after year the AIFLD grant and contract agreements signed with AID contain exactly the same wording.

Peter Romano, the director of the Labor Program Division of AID's Latin America and Caribbean (LAC) office, said that "AIFLD receives about $20 million a year from all spigots of AID." Half of this amount is in the form of a grant that is channeled to AIFLD through the LAC office in Washington.[11] (See accompanying table.) Besides the regional grant, $10 million more from AID goes to AIFLD in the form of operational program grants (OPGs) and technical service contracts for different AIFLD country programs, such as the institute's support for agrarian reform in El Salvador.

1986 LAC Grant to AIFLD
($9.7 million)

Educational Dept. $0.4 million	Washington Office $1.5 million	George Meany Center $1.6 million
International Trade Secretariats $1.1 million	AUDD (Agricultural Program) $0.7 million	Country Offices $4.4 million

The reported $20 million figure does not represent all the U.S. government funding available to AIFLD. It excludes the money funneled to AIFLD through the National Endowment for Democracy (NED) and the Free Trade Union Institute (FTUI). In 1984, AIFLD received at least $5 million from those two funding channels. AIFLD also receives grants from AID and the Inter-American Development Bank (IDB) for housing and other social projects that benefit AIFLD-associated unions.

COUNTRY PROGRAMS IN CENTRAL AMERICA

AIFLD is best understood in the context of its specific activities in individual countries. In the name of building democracy and protecting the region from encroaching communism, the AFL-CIO and Washington have stepped up their labor programs throughout Central America since 1979.

Guatemala

The origins of AIFLD in Guatemala can be traced back to AFL's and ORIT's support for the 1954 coup. AFL said that it "rejoiced over the downfall of Arbenz" and hailed the new "liberation" government headed by Colonel Castillo Armas. AIFLD's current inability to attract many workers or peasants is at least partially attributable to this tainted past.

Union organizing became a subversive activity in Guatemala, although the association formed by AFL's "labor ambassador" Serafino Romualdi was able to operate relatively free of the brutal repression that other unions suffered. During the last decades of almost unbroken military rule, the AFL-CIO and AIFLD have only mildly protested military repression, which has been responsible for the deaths of over 100,000 civilians including hundreds of union leaders.

AIFLD left Guatemala in the late 1970s when the military's counterinsurgency campaign was picking up steam and disappearances of union activists were an everyday affair. The institute had a difficult time operating under those conditions. It was reluctant to criticize the widespread state terrorism for fear of giving support to the building revolutionary movement. The local AIFLD-backed union had little influence or credibility— emphasized by the fact that even the conservative ORIT regional federation rejected the union because of its close relationship with the military regime.[12]

Both Washington and AIFLD viewed the military coup of 1982 that put General Efraín Ríos Montt in the National Palace as a good opening for increased U.S. influence in Guatemala. AIFLD reentered the country that year and in May 1983 founded a new labor confederation called the Confederation of Guatemalan Union Unity (CUSG). Ríos Montt welcomed AIFLD and pointed to the new labor federation as evidence that his regime was installing democracy in the country. In a 1983 report, the U.S. labor attaché stated that the "decision to reinstall a full-time, permanent AIFLD director in Guatemala has markedly helped to rejuvenate the democratic trade union movement in Guatemala."[13]

The creation of CUSG served economic as well as political purposes. Both Ríos Montt and President Reagan wanted U.S. economic aid (which was cut off during the Carter administration) to start flowing again. To qualify as a beneficiary of funds from the Caribbean Basin Initiative (CBI), it was required that a country at least give the appearances of allowing union organizing—a condition that was satisfied by the formation of the AIFLD-supported federations.

CUSG along with several other AID- and USIA-sponsored Guatemalan organizations were involved in preparations for the elections. With funds from NED (channeled through an AFL-CIO branch organization called the Free Trade Union Center), CUSG sponsored mobilization and get-out-the-vote drives in 1985 through its affiliated Study Center.

CUSG had more success getting out the vote than it has had organizing workers. The U.S. embassy has made the wild claim that CUSG represents 75 percent of the country's work force, but the truth is that it is a cardboard creation of AIFLD with little support among Guatemalan workers.[14] Its main work involves leadership training courses, not actual workplace organizing. AIFLD claims that the Study Center annually trains about 50 unionists in "advanced leadership and democratic values," and about 250 rank-and-file members receive special instruction in leadership and economic development. AIFLD has also teamed up with the Israeli embassy and the Histadrut Workers Central Council of Israel to sponsor joint seminars for small farmers and unionists.

As elsewhere in Central America, AIFLD also tried to establish a conservative base in rural areas. Antonio Alfaro, the director of CUSG's Study Center, said the main focus of their organizing work was "to build cooperatives rather than unions" and to support self-help projects in the countryside. While most of AIFLD's own rural organizing work has taken place in southeastern Guatemala, the institute also works with AID in rural development programs in the northwestern reaches of the Altiplano. The increasing emphasis on rural operations in Guatemala conforms to AIFLD's efforts throughout the region to create a network of conservative associations of small farmers that undermine the development of progressive rural unions.

Although the institute's formation of CUSG was an important component of the economic and political stabilization process, it has not been able to obstruct the rise of militant labor unions and *campesino* movements. AIFLD-sponsored organizations have criticized *campesino* demands for agrarian reform and invasions of idle land as being "antidemocratic," supported unpopular economic austerity programs, and in 1986 refused to join with the country's two other labor federations in the first May Day march since 1980. While the other unions were out in the streets, CUSG celebrated May Day at an indoor meeting attended by the president. Despite ample funding from USIA and AID, CUSG failed to develop a substantial trade union base. Its access to foreign "rural development" funds did, however, give the union a base in the countryside. Initial CUSG support for the Christian Democratic government turned sour by late 1986, and the AIFLD union joined other confederations protesting the government's economic policies. As the union movement grows in Guatemala, the CUSG's early prominent position in the labor movement is being swept aside by other private and public-sector unions not dependent on U.S. funds.

Honduras

AIFLD regards Honduras as a major success story, having been able to maintain a hold on a significant part of organized labor and to keep a united, progressive labor movement from developing. Its relatively strong position in Honduras can be traced to the pivotal 1954 banana strike during which ORIT gained control of United Fruit and Standard Fruit unions. Once again, Serafino Romualdi played a pivotal role in establishing a trade-union confederation that included both banana workers and urban workers. The banana companies, the church, the U.S. embassy, and the country's security forces all stood behind Romualdi's efforts to reduce the influence of leftist unions.

When AIFLD came to Honduras in 1962, it associated itself with the ORIT-affiliated federation FESITRANH, formed a new rural association called ANACH, and established a national confederation of urban and rural democratic unionists that is still known as the Confederation of Honduran Workers (CTH). Ever since, these AIFLD-sponsored labor organizations have been struggling to combat the influence of the country's Christian Democratic and leftist labor confederations, but with diminishing success.

Through its programs in Honduras, AIFLD tries to politically and economically prop up the U.S.-backed government. The institute pledges union "participation in future development plans for the country." Those plans concern efforts to increase nontraditional agroexports and to expand export-directed manufacturing in the free trade zones. In return for its support, AIFLD expects to be allowed to organize "democratic" unions in the new textile and electronics plants and to continue receiving the government's blessing for its rural organizing work.

In other areas of Honduras, where the main social issue is landlessness, AIFLD is trying to put the lid on an increasingly militant *campesino* movement. One component of this effort is the distribution to *campesinos* of a weekly newspaper *El Agricultor,* which is published by a Honduran organization called *Avance. Avance* receives funds from AID and the Simon Bolívar Foundation, a U.S. group supported by conservative corporations.

Through its associated unions, AIFLD also attempts to build popular support for U.S. foreign policy in Honduras. One example of this was a 1983 rally organized by AIFLD to express labor's approval of the U.S. and Honduran military. Bernard Packer, AIFLD country director at the time, spoke at the rally. He and other AIFLD speakers called for labor support of the Honduran government, invited the private sector to unite with labor to improve the economy, and expressed approval of the increased professionalization of the armed forces. The rally also endorsed the establishment of a U.S. military training center in the country.

AIFLD also tries to deter progressive unions from rising to the forefront of the Honduran labor movement. In its *Country*

Labor Plan, 1977–1981, it warned of the "new danger" of militant union leadership. It pledged "to actively seek to counteract the negative action and the danger of political and ideological infiltration as represented by anti-democratic forces." Moreover, it promised to "assist the membership of many unions [that] presently are under non-democratic leadership in re-establishing trade union democratic processes."[15]

Nowhere else in Latin America has AIFLD devoted such constant attention to "democratic" unionism. Despite over thirty years in Honduras, AIFLD and its predecessors have not created unions capable of improving conditions for peasants and workers. It has, however, helped prevent the emergence of a worker-peasant alliance, and it has helped create a conservative sector of small farmers. But given that Hondurans remain among the poorest and most malnourished people in the hemisphere, it is doubtful that revolutionary change can be postponed another three decades.

El Salvador

One of the saddest chapters in the history of U.S. labor's foreign policy has been played out in El Salvador. It would be hard to find another country where the AFL-CIO's foreign operations have been so integral to repression, counterinsurgency, and U.S. intervention in the underdeveloped world. During the 1960s and 1970s, AIFLD closely collaborated with military regimes to contain the growing politicization and militancy of workers and peasants. Instead of serving as an advocate for democracy, AIFLD spread the message of anticommunism. Oligarchs and generals latched on to the ideology to justify their repression against all dissidents, including those advocating political democracy for El Salvador. AIFLD failed to protest the widening repression and contributed to this antidemocratic atmosphere by helping to establish unions and associations supportive of the military.

The U.S. labor bureaucracy's involvement in El Salvador

began in the early 1950s when Serafino Romualdi came to the country at the request of the military to develop an anticommunist trade union front that would undercut the developing progressive union movement. Romualdi hailed the military governments of this era as reformers who "set their mind and enthusiasm to remake El Salvador into a modern, developing country, with constitutional guarantees for all citizens and a favorable climate for the investment of domestic and foreign capital."[16] During the 1960s and 1970s, ORIT and AIFLD supported the Salvadoran General Confederation (CGS), a trade union that counted on the blessing of the military regimes at a time when all organizing was repressed.

In the 1960s, AIFLD also became involved in the Salvadoran countryside. Concerned that poverty and landlessness in rural El Salvador would lead to revolutionary upheaval, the military government in 1962 signed a contract with AIFLD to start rural education and development work with *campesinos.* In 1968, AIFLD founded the Salvadoran Communal Union (UCS), an organization of small farmer cooperatives.[17]

During the 1960s, the Salvadoran military regimes adopted a reformist strategy in line with the Alliance for Progress. By the early 1970s, as worker and peasant organizing increased, the military regime had dropped most of its reformist pretensions. Repression rather than reform reigned in El Salvador. The oligarchy asserted that the Alliance for Progress reforms were opening the country to revolutionary organizing rather than pacifying it. Many in the right-wing elite even labeled UCS members as "communists." Accordingly, AIFLD was expelled from El Salvador in 1973 and did not officially return until 1979.[18]

During the 1970s, the pro-government and AIFLD-associated CGS trade union federation lost the small base that it had previously counted on.[19] Concerned by the rapid growth of left-led rural and urban organizations, AIFLD attempted to reenter the country in 1977. But it was not until the regime of Carlos Humberto Romero was on the verge of collapse that

AIFLD was called back into El Salvador to take direct control of UCS. In early 1980, AIFLD staff set up headquarters in the top two floors of the Hotel Sheraton in San Salvador. The immediate task was to design an agrarian reform that would give landless peasants (the base of the burgeoning FMLN guerrilla army) a stake in the new government. The program also aimed to reduce the power of the landed elite while creating a base of popular support for the new junta.

While working in El Salvador, AIFLD representatives Michael Hammer and David Pearlman fell victim to right-wing violence when they were gunned down at the Sheraton Hotel in January 1981. Their murders raised questions about the role of AIFLD in El Salvador. Hammer was suspected of having intelligence connections dating from his student days at the School of Foreign Service at Georgetown University when he began working with AIFLD. He was given a state funeral at Arlington National Cemetery, indicating that he was more than just an AIFLD organizer. During a Supreme Court hearing shortly after the murders, U.S. Solicitor General Wade H. McCree, Jr. blurted out: "the two Americans who were recently killed in El Salvador were undercover."[20]

Besides implementing the agrarian reform it had helped design, AIFLD set out to help build a "democratic center" in El Salvador by creating a base of support for the Christian Democratic Party among rural and urban unions. After the 1979 coup that brought a reformist military-civilian junta to power, AIFLD jumped into politics, using its ties with urban and rural labor organizations to gain popular support for El Salvador's so-called democratic center. AIFLD helped form the Popular Democratic Unity (UPD) in early 1980 to offer peasant and worker support for Washington's "democratization" strategy in El Salvador. With generous financial support from AID and AIFLD, UPD promoters organized a door-to-door canvassing campaign in support of Christian Democratic candidate José Napoleón Duarte. During this period before the 1984 presidential elections, UPD leaders were often whisked off to Washington to tell Congress that strong popular support existed for agrarian reform, the electoral process, and the Christian Democrats.

José Napoleón Duarte was elected president in May 1984—a victory largely attributable to the AIFLD-orchestrated social base organized by UPD. Duarte did fulfill his promise to appoint UPD leaders to government ministries, but the rest of the social pact was ignored. Despite almost weekly meetings with UPD leaders—which state-owned television presented as evidence that the president was listening to the common people—the new Duarte government refused to follow through with the rest of the reform package.

As a result of Duarte's failure to follow through with the agrarian reform and negotiate a peace settlement, the UPD grew critical of the Christian Democratic administration and the control that Washington exercised over the government. One UPD leader, Miguel Angel Vasquez, said that the UPD had been used as a trampoline to get Duarte into the National Palace, but once there he had forgotten about the workers and peasants who put him there.[21] Because of UPD's criticism of Duarte and its call for peace dialogues, AIFLD distanced itself from the federation. "The UPD played a useful role," explained AIFLD's public relations director John Heberle, "but it was off to the left of Duarte."[22]

The next stage in the country's dynamic union movement came in February 1986 when workers, peasants and human rights organizations created the National Unity of Salvadoran Workers (UNTS).[23] UNTS, which represented some 300,000 workers and *campesinos,* organized its first demonstration in February 1986 and followed with a huge May Day protest, despite the military's attempt to undermine the latter march with psychological-operations techniques. From U.S.-supplied Cessna observation planes, the military dropped leaflets telling workers that their decision to go back to their jobs would be "the best rejection of the terrorist element of the FMLN."

AIFLD also joined the effort to discredit UNTS. Two days

before the May Day protest, AIFLD and Freedom House (a conservative organization funded by the USIA) held a press conference to release documents allegedly captured from the FMLN that AIFLD said revealed a secret guerrilla plan to manipulate the union movement. William Doherty, AIFLD's executive director, charged that Marxist-Leninist guerrillas had infiltrated the union movement to foment discord between labor and the Duarte government. He said that some leaders of the new labor movement were "ideologically friendly to the guerrillas."[24] The U.S. embassy joined in the attempts to undermine UNTS, dismissing UNTS as "a political, not a labor group" because "real trade unions" concern themselves with wages, not questions of peace and dialogue.[25] UNTS organizers dismissed the statements as "psychological warfare."

UNTS offered a strong challenge to the political and economic policies of the Duarte government. While not allied with the FDR/FMLN, UNTS had become a center-left coalition in firm opposition to Duarte. UNTS also took a strong stance against AIFLD. Its platform called for the "expulsion of AIFLD from the country for its shameful practice of dividing the unions and associations of Salvadoran workers."[26] To provide a conservative counterweight to UNTS, AIFLD in early 1986 hastily organized a competing coalition called the National Union of Workers and Campesinos (UNOC), which used the institute's funds to organize a rally supporting Duarte's policies shortly after the UNTS' February 1986 demonstration.

In several aspects, AIFLD's achievements in El Salvador have been considerable. Its ideological instruction and union-building activities instilled anticommunism into the Salvadoran labor movement and undermined attempts to forge labor unity. Agrarian reform, while commonly regarded as an economic failure, did pacify key elements of the rural community and gave the Salvadoran government a reformist image in the U.S. Congress. Without AIFLD's support for the rural associations that helped organize popular backing for the program, agrarian reform would have been even less credible and probably would have flopped immediately. But AIFLD's crowning achievement was its campaign to mobilize voters for Duarte and the Christian Democrats. If Washington had been unable to put at least a token centrist government in the National Palace, its ability to win congressional support for increasing sums of aid would have been seriously undermined.

AIFLD played a key role in low intensity conflict in El Salvador by mobilizing popular support for the civilian government, directing the shallow agrarian reform program, and attempting to set the agenda of worker and peasant associations. Through congressional testimony, AIFLD helped ensure that large sums of U.S. aid continued to flow to the country to fuel the counterinsurgency efforts.

FUNDING FOR DEMOCRACY AND COUNTERREVOLUTION

The 1980s brought top AFL-CIO officials into a powerful new alliance with the New Right, Cold War liberals of the Democratic Party, neoconservatives, and the Reagan administration. This new alliance revolves around a U.S. government campaign called Project Democracy aimed at countering left-led revolutionary movements and at creating pro-U.S. organizations outside the United States.

In a speech before the British Parliament on June 8, 1982, President Reagan announced Project Democracy. The United States, he promised, would launch a major effort to help "foster the infrastructure of democracy—the system of a free press, unions, political parties, and universities—which allows a people to choose their own way, to develop their own culture, to reconcile their own differences through peaceful means." AIFLD and the AFL-CIO leadership played prominent parts in both the development and implementation of Project Democracy.

Shortly before Reagan's speech to the British Parliament, the

American Political Foundation (APF)—a coalition of labor, business, political and academic leaders formed in the late 1970s—proposed to the president that he commission a study to examine how the United States could better promote democracy in foreign countries. The APF said that such a study should examine how a bipartisan program could maintain "friendly relations with current governments while sowing the seeds of democratic successors" and "encourage domestic pluralistic forces in totalitarian countries."

Immediately following Reagan's trip to Britain, APF received $250,000 from AID for its Program Democracy study. Continuing the tripartite alliance (labor-business-government) begun by AIFLD, the executive board for this study included Lane Kirkland, William Brock (then International Trade Representative and later Labor Secretary), Charles Manatt (then chairperson of the Democratic National Committee), Frank Fahrenkopf (chairperson of the Republican National Committee) and Michael Samuels (vice-president of the U.S. Chamber of Commerce). In 1983, APF recommended the establishment of the National Endowment for Democracy (NED) as part of a two-pronged (private and public sector) campaign to promote "democracy" around the globe.

Two pieces of legislation were passed in 1983 to implement the recommendations of Project Democracy. One authorized increased funding for AID, USIA, and the State Department for support of democratic institutions, and the other directed the USIA to spend $18 million for the creation of NED to promote private-sector efforts to build democracy and fight communism.

Carl Gershman, who had served as chief aide to former UN Ambassador Jeane Kirkpatrick, was selected as NED's executive director. Before his work at the United Nations, he was a resident scholar at Freedom House, a neoconservative group that receives NED funding. From 1974 to 1980, Gershman served as the executive director of the Social Democrats USA

(SDUSA), an anticommunist organization closely linked with the AFL-CIO's International Affairs Department.[27] Gershman flatly denied any CIA involvement in NED, but he does acknowledge that NED is now responsible for operations that used to be handled by the CIA. He told the *Washington Post* that the organization was created to provide an overt funding channel to foreign organizations which in the past would have been secretly backed by the CIA.[28]

When NED was created in 1983, AFL-CIO chief Lane Kirkland said the new organization would "considerably strengthen the international programs of the American labor movement." According to Kirkland, it made sense to give U.S. labor an important role in NED. "Of the four entities composing NED—labor, business, and the two political parties—labor has the longest track record on the international scene," he said, as well as having the "clearest philosophical rationale" in democratic freedoms.[29] Kirkland sees NED as a way that private sector organizations can openly support the type of political forces that have in the past received covert CIA backing. "Democratic institution-building," he said, "is not the proper mission of the CIA, even if it were equipped for the task. The promotion of democratic institutions should not be a covert activity. It should be a proudly proclaimed goal of American foreign policy."[30]

Coordinating Covert and Overt Operations

At the same time that the APF study group was looking at the best way to involve the private sector, the CIA-dominated National Security Council (NSC) was discussing a public diplomacy program with four components: information dissemination, political support, covert action, and the creation of a quasi-government institute. A secret document prepared by Mark Palmer of the State Department stated that the CIA and the National Security Planning Group would be responsible for the covert action involved in this new anticommunist initiative.[31] Palmer had also written Reagan's speech about Project Democracy a year before.[32]

Project Democracy had other links to the NSC and covert operations. National Security Decision Document 77 (NSDD 77), issued in January 1983, defined public diplomacy as "comprised of those actions of the U.S. government designed to generate support for our national security objectives." NSDD 77 created the International Political Committee "to build up U.S. government capability to promote democracy, as enunciated in the President's speech in London on June 8, 1982."[33]

As the Irangate scandal unfolded, it was revealed that Project Democracy included a covert side that paralleled its overt operations. Authorized by NSDD 77, this covert component was coordinated by the NSC and supervised by Lieutenant Colonel Oliver North. It encompassed an elaborate network of bank accounts, front companies, secret envoys, and communications and transportation systems that, among other things, passed money and arms to the contras.[34]

Lawrence Eagleburger, undersecretary of state for political affairs, acknowledged that several "option papers" proposed CIA participation. However Eagleburger, currently a trustee of anticommunist Freedom House, said that "a firm, flat decision was made at very senior levels that there would be no CIA involvement."[35] William C. Casey, who at that time headed the CIA, participated in NSC discussions about the possibility of directly involving the CIA in NED. The NSC decided against this option, but did not rule out close collaboration between the covert and overt sides of Project Democracy.

Rather than the CIA, the USIA is now financing foreign private operations. Between 1984 and 1986, NED channeled over $53 million in USIA grants to U.S. and foreign private organizations around the world. The main recipient of these funds was the Free Trade Union Institute (FTUI), an offshoot of the AFL-CIO's International Affairs Department. During

NED's first two years, FTUI received nearly 70 percent of NED's grants. Most of the balance was spread among CIPE (the Center for International Private Enterprise, a 1983 creation of the U.S. Chamber of Commerce) and the two international institutes of the Democratic and Republican Parties. The accompanying diagram illustrates the flow of NED funds.

Resurrection of the Free Trade Union Committee

AIFLD and the two other regional labor institutes receive NED grants through FTUI, the reincarnation of the AFL-CIO's Free Trade Union Committee (FTUC) that was an old haunt of CIA collaborators. The AFL-CIO says that FTUI was created in 1979 as "an outgrowth of the AFL-CIO's historic commitment to democracy and human rights."

When asked what differences there were between FTUI and AIFLD, Thomas Melia, a FTUI official answered, "We are them. In Central America, there are no FTUI projects that are not AIFLD. What AIFLD is doing is what we are doing." Melia explained that both AIFLD and FTUI are "creatures of the AFL-CIO and Lane Kirkland." FTUI's executive director is Eugenia Kemble, who also served as a director of the APF study group that proposed the formation of NED.

The operations of FTUI and AIFLD in Central America have received widespread support from both political parties, the business community, and even the right wing. Orrin Hatch, a senator from Utah, is a NED board member who enthusiastically backs the AFL-CIO's international programs.

PRODEMCA: Democracy's Dubious Friends

In late 1984, the Friends of the Democratic Center in Central America (PRODEMCA), a NED grantee, announced its formation at a Washington news conference. (The organization was actually founded in 1981 under the name Citizens Committee for Pro-Democratic Forces in Central America.) The

Funds for Democracy in Central America

Congress
The 1983 National Endowment for Democracy Act authorized the creation of NED. Congress appropriated $18 million for 1984, $18.5 million for 1985, and $17.2 million for 1986.

United States Information Agency (USIA)
Funds for NED are channeled through the USIA as part of the Project Democracy program.

National Endowment for Democracy (NED)
A private organization created to channel USIA funds for democracy-building projects. Its directors represent the two political parties, AFL-CIO, and the U.S. Chamber of Commerce.

Free Trade Union Institute (FTUI)
This branch of the AFL-CIO received $25 million in 1984–1985 to support free trade unions.

U.S. Chamber of Commerce
The Center for International Private Enterprise (CIPE), a branch of the U.S. Chamber of Commerce, received $4.2 million in 1984–1985 for programs to promote political involvement by business communities.

Political Institutes
The National Republican Institute for International Affairs (NRI) and the National Democratic Institute for International Affairs (NDI) receive NED funds to promote "democratic political ideas and forces."

er FTUI funds channeled to the an-American e Labor Institute, African-Ameri- Labor Center activities of the L-CIO's Interna- al Affairs partment.

(AIFLD) American Institute for Free Labor Development
AIFLD backs pro-government unions in Costa Rica, Honduras, Guatemala, and El Salvador and anti-government unions in Nicaragua.

Miscellaneous Groups
Other organizations received $3.1 million in 1984–85. These include PRODEMCA, Freedom House, American Friends of Afghanistan, and A. Philip Randolph Institute.

International Policy Forum sponsors political forums for business owners in El Salvador and Guatemala.

Caribbean/Central American Action (CCAA), a U.S. corporate group receiving AID grants, funds the Political Study Center (CEDEP) in Guatemala.

The Pan American Development Foundation (PADF) funded a study of the counterrevolutionary political potential of small business owners and vendors in Nicaragua.

The Center for International Private Enterprise has contributed funds for a conference of Central American employers' organizations.

NRI funds the Association for Defense of Costa Rican Liberty and Democracy.

NRI supports "civic education and leadership training courses" at the Conservative Institute for Nicaraguan youth.

NRI supports "political party development programs that strengthen the grassroots organizations of democratic political parties in Nicaragua."

NRI and NDI sponsor joint training seminars with similar Venezuelan institutes active in Central America.

NRI assists a campaign by Rotary Clubs of Guatemala to develop a "multimedia campaign to promote the democratic process among the campesino population."

NRI sponsors a Political Activist Training Program for moderate and conservative parties.

Freedom House operates the Freedom Exchange program which circulates anti-Sandinista articles around the world.

PRODEMCA supports the anti-Sandinista Permanent Commission on Human Rights and funded the creation of the Nicaraguan Center for Democratic Studies, which is run by contra leadership.

PRODEMCA has supported La Prensa in Nicaragua.

Delphi Associates received a 1986 grant from NED to help La Prensa (if it resumes publishing) by forwarding supplies from the United States.

Freedom House funded Libro Libre in Costa Rica to publish a book about Miskitos in Nicaragua.

1984 press conference featured Nicaraguan counterrevolutionary leader Arturo Cruz and was hosted by two PRODEMCA founders, William Doherty and Angier Biddle Duke. The organization acknowledged that right-wing oligarchs and their armed supporters are a threat to Central American democracy. But "even more dangerous," says the group, is "the threat from the local totalitarian left in Central America which, with Soviet and Cuban support, is now tightening its hold on Nicaragua, carrying out guerrilla and terrorist attacks in other countries of the region, and building unprecedented military forces."[36]

In June 1985 and March 1986, PRODEMCA took out full-page ads in the *Washington Post* and *New York Times* requesting tax-deductible contributions for its work in Central America. The June 1985 ad, entitled "Democracy is the Issue in Nicaragua," asked readers to "help us build a movement of support throughout the United States for those in Nicaragua who, at great risk, are standing up for democracy." The PRODEMCA ad in March 1986 was more forthright in defining its support for democracy. The ad called for reader support for "military assistance to the Nicaraguans fighting for democracy."[37] PRODEMCA's administrative director is Adrianne Doherty, the daughter-in-law of AIFLD director William Doherty. Members of its executive committee include FTUI executive director Eugenia Kemble and her neoconservative brother Penn Kemble.

PRODEMCA went beyond placing ads in its campaign to support the "democratic" opposition to the Nicaraguan government. It sponsored visits by contras to Washington, and it hosted trips to contra camps in an effort to increase U.S. aid to the counterrevolutionary armies. Within Nicaragua, PRODEMCA funded the anti-Sandinista newspaper *La Prensa* and the Permanent Commission on Human Rights, an anti-Sandinista group that concentrates on exposing alleged violations by the Nicaraguan government while totally ignoring the activities of the contras.

Freedom House: "Freedom's Advocate the World Over"

Another NED grantee, Freedom House, has strong AFL-CIO connections. A conservative human rights organization, Freedom House received over three-quarters of a million dollars from 1983 to 1986 from NED. A large part of these funds helped establish "a network of democratic opinion-leaders . . . to end the isolation of democratic-minded intellectuals and journalists in the Third World who want to participate in democratic discourse with the countries of North America and Western Europe." Freedom House uses NED money to photocopy anticommunist and pro-U.S. articles and circulate them in what the director calls the "international idea circuit."[38]

In 1984, the AFL-CIO's Department of International Affairs called upon Freedom House members to form part of the AFL-CIO team of election observers during recent elections in Guatemala and El Salvador. Included in the nine-person AFL-CIO delegation to observe the 1984 elections in El Salvador were three Freedom House representatives. Together with AIFLD, Freedom House published a report in 1986 that purported to show manipulation of the Salvadoran labor movement by leftist guerrillas. The report asserted that labor organizations that have formed outside of AIFLD control "are dominated by the FDR/FMLN apparatus."

When infatuation is mutual, interlocks develop and favors are reciprocated. Freedom House is listed among the few recipients of AFL-CIO contributions to private organizations. Bayard Rustin, while chairperson of Freedom House, served as the chairperson of the anticommunist labor organization, Social Democrats USA (SDUSA). Rustin also conveniently sat on the board of directors of the Coalition for a Democratic Majority, the International Rescue Committee, the AFL-CIO Labor Studies Center, and PRODEMCA.

The launching of Project Democracy, through the creation

of organizations like NED and PRODEMCA, gave hardline anticommunists within the AFL-CIO an expanded role in U.S. foreign policy in Central America. The inclusion of Lane Kirkland and Albert Shanker on NED's board, the priority funding given by NED to AFL-CIO's international programs, and the prominent position of William Doherty in PRODEMCA are signs of the leading part the AFL-CIO is playing in Washington's anticommunist assault on Central America.

The Contradictions of Project Democracy

President Reagan promised that Project Democracy would build democratic institutions so that people could choose to change their countries using peaceful means. Project Democracy showed itself to have little to do with democracy. With funds provided by the USIA, "private" organizations like AIFLD have set out to foster an infrastructure of U.S.-controlled institutions and associations that form a bulwark against progressive change in Central America. Instead of promoting peaceful solutions, organizations like PRODEMCA and labor representatives like William Doherty backed counterrevolutionary and counterinsurgency wars in Nicaragua and El Salvador. In Central America, the real function of Project Democracy, the National Endowment for Democracy, PRODEMCA, and the many other associated organizations that proclaim democratic principles, is not to support self-determination but to ensure that the United States keeps its political and economic hold on the region. The tripartite alliance of labor, business, and government that began with the founding of AIFLD in 1961 is still going strong in the 1980s. NED, and the interventionist coalition gathered around it, is the latest manifestation of this dubious alliance to further U.S. hegemony.

For over four decades, the AFL-CIO's foreign policy has been in the hands of a narrow elite that directs its extensive foreign operations. The federation's International Affairs Department, which controls a budget larger than that of its domestic operations, has been the domain of Cold War warriors who have worked closely with U.S. intelligence services. The ideology propagated by this department and AIFLD is a harsh blend of liberal capitalism and anticommunism. AIFLD has backed military dictators out of fear that a more democratic society might lead to a resurgence of left-led unions and other popular movements. So busy is AIFLD in propagating its ideology that it accomplishes very little labor organizing. As a result, AIFLD-backed confederations are continually disintegrating. AIFLD's ability—thanks to AID—to keep passing out the almighty dollar is the only way it keeps the "free" trade union movement alive in many countries. AIFLD has never been able to sort out its priorities between fighting communism and bolstering its brand of unionism.

There is little that is "free" or "democratic" about the AFL-CIO's foreign operations to support "free trade unionism." The overriding purpose of AIFLD is not to support efforts by workers and peasants to achieve a better life in their own countries but to serve as an instrument of U.S. foreign policy.* It does this by creating paper organizations and financing conservative unions that support U.S. intervention, while attempting to undermine more progressive unions. In Central America, operations sponsored by the AFL-CIO form a front line in the ever expanding U.S. effort to maintain tight political and economic control of the isthmus.

---

*As U.S. involvement in Central America deepened, the dominance of pro-interventionist forces with the labor federation began to be challenged by a coalition of progressive, noninterventionist unions and labor leaders in the United States. The formation of the National Labor Committee in 1981 marked a shift in the balance of forces within the AFL-CIO. The committee, which represented the majority of unionists affiliated with the AFL-CIO, directly challenged the Cold War framework of U.S. policy in Latin America. In opposing Washington's Central America policy, the National Labor Committee set off a storm of debate within the AFL-CIO itself. It is a debate promoted not only by the rank-and-file members but also by national union leaders—nine of whom sit on the 33-member AFL-CIO executive council.

CHAPTER **10** Conclusion

The political foundations of U.S. economic aid policy are transparent—probably more so in Central America than anywhere else in the world. The Kissinger Commission recommended that U.S. military aid programs form a "shield" behind which U.S. economic assistance could go about solving the region's economic and political problems. But the distinction between military aid and economic aid has become increasingly muddled in Central America. Like military aid, nonlethal assistance is mainly used to stabilize "friendly" governments, back counterrevolutionary armies, and contain popular rebellion. Like military aid, U.S. economic support is used to reward friends and punish enemies.

Another key trait of the U.S. foreign aid program is its self-interested nature: the aid serves the "national interest" of the United States. Instead of considering a long-term global reordering, the national interest is defined over the short term and designed to benefit narrow economic, political, and military sectors in the United States. A country's voting pattern in the United Nations, its openness to U.S. investment, and its willingness to host military bases are the criteria Washington uses to determine who should get aid and how much.

The self-interested motivation of U.S. economic aid can be easily observed in the way AID uses its assistance to push for alterations in a nation's economic policies. AID-imposed stabilization programs loosen restrictions on imports, decrease the price of exports, encourage foreign investment, and establish debt repayment schedules. In this manner, the agency serves as the self-appointed guardian of the private sector and the international banking community.[1] AID uses its development assistance in similar ways—funding projects that promote the production of cheap exports to the United States, facilitate foreign investment, and encourage the purchase of U.S. products. While foreign aid does undeniably benefit the U.S. economy in some ways, a foreign aid policy based on a broader and more long-term conception of U.S. national interest would also benefit U.S. citizens. It could mean a lower tax burden, and such a policy could result in more productive and politically stable third world countries that would purchase more U.S. products. Fewer families would migrate from these developing nations, and the higher wage rates would mean that fewer U.S. factories would be closing down to seek cheap labor outside U.S. borders. Most economic aid comes boomeranging back to the United States.

The fact that U.S. assistance bolsters the elites in recipient countries is consistent with the U.S. government's practice of supporting those who back U.S. foreign policy and corporate investment. It is not surprising that Washington has found its most enthusiastic supporters, measured by a commitment to unrestricted private enterprise and to counterrevolution, among the members of the business elite. By channeling aid through governments that serve this privileged class, AID contributes to the strengthening of established power structures. This is as true on a local level as it is on a national one. Because AID makes little effort to direct its assistance to independently organized community groups, its funds generally flow into the hands of the most privileged members of a community. Those with the most commercial experience, education, and experience with government institutions are the ones who usually derive the greatest benefits from AID's development programs.

At the same time that U.S. assistance strengthens the Central American elite, it undermines the power of the popular sectors. It does this by sponsoring organizations like AIFLD to keep the labor movement weak and disorganized. AID also finances the formation of government-linked cooperatives that compete with independently organized peasant and worker groups, which seldom receive AID funds. A lack of resources hampers the influence of grassroots organizations while government repression decimates their ranks. In contrast, business associations, whose interests are often diametrically opposed to those of the popular sector, receive generous U.S. support and benefit from alliances with the government and military.

A more accurate label for AID might be the Agency for International Dependency. In its view, the path to development in the third world must be outward-oriented. Through its aid agreements and policy dialogues with recipient nations, AID encourages countries to look outside their borders for capital, investment, technology, and markets. AID also pushes countries to open up their economies to imports (especially those from the United States) and to prime their economies for increased export production (especially to the United States). It pressures them to adopt technology, consumption patterns, and diets that make them ever more dependent on the United States.

This abuse of economic aid clearly enhances U.S. corporate interests. It keeps Central American nations always looking to the developed countries for economic solutions instead of searching within their own country and region for development options. Their indigenous material and human resources are exploited by outsiders rather than harnessed for domestic advantage. Development strategies that call for increased exports and liberalized imports argue that countries must follow the dictates of comparative advantage. In the case of Central America, this means producing cheap exports based on cheap labor and importing manufactured goods from the industrialized world. While countries do need to be cognizant of their comparative economic advantages, it makes little economic sense to orient production exclusively toward foreign markets at a time when those markets are shrinking, commodity prices are falling, and new protectionist barriers are being erected. Only in boom times would this course of development possibly work— and even then it would mean relying on a low-paid, repressed work force. And even when traditional and non-traditional exports do increase, the income flows to a small elite, not the poor. The main condition for real economic progress is the increase in the income levels of the poor majority, making them consumers as well as laborers.

In Central America, AID contends that its contributions are helping to stabilize the region. Yet the injection of large sums of aid, while providing short-term stability, is deepening the region's dependency on outside capital. When this aid dries up, it will leave economies and governments weaker than ever. AID's stabilization strategy is doing more to ensure the long-term destabilization of Central America than it can possibly achieve in steadying the region in the short term.

Yet another aspect of AID's dependency-building behavior is its preference for bilateral instead of multilateral or regional links. This emphasis on bilateral aid keeps countries divided and competing with one another. AID encourages each small nation to devise its own development plan rather than using the assistance as an instrument to create regional economic solutions. In its bilateral agreements with recipients, AID obligates countries to follow certain economic policies dictated by Washington. These policies not only serve the perceived interests of the United States but also those of global capital. In some cases, AID has withheld its assistance until countries comply with austerity and monetary measures recommended by the IMF and World Bank. These measures, while purported to be in the best interests of the countries themselves, are thinly disguised efforts to protect the loans and trade of the international banking community and private sector. Austerity policies invariably squeeze money out of the poor majority while leaving the elite relatively unscathed.

During the 1970s, AID and the IFIs responded to criticism of development aid by adopting new rhetoric and by launching new types of development projects. AID embarked on a strategy to promote economic growth and help distribute the benefits to the poor. Its programs in integrated rural development formed part of this new effort. In response to increasing unemployment, AID supported food-for-work projects and financed industrial parks to attract labor-intensive manufacturing plants.

AID can point to some improvements in socioeconomic conditions since the launching of the new programs. Overall, however, the relative economic position of the poor declined. In most cases, Central American societies have experienced an absolute decline in income of the poorest sectors since 1970. The central reason for this failure is that AID does not recognize the phenomenon of unequal development. Unless there are measures taken—such as strong labor laws, agrarian reform, state control over certain areas of the economy, progressive taxation, international agreements to guarantee fair prices for commodity exports—economic growth for some will mean continued impoverishment for most.

Since 1980, billions of dollars in U.S. economic aid have flowed to Central America, yet there has been no economic development nor improvement in the conditions of the poor. While economic aid has soared to higher levels each year, regional trade has ground almost to a halt, exports continue to decline, the numbers of unemployed or underemployed approach 40 percent in most countries, and per capita income is sinking every year. The distorted priorities of AID contribute to this lack of development. Yet even with altered priorities, development aid would have few positive results in the conditions of war that exist in Central America.

In Central America, there are no ready-made solutions to underdevelopment. Economic aid, instead of being an answer, has proved to be a serious obstacle to broad-based development. True growth must come from within; it can never be imposed from the outside. Likewise, meaningful development cannot come from the top down, but must start with grass-roots initiatives. Trying to meet basic needs with international charity is not a lasting solution. Supporting popular organizations that are struggling for land reform, more government services, and better labor laws would yield far more beneficial long-term results. If economic aid is to stimulate development, it needs to be an instrument of empowerment, not one of dependency and pacification. If foreign donors are truly concerned about helping the poor, assisting small farmers, and creating equitable growth, then their aid should primarily flow to those governments that share those priorities. Aid should come with conditions that countries enforce agrarian reform, guarantee human rights and the right to organize, and seek to broaden income distribution.

Similarly, economic aid should go first to those countries struggling to establish their economic independence. As it is, funds are usually cut off as soon as countries take measures to reduce their dependency on U.S. trade, investment, and financing. AID rails against import-substitution schemes that aim to reduce imports through domestic manufacturing. Yet import-substitution, especially when it involves the production of basic goods and the use of local materials, is a necessary element in development, recognized even by AID itself in its younger days. Economic aid could be put to better use on regional investment projects that produce necessary items like fertilizer and chicken feed than on those that grow snow peas or assemble jeans for export.

Unfortunately, there are few examples of official economic aid that are not self-serving. Foreign aid projects backed by the governments of the Netherlands and the Scandinavian countries come closest to supporting economic independence, self-reliance, and popular empowerment. Among private donors there are more examples of foreign aid being used to meet local development priorities. The Oxfam organizations are models in this regard. Union-to-union solidarity, like that exhibited for the Coca-Cola workers in Guatemala, also serves an an example of beneficial foreign support. The most effective private development groups are those that try to avoid paternalism while seeking to instill dignity, promote self-sufficiency, spur critical thinking, and support independent organizing. Groups like

Pueblo to People, which enhance cooperatives through the marketing of Central American crafts, show that development assistance does not have to be paternalistic, but can instill dignity and promote self-sufficiency.

The U.S. national interest needs to be redefined to allow room for economic aid programs that support empowerment not pacification, self-determination not dependency, and development for the many not just the few. Overhauling the U.S. foreign aid program should be part of this redefinition process. Central America is a good place to start. Both sides of the aisle in Congress have justified their support for increased U.S. economic aid on the grounds that this assistance promotes democracy and development. But the facts are otherwise. In the politically tense atmosphere of Central America, U.S. economic aid, like military aid, is essentially interventionist and counterrevolutionary. It throws money at our "friends" while trying to control the hearts and minds of the popular sectors. It is used to back low intensity conflicts that are in fact very high intensity for those who live in the region. Economic aid is not, as widely believed, addressing the root causes of the crisis in Central America. It is, instead, a misuse of tax revenue, an abuse of U.S. citizens' goodwill, and a less prominent but perhaps more destructive side of the war in Central America.

Reference Notes

Chapter One:
Promises and Illusions

1. In 1986, U.S. economic aid per capita was $12.32 for Central America while only $1.61 for Africa and 38 cents for Asia. Statistics from Overseas Development Council, "U.S. Foreign Aid in the 1980s," No. 4.
2. Quoted in *Help Yourself: The Politics of Aid* (London: Third World First, 1984), p. 3.
3. Ronald Brownstein and Nina Eaton, *Reagan's Ruling Class* (Washington, D.C.: Presidential Accountability Group, 1982), p. 607, quoting an AID brochure.
4. There have been numerous studies of the CIA involvement in the 1954 coup. The best of these are: R. Immerman, *The CIA in Guatemala: The Foreign Policy of Intervention* (Austin: University of Texas, 1982) and Steven Schlesinger and Steven Kinzer, *Bitter Fruit: The Untold Story of the American Coup in Guatemala* (New York: Doubleday, 1983).
5. Speech by President Kennedy, March 13, 1961. *Public Papers of the Presidents of the United States, 1961* (Washington: U.S. Government Printing Office, 1962), pp. 170–81.
6. Ibid., p. 223.
7. Jenny Pearce, *Under the Eagle* (London: Latin American Bureau: 1981), p. 41.
8. Statement by Robert McNamara, *Hearings on the Foreign Assistance Act of 1962,* House Committee on Foreign Affairs, pp. 267–68.
9. Nelson Rockefeller, *Rockefeller Report on the Americas* (Hearing before the Subcommittee on Western Hemisphere Affairs, Committee on Foreign Relations, U.S. Senate, Nov. 20, 1969. p. 61).
10. Quoted in Walter LaFeber, *Inevitable Revolutions: The United States in Central America,* (New York: W.W. Norton and Co., 1984) p. 152.
11. From 1962 to 1979, the United States sent over $150 million in military and police aid to Central America, and trained more than 21,000 members of Central America's police and military. A large part of the security force training was paid for by economic aid funds through AID's Office

263

of Public Safety (OPS), which focused on ideological instruction and counterinsurgency training. In countries where there were incipient guerrilla movements, like Guatemala and Nicaragua, AID closely coordinated its development programs with counterinsurgency operations directed by the military. AID's police training program under the Office of Public Safety was shut down by Congress in 1975 because of evidence that the training and supplies were being used for torture and repression. In 1976 the General Accounting Office (GAO) produced the report *Stopping U.S. Assistance to Foreign Police and Prisons,* concluding that "commodities furnished to police units under the public safety program are now being provided to the same units under the Narcotics Program." The GAO study stated that both programs provided radios, vehicles, revolvers, handcuffs, cameras, binoculars, and office equipment to foreign police.

12. In the first five years of the Alliance, there were 13 cases of military-supported coups in Latin America: Ecuador (November 1961), Dominican Republic (January 1962), Argentina (March 1962), Peru (July 1962), Guatemala (March 1963), Ecuador (July 1963), Dominican Republic (September 1963), Honduras (October 1963), Brazil (March 1964), Bolivia (November 1964), Dominican Republic (April 1965), Ecuador (March 1966), and Argentina (June 1966). *Survey of the Alliance for Progress: The Political Aspects,* September 18, 1967. A study prepared at the request of the Subcommittee on American Republic Affairs, Staff of the Committee on Foreign Relations, U.S. Senate.

13. Gary W. Wynia, *Politics and Planners: Economic Development Policy in Central America* (Madison: University of Wisconsin Press, 1972), p. 103.

14. John F. McCamant, *Development Assistance in Central America* (New York: Praegar, 1968), p. 35.

15. Quoted in LaFeber, op. cit., p. 174.

16. AID, *Congressional Presentation FY 1966.*

17. Organization of American States (OAS), *Informe final del subcomité del CIAP sobre Nicaragua* (Washington, 1967), p. 31.

Chapter Two:
Stabilization Not Development

1. Department of State, *Congressional Presentation of Security Assistance Programs FY 87.*

2. Closely related to Title I assistance is a food program of the Commodity Credit Corporation (CCC), a division of the United States Department of Agriculture (USDA). CCC offers credit at low interest rates to foreign

nations for the purchase of U.S. food commodities. This arrangement allows countries to import U.S. food even when they do not have the cash to pay for it or the ability to secure private financing. Because it does not require prior congressional approval, CCC offers a discreet way for Washington to assist controversial governments. In Central America, CCC guarantees increased from zero in 1979 to over $120 million in 1984. Significantly, the CCC's major recipients are El Salvador and Guatemala—the two countries beset by guerrilla insurgency.

3. AID, Latin American Bureau, *Regional Strategic Plan for Latin America and the Caribbean,* December 1983, p. 25.
4. GAO, *Political and Economic Factors Influencing Economic Support Fund Programs,* April 18, 1983, p. 3.
5. *Christian Science Monitor,* May 9, 1985.
6. Quoted in the *Miami Herald,* May 19, 1986.
7. *Central America Report,* October 18, 1985.
8. Interview by authors, August 1984.
9. Testimony of Frank C. Conahan, Director of the National Security and International Affairs Division, at hearings before the Senate Subcommittee on Foreign Operations of the Committee on Appropriations, March 14, 1984.
10. Interview by authors, August 1984.
11. Until 1985, AID did require that the cash transfers be used solely for U.S. imports. That regulation was then modified to cover limited purchases from other Central American nations. One reason for the change was that recipient countries were actually accumulating more dollars than they needed for U.S. purchases.
12. According to the GAO, "The recipient country is responsible for determining who will receive foreign exchange and what it will be used for and for limiting illegal foreign exchange practices, such as capital flight." GAO, "U.S. Economic Assistance to Central America," March 1984.
13. Report by Congressional Research Service, "Capital Flight from Central America," *Foreign Assistance and Related Programs Appropriations FY 85.* Hearings before a subcommittee of the House Committee on Appropriations, March 7, 1985.
14. Representative Jim Leach, Representative George Miller, and Senator Mark O. Hatfield, "U.S. Aid to El Salvador: An Evaluation of the Past, A Proposal for the Future," *A Report of the Arms Control and Foreign Policy Caucus,* February 1985.
15. *Wall Street Journal,* September 9, 1985.
16. AID, "Policy Planning and Administration Improvement: Costa Rica 1983–84."

17. Department of State, "Sustaining a Consistent Policy in Central America: One Year After the National Bipartisan Commission Report," *Special Report No. 124*, April 1985.

Chapter Three:
Expensive Magic

1. *Foreign Assistance Legislation, FY 1986 and 1987,* House Committee on Foreign Affairs, p. 247, Part I, Feb. 19, 20, 21, 26, Mar. 7, 1985 AID Administrator McPherson came to AID with a background in business affairs. Before serving as general counsel for the Reagan transition team in 1980, he worked as an international and corporate tax specialist.
2. *The Nation,* October 5, 1957, p. 214; John Hollister, ICA director under Eisenhower, noted that one of the main objectives of foreign aid was "to encourage private U.S. investors to go into newly developed countries."
3. Statement of Theodore W. Galdi, Specialist in International Political Economy, Congressional Research Service, to the Subcommittee on Foreign Operations, House Committee on Appropriations, March 20, 1985.
4. The CBI became effective on January 1, 1984, and excluded Nicaragua.
5. Bureau of Private Enterprise, *Progress Report 1984.*
6. *Front Lines* (AID), March 1986.
7. Eximbank's financial exposure in Central America was about $120 million as of September 1984. This figure includes $19.9 million in loans and insurance from past U.S. trade with Nicaragua. The last year for Eximbank financing of Nicaraguan importers was 1981, when the total financing was only $11,514.
8. In addition to its investment insurance program, OPIC finances U.S. investors through direct loans and guarantees.
9. Comisión Económica para América Latina (CEPAL), *Satisfación de las necesidades básicas de la población del Istmo Centroamericano,* November 23, 1983, p. 8.
10. U.S. Department of Commerce, *Caribbean Basin Information Starter Kit,* October 1984, p. 16.
11. Statement of Loret Miller Ruppe, *Foreign Assistance and Related Programs Appropriations, FY 1984,* House Committee on Appropriations, September 2, 1984, pp. 58–80.
12. From a report by the U.S. State Department on the Caribbean Basin Initiative, September 1985. The following are the main AID-sponsored business organizations in Central America: Costa Rica: Costa Rican

Coalition for Development Initiatives (CINDE); El Salvador: Salvadoran Economic and Social Development Foundation (FUSADES); Guatemala: Free Business Chamber (CAEM); Honduras: Foundation for Business Development and Investigation (FIDE); and Panama: Panama Economic Development Association (ADEPA). In the years immediately following the 1979 Sandinista victory, AID supported the COSEP and FUNDE until aid was cut off to Nicaragua by the Reagan administration.

13. *El Dia Internacional,* January 29, 1985.
14. *Foreign Assistance Legislation, FYs 1986 and 1987,* Part 1, House Committee on Foreign Affairs, pp. 262–263.
15. "Who Does Foreign Aid Really Help?" *Farm Journal,* May 1985.
16. Department of Commerce, *Caribbean Basin Initiative Business Bulletin,* June 1985.
17. Overseas Development Council, "Caribbean Basin Initiative Update," *Policy Focus,* No. 3, 1985.
18. U.S. Department of Labor, Bureau of International Labor Affairs, *Trade and Employment Effects of the Caribbean Basin Recovery Act* (1985). This percentage for 806 and 807 imports is higher than anywhere else in the world.
19. Statement of Lawrence Theriot, CBI Center, U.S. and Foreign Commercial Services, International Trade Administration.
20. Memo from the president to all department and agency directors, December 5, 1984.
21. Richard S. Newfarmer, "The Private Sector and Development," in John P. Lewis and Valeriana Keillab, eds, *U.S. Foreign Policy and the 3rd World Agenda 1983* (New York: Praegar, 1983), pp. 117–38.
22. Ibid.
23. Ibid.

Chapter Four:
Plantation Development

1. Report of the Joint Economic Committee. Cited in James Petras, *Cultivating Revolution: The United States and Agrarian Reform in Latin America* (New York: Random House, 1971).
2. *El Imparcial,* January 5, 1968.
3. AID, *Regional Strategy Statement 1986,* April 1984.
4. Jack Corbett and Ronald Ivey, *Evaluation of Latin American Agribusiness Development Corporation* (Washington: Checchi and Co., July 31, 1974).

5. Checchi and Co., *Evaluation of LAAD de Centroamerica* (Washington: November 23, 1977); Frances Moore Lappé, Joseph Collins, David Kinley, *Aid as Obstacle: Twenty Questions about our Foreign Aid and the Hungry* (San Francisco: Institute for Food and Development Policy, 1981), pp. 66–68.

6. *Evaluation of the Agribusiness Employment/Investment Promotion Project Implemented by the Latin American Agribusiness Development Corporation de Centroamerica* (Washington: Checchi and Co., November 1983).

7. Ibid.

8. ROCAP (AID's Regional Office for Central America and Panama) *Agribusiness Employment/Investment Promotion,* September 30, 1984, p. 29.

9. Interviews by authors, August and September 1984.

10. AID/Guatemala, *Small Farmer Diversification Systems,* 1981.

11. AID/Guatemala, *Country Development Strategy Statement, FY86,* 1984.

12. Interview by authors, June 1984.

13. Interview by authors, June 1984.

14. AID, *Regional Strategy Statement 1986,* April 1984.

15. The authors acknowledge that many of the concepts presented in this section on Rural Development and Basic Needs come from the insightful work of Alain de Janvry. For an excellent examination of agrarian issues in Latin America, see: Alain de Janvry, *The Agrarian Question and Reformism in Latin America* (Baltimore: Johns Hopkins University Press, 1981).

16. Ibid, p. 229.

17. See: AID, *Agricultural Development Policy Paper,* June 1978, and *AID Policy on Agricultural Asset Distribution: Land Reform,* January 1979.

18. *Front Lines* (AID), August 1984.

19. The preamble to the Agricultural Trade and Assistance Act of 1954 (Public Law 480) stated: "The Congress hereby declares it to be the policy of the United States to expand international trade; to develop and expand export markets for U.S. agricultural commodities; to use the abundant agricultural productivity of the United States to combat hunger and malnutrition; and to encourage economic development of the developing countries. . . ." The third and fourth objectives were not added until a 1966 amendment.

20. Hubert Humphrey, quoted in *Family Farm* (undated), a newsletter of the Wisconsin Farm Unity Alliance.

21. *Foreign Agriculture,* February 1984.

22. GAO, *Disincentives to Agricultural Production in Developing Countries*

(Washington: November 6, 1975); summary of document's conclusions in *Feeding the World's Population: Developments in the Decade Following the World Food Conference of 1974,* a report prepared by Congressional Research Service for the House Committee on Foreign Affairs, October 1984, p. 418.

23. Ibid.
24. For a good critique of PL480, see: Oxfam America's "The Appropriateness of PL480 as a Development Tool," testimony prepared for the Senate Committee on Agriculture, Nutrition, and Forestry, April 4, 1985.
25. AID, *Congressional Presentation FY 1987,* Main Volume, p. 178.

Chapter Five:
Low Intensity Battlefield

1. Paul Harvey, broadcast of October 25, 1986.
2. Statement of General Paul Gorman, Commander in Chief, U.S. SOUTH-COM, at hearings before the Senate Committee on Armed Services, Department of Defense, *Authorization for Appropriations for FY 1986,* February 27, 1985, pp. 1209–10.
3. David L. Caldon, "The Role of Security Assistance in the Irregular Conflict Ongoing in the Caribbean Basin Today: Prevention-Deterrence-Counteraction," *The DISAM Journal,* Vol. 5, No. 2, Winter 1982–83, p. 31.
4. Frank Barnett, B. Hugh Tovar, and Richard H. Shultz, eds., *Special Operations in U.S. Strategy* (Washington: National Defense University Press, 1984), p. 1.
5. Quoted in William Robinson and Kent Norsworthy, *David and Goliath: the U.S. War Against Nicaragua* (New York: Monthly Review Press, forthcoming).
6. John W. Waghelstein, "Post-Vietnam Counterinsurgency Doctrine," *Military Review,* May 1985.
7. Richard Armitrage in *Defense 85,* October 1985.
8. TRADOC Pam 525–44, *Military Operations: U.S. Army Operational Concept for Low Intensity Conflict,* October 1985.
9. Fred Ikle, "Small Wars in Many Regions," *Proceedings of the Low Intensity Warfare Conference,* January 14–15, 1986.
10. Sam Sarkesian, "Low Intensity Warfare: Threat and Military Response," *Proceedings of the Low Intensity Warfare Conference,* January 14–15, 1986.

11. Jeane Kirkpatrick, "The Role of the Soviet Union in Low Intensity Warfare," *Proceedings of the Low Intensity Warfare Conference,* January 14–15, 1986.

12. U.S. Army, *Field Manual 100–5 Operations,* 1982.

13. J. Michael Kelly, "Economic/Security Assistance and Special Operations," in *Special Operations in U.S. Strategy,* p. 223.

14. George K. Tanham, "Organizational Strategy and Low Intensity Conflicts," in *Special Operations in U.S. Strategy,* p. 295.

15. Office of the Assistant Secretary of Defense for National Security Affairs, "U.S. Policies Toward Latin American Military Forces," February 25, 1965.

16. Douglas Blaufarb, "Economic/Security Assistance and Special Operations," in *Special Operations in U.S. Strategy,* p. 209.

17. Dr. Michael W. S. Ryan, "Security Assistance: Planning for Low Intensity Conflict," *DISAM Journal,* Summer 1985.

18. Caspar Weinberger, Secretary of Defense Memorandum, "DOD Task Force on Humanitarian Issues," January 12, 1984, p. 1.

19. Department of Defense, *Task Force Report on Humanitarian Assistance* (approved by the Secretary of Defense, June 19, 1984).

20. Department of Defense humanitarian activities have traditionally been limited to those construed as integral parts of defense. DOD is bound by a law that states: "Appropriations shall be applied only to the objects for which the appropriations were made." (Douglas Blaufarb, "Economic/Security Assistance and Special Operations," in *Special Operations in U.S. Strategy,* p. 209.) Because Congress authorizes the DOD to carry out only defense functions, relief and development projects are normally prohibited. Only when area commanders determine that (1) nonmilitary activities, like medical outreach, are somehow related to DOD's defense functions, or (2) there is an immediate threat to public health, can DOD initiate humanitarian operations. However, DOD participation in humanitarian assistance is also permitted following explicit requests by AID and the State Department—the government agencies that have the prime responsibility for economic aid.

21. Interview by authors, August 1985.

22. John Marsh, Secretary of the U.S. Army, "Introduction" in *Special Operations in U.S. Strategy,* p. 24.

23. Tom Barry, Deb Preusch, and Beth Sims, *New Right Humanitarians* (Albuquerque: Resource Center, 1986).

24. M. Forbes, Jr., "Forbes Comment," *Forbes,* February 25, 1985.

25. *Texas Observer,* September 27, 1986.

26. *The Nation,* March 9, 1985.

27. Geneva Conventions of 1949, Article 9.

28. Joseph Mitchell quoted in *Oxfam Legislative Update,* March 1986.

29. Department of Defense, *Task Force Report on Humanitarian Assistance,* (June 19, 1984).

30. R. W. Komer, *The Malayan Emergency in Retrospect: Organization of a Successful Counterinsurgency Effort* (Santa Monica: Report prepared for Advanced Research Projects Agency, Rand, February, 1972), p. 54; Lennox Mills, *Malaya: A Political and Economic Appraisal* (Minneapolis: University of Minnesota, 1958), p. 63.

31. Ibid., Komer, p. 54.

32. Major General Edward Lansdale, *In the Midst of War: An American's Mission to Southeast Asia* (New York; Harper and Row, 1972), p. 213.

33. Statement by President Kennedy, March 13, 1961, quoted in Willard F. Barber and Neale Ronning *Internal Security and Military Power* (Columbus: Ohio State University Press, 1966), pp. 27 and 73.

34. Civic action is designated, along with public safety (police support and training) as a "specific counterinsurgency program." See AID Memo: "AID Supported Counter Insurgency Activities", dated July 18, 1962, To: Members of Special Group CI, from Frank Coffin, classified SECRET.

35. Willard F. Barber and Neale Ronning *Internal Security and Military Power* (Columbus: Ohio State University Press, 1966), p. 229.

36. Don L. Etchinson, *The United States and Militarism in Central America* (New York: Praeger, 1975), pp. 108–09.

37. John S. Pustay, Major, USAF, *Counterinsurgency Warfare* (New York: The Free Press, 1965), pp. 170–71. Pustay is currently division director of the Analytical Science Corporation, a member of the DOD's Special Operations Policy Advisory Group, and a member of the National Defense University.

38. "Nuevo Capitulo de la Labor de los Amigos de las Americas," *Revista Militar* July-September 1970.

39. Barber and Ronning, op. cit., p. 127.

40. Richard Millett, *History of the Guardia Nacional de Nicaragua, 1925–1965* (Ph.D. dissertation, University of New Mexico, 1966), pp. 460–61.

41. U.S. Southern Command, *The U.S. Army and Civic Action in Latin America: July 1967–July 1969,* Volume 4, p. 32.

42. Millett, op. cit., p. 456.

43. Robert Elan, *Appeal to Arms: The Army and Politics in El Salvador,* (Ph.D. dissertation, University of New Mexico, 1969), p. 166.

44. Ibid., p. 167.

45. Robert S. Perry (Captain U.S. Army), "Civic Action and Regional Security," *DISAM Journal,* Vol. 5, No. 3, Spring 1983, pp. 34–36.

46. Ibid.
47. This view was also clearly stated by two staff officers at the U.S. Army Training and Doctrine Command, Major General Donald Morelli and Major Michael Ferguson: "Army engineering construction of a reservoir, Peace Corps efforts at irrigation farming and an agriculture plan for fish breeding should be coordinated closely and executed concurrently rather than as separate projects over a protracted period." Major General Donald R. Morelli (Retired) and Major Michael M. Ferguson, "Low Intensity Conflict: An Operational Perspective," *Military Review*, November 1984.
48. Captain John W. Athanson, "Aiding Our Neighbors," *Proceedings*, February 1985, p. 51.
49. Ibid., p. 53.
50. "Counterinsurgency and Development" was the name of one of the courses taught to the country's civil guard at a training session in Honduras. *Mesoamerica*, June 1985.
51. *The Nation*, October 5, 1985.
52. Eva Gold, "High Stakes," *Sojourners*, August 1984.
53. Information from material on the seminar program supplied by U.S. SOUTHCOM, February 1986.
54. Interview by authors, January 1986.
55. Information from correspondence supplied by Project Handclasp.
56. Lieutenant Colonel James A. Taylor, "Military Medicines's Expanding Role in Low Intensity Conflict," *Military Review*, April 1985.
57. Ibid.
58. Colin Danby, "U.S. Military Health Programs Criticized," *Honduras Update*, September 1984.
59. *Washington Post*, September 2, 1985.
60. Letter from Lewis Brodsky, Chief, Public Affairs Office, Department of the Army, March 20, 1986.
61. Statement of General Paul Gorman, at hearings before the Senate Committee on Armed Services, Department of Defense, *Authorization for Appropriations for FY 1986*, February 27, 1985, p. 1232–33.
62. Colonel James R. Compton, U.S. Army Reserve, "CIMC: A Force Multiplier for the Combat Commander," *Military Review*, February 1982.
63. Statement of General Paul Gorman, Commander in Chief, SOUTHCOM, on *The Role of the U.S. Southern Command in Central America*, at hearings before the Subcommittee on Western Hemisphere Affairs of the House Committee on Foreign Affairs, August 1, 1984, p. 10.

Chapter Six:
Terror and Development in Guatemala

1. A civilian government headed by Julio Cesár Méndez Montenegro ruled Guatemala from 1966 to 1970. Like Cerezo, he came to the National Palace with little control, having signed a 16-point agreement with the military that severely limited his power. An estimated 6,000 to 8,000 people were killed during a counterinsurgency campaign under his civilian government. It was also about this time that death squad operations became frequent. During Méndez Montenegro's term, there was a rapid increase in the presence of U.S. military advisers and in U.S. economic assistance for pacification.

2. Stephen Schlesinger and Stephen Kinzer, *Bitter Fruit: The Untold Story of the American Coup in Guatemala* (New York: Doubleday, 1982).

3. Susanne Jonas and David Tobis, *Guatemala* (Berkeley: NACLA, 1974), p. 44.

4. Charles Hillinger, "Guatemala Booms Under New Rule," *Los Angeles Times,* June 30, 1957.

5. Susanne Jonas, *Guatemala: Plan Piloto Para El Continente,* (San José: Educa, 1981), p. 205.

6. Gordon L. Bowen, "U.S. Policy Toward Guatemala 1954–1963," *Armed Forces & Society,* Winter 1984, p. 168.

7. *Foreign Assistance and Related Agencies Appropriations for 1968,* hearings before a subcommittee of the House Committee on Appropriations, April 24, 1967, Part 2, Economic Assistance," 1967, p. 1515.

8. William and Elizabeth Paddock, *We Don't Know How: An Independent Audit of What They Call Success in Foreign Assistance* (Ames: Iowa State University Press, 1973).

9. Eduardo Galeano, *Guatemala: Occupied Country* (New York: Monthly Review, 1967), p. 79.

10. "Prufen sie die geschichte der menschheit," *Der Spiegel,* April 1970, which was cited in Brian Jenkins and Caesar D. Sereseres, "U.S. Military Assistance and the Guatemalan Armed Forces," *Armed Forces and Society,* August 1977, p. 580.

11. Junta Militar de Gobierno, *Objectivos Nacionales Actuales,* March 23, 1982; Estado Mayor General del Ejército, *Plan Nacional de Seguridad y Desarrollo,* Anexo H (Ordenes permanentes para el desarrollo de operaciones contrasubversivas) al plan de campaña Victoria 82, July 16, 1982. Quoted in George Black, "Under the Gun," *NACLA Report on the Americas,* November/December 1985, p. 11.

12. The military added the Civilian Affairs and Community Development section to those of Intelligence, Logistics, Operations, and Personnel.

13. Until 1978, the assistance from the World Food Program was coordinated by the Ministry of Health. In 1982, just as the counterinsurgency campaign was gaining steam, the program was transferred to the CRN.
14. "Operacion Ixil," *Revista Militar,* September-December 1982.
15. *Development Poles, Polos de Desarrollo,* (Guatemala City: Editorial del Ejercito), February 1985, p. 85.
16. Ibid., p. 13.
17. *Enfoprensa,* September 14, 1984.
18. Department of Defense, *Foreign Assistance Legislation for FY 86–87, Part 6.* Close observers of the Guatemalan military note that the army has consistently refused to use its helicopters for medical evacuation even when they were available.
19. "Labor Trends in Guatemala, 1983," Prepared by the American Embassy (Guatemala), p. 6.
20. AID *Annual Budget Submission, FY 1984, Guatemala* (June 1982), pp. 2–3.
21. Testimony of M. Peter McPherson, Administrator of AID, at a subcommittee of the House Committee on Appropriations, April 19, 1983, p. 86.
22. The 1984 annual report of ACNI explained that a fund of 2 million quetzales (equivalent at that time to $2 million) set up by the Guatemalan government as part of an agreement with AID financed most of its joint programs with PVOs that year. Area de Cooperacion Nacional e Internacional de CRN, *Informe Anual de Actividades 1984.* AID agreement 520-K-036.
23. Quoted in Alvaro Galez, "Ayuda Norteamericana," *Prensa Libre,* December 20, 1985.
24. Letter to Senator Patrick J. Leahy from Jay F. Morris, AID, March 6, 1985.
25. Ibid.
26. Interview by authors with Robert Queener, Aid, Washington, October 1984.
27. One AID official noted that Bandesa loans were not being repaid because "cooperative leaders kept disappearing." Channeling the credit through private financial institutions caused interest rates to jump from 8 to 12 percent. "That has resulted in our credit going to slightly better off buyers," admitted AID's Gary Vaughn, "but the investment should be more productive."
28. These include the Business Chamber (CAEM), Foundation for Development (FUNDESA), and the Guatemalan Association for Nontraditional Exports (GEXPORT).

29. National Endowment for Democracy, *Annual Report 1985.*

30. WFP, "Project Summary: Guatemala," Seventeenth Session, 1983. In 1985, AID said that WFP's program "is closely coordinated with AID's plans to add new activities worth some $20 to $25 million."

31. A WFP official in Guatemala readily acknowledged that its donations were being used by the military as part of its pacification and counterinsurgency plan in the Altiplano. "But you need to understand," he added, "that the United Nations judges its food aid not by politics but by need, and there's a lot of hunger in the highlands."

32. Nancy Peckenham, *Guatemala 1983,* (Philadelphia: American Friends Service Committee, 1983), p. 17.

33. Americas Watch, *Guatemala: A Nation of Prisoners: Social and Economic Consequences of Repression,* January 1984.

34. A review of the activity of Caminos Rurales and INTA shows that the overwhelming amount of new rural road construction has occurred in either the highlands or the Franja Transversal de Norte. Hundreds of kilometers of roads have been built in the development poles and leading to the model villages. Over half of the construction by Caminos Rurales since 1978 has occurred in Huehuetenango and Quiché—the two provinces most affected by the counterinsurgency war. Roads built by the government extend into the development poles of those two provinces.

35. AID, *Highlands Agricultural Development Project,* 1984.

36. Like AID, the Guatemalan government has given rural roads in the highlands top priority. In 1985, the AID Mission observed: "At a time when other government ministries are being requested to reduce their budgets, the government is increasing its roads program." This emphasis given to road building by the military government of Mejía Víctores demonstrated "the government's commitment to provide access roads to needy farmers." The AID Mission made no mention of the obvious military implications of improved rural transportation. AID, *Highlands Agricultural Development Project,* p. 4.

37. AID, *Small Farmer Development Project,* 1984.

38. Since 1978, AID-sponsored projects have resulted in over 600 kilometers of road. The agency has now set in motion a project that will pay for the maintenance of 1300 kilometers of roads in the Altiplano. Called the Farm-to-Market Access Roads, AID's latest rural roads program provides $10 million for the construction and rehabilitation of 800 kilometers of roads in the highlands. AID predicted that the project would "provide more than 150,000 rural inhabitants with roads to market centers, providing incentives to produce higher value cash crops." Judy Van Rest, "AID in Guatemala," *Frontlines* (Washington: AID), November 1985.

39. Gary Smith, "Abbreviated Economic Analysis of the Small Farmer Development Project," (AID: Office of Rural Development, Report No. 6), May 1983.
40. *Development Poles, Polos de Desarrollo,* p. vii.; AID rejects suggestions that its road-building program is related to pacification in Guatemala. "If there is ever a tendency that the road will help anything other than the small farmer, we don't touch it," declared Lawrence Hill of the AID Mission in Guatemala. However, interviews with officials from Caminos Rurales and INTA conflicted with AID statements. In 1983, Minister of Communications Hugo Solares said that AID gave the military government funds to construct roads in the isolated areas of the northwestern highlands, including the sites of the new model villages. In 1984, Julio Galicia of Caminos Rurales said that virtually all rural road construction and maintenance projects in the highlands were backed by AID, including the roads that lead directly to the model villages and provided access to the development poles.
41. Interview by authors, source wished to remain anonymous, January 1987.
42. Interview by authors, source wished to remain anonymous, January 1987.
43. Interview by authors, source wished to remain anonymous, June 1984.
44. Quoted in *Central America Report,* November 21, 1986.
45. Guatemala Church in Exile, *Development: The New Face of War,* April 1986, p. 39.
46. Ibid.
47. Cited in *Inforpress, Guatemala 1986: El Año de Las Promesas,* February 1987.

Chapter Seven:
The Other War in El Salvador

1. The term "other war" was first used by members of the Johnson administration to describe the nonmilitary aspects of the war handled mostly by AID, PVOs, and military civic action teams.
2. These figures do not include the many millions that AID pumped into El Salvador through its regional programs. Programs funded by AID's Latin American and Caribbean Office and its Regional Office for Central America and Panama (ROCAP) direct funds to regional projects, such as the Central American Bank of Economic Integration and the American Institute for Free Labor Development (which is also funded through country programs).

3. Roy Prosterman and Mary Temple, "Land Reform in El Salvador," *AFL-CIO Free Trade Union News,* June 1980, p. 1.
4. Ibid., p. 4.
5. *New York Times,* March 13, 1980.
6. The eventual subdivision of Phase I estates was discussed early on by Prosterman and other advocates of small owner-operator farms. Prosterman and Temple wrote in 1980 that "experiments with subdividing and smaller-scale cultivation will probably get underway in early 1981." op. cit., p. 4.
7. Ibid., p. 2.
8. AID's Regional Inspector General for Audit (Latin America), *Agrarian Reform in El Salvador: A Report on its Status,* 1984.
9. Ibid.
10. Laurence R. Simon and James C. Stephens, *El Salvador Land Reform 1980–81, Impact Audit* (Boston: Oxfam, 1982).
11. Laurence R. Simon, "The Dismal Legacy of Land Reform," *In These Times,* July 11, 1984.
12. *New York Times,* June 30, 1984.
13. *Time,* June 4, 1984.
14. In a gambit aimed at increasing his popularity among peasant associations, Duarte in late 1986 promised to press forward with Phase II in 1987. The announcement was greeted with predictable fury by business associations like the National Association of Private Enterprise and the Salvadoran Coffee Growers Association. Even in the unlikely event that Phase II is finally enforced, the redistribution will have little impact on the rural poor. Most landowners have already sold off or arranged title transfers for property over the 605 acre minimum. "We're not talking about much land anymore," observed AID's Tom King in December 1986.
15. AID, "El Salvador: Agrarian Reform Accomplishments," June 20, 1985.
16. Department of State, *Report on the Situation in El Salvador,* January 16, 1984, p. 53.
17. *Newsweek,* March 21, 1983.
18. *USAID El Salvador,* AID San Salvador, July 1985.
19. AID backed the National Plan with funds for community infrastructure like clinics and town halls, food-for-work projects, resettlement projects, civic action programs, and the government institutions that carried out the plan. In its 1988 budget for El Salvador, AID said it was "giving increased priority to the carrying out of development activities in newly secured areas" in association with the National Plan. AID underwrites the National Plan with development assistance, food aid, and local currency generated from Title I and ESF programs.

20. *Informador Guerrillero,* November 7, 1983.
21. Hearings before the Subcommittee on Western Hemispheric Affairs, House Committee on Foreign Affairs, March 1, 1983, p. 84.
22. *Christian Science Monitor,* December 12, 1983.
23. Ignoring the National Plan's shortcomings, President Duarte in late 1984 expressed his government's commitment to continue its extensive pacification programs and even expand the work of CONARA into five additional provinces. Besides San Vicente and Usulután, the National Plan affected the provinces of La Unión, Morazán, Cabañas, Cuscatlán, and Chalatenango. The Duarte government hoped to use the National Plan as a way to extend the influence of the Christian Democratic Party by putting party people in charge of food distribution and work programs.
24. *NACLA's Report on the Americas,* January–March 1986, p. 22.
25. One of the first signs of this proposed unification of resources under military control was the creation of the Vice-Ministry of Public Security in June 1984, a measure that brought all security and police forces under military jurisdiction.
26. Interview by authors, October 1986.
27. *El Boletín,* ACEN-SIAG (Mexico City), August 18, 1986.
28. Interview by authors, August 1986.
29. Interview by authors, August 1986.
30. Interview by authors, December 1985.
31. Interview by authors, December 1985.
32. Ibid.
33. *Washington Post,* December 27, 1984.
34. USIA, Description of Country Operations in Central America, 1985.
35. Jack Anderson, United Features Syndicate, February 23, 1983 and March 4, 1983.
36. Jack Anderson, "Soccer Balls, Subtle Threats Win Some Over in El Salvador," *Albuquerque Journal,* February 9, 1985.
37. *Washington Post,* August 5, 1985.
38. *Miami Herald,* July 14, 1985.
39. *Washington Post,* August 5, 1985.
40. The number of internal refugees has steadily escalated since 1980. From an estimated 85,000 registered displaced persons in 1980, the figure jumped to 250,000 in 1982 and over 525,000 in 1985. By late 1986, estimates of the number of displaced ran as high as 700,000—14 percent of the entire population. Together with the estimated 500,000 refugees living outside the country, almost a quarter of the Salvadoran population has been displaced because of the war. In contrast, 8 percent of South Vietnam's population was displaced during the period of U.S. intervention.

41. For more information on the air war, see: Americas Watch, *Free Fire: A Report on Human Rights in El Salvador,* August 1984.

42. Washington provided the money, hardware, and technical assistance that made the air war possible. Between 1980 and 1986, the United States gave the Salvadoran military nearly $600 million in direct military aid—much of which was used to enhance its small Air Force. By late 1986, the Air Force had at its command more than 60 combat-equipped helicopters and 40 attack planes. This buildup was reflected in the number of air strikes, increasing from 111 air strikes in 1982 to 1,081 in 1985.

43. *Christian Science Monitor,* March 26, 1984.

44. Americas Watch, *Free Fire,* op. cit., p. 35.

45. Robert Parry, "Salvadoran Escalation," *Associated Press,* May 31, 1984.

46. Mary Jo McConnahay, "Rescue or Capture?—Forced Evacuations Now Key Government Tactic in Salvadoran Countryside," *Pacific News Service,* July 3, 1985.

47. *CBS Evening News,* August 21, 1985. Even when the supplies were given to those needing it, the unspoken motives were apparent. An observer reported, "When the army finally comes to town, they arrive with bags of U.S.-donated food and give a self-promotion speech before handing the food out."

48. *Christian Science Monitor,* January 1, 1984.

49. Ibid.

50. AID initially offered its assistance only to registered refugees in areas of government control. Criticism of this policy, combined with a recognition that excluding the nonregistered population limited government influence, pressured AID in 1985 to promise to adjust its procedures. But AID failed to develop a workable program to reach the nonregistered. In fact, it proceeded with Project Hope's medical services and other programs that were not available to the nonregistered.

51. *Miami Herald,* December 17, 1984.

52. Ibid.

53. *Central America Bulletin,* May 1984.

54. U.S. General Accounting Office, *Funding of International Election Observers for El Salvador,* June 25, 1985.

55. *New York Times,* May 13, 1984; *Washington Report on the Hemisphere,* May 29, 1984. Some of the CIA support for the Christian Democratic Party was thought to have been laundered through the Konrad Adenauer Foundation, a West German foundation that contributes to IVEPO (Venezuela Institute of Popular Education), which helped finance the elections.

56. *Report of the Interdepartmental Subcommittee on Police Advisory Assistance,* June 11, 1962. See Michael McClintock, *The American Connection: State Terror and Popular Resistance in El Salvador* (London: Zed Press, 1985) for an excellent description of the OPS program.
57. Among OPS graduates were death-squad leaders like Roberto D'Aubuisson, Colonel Roberto Staben (implicated in the 1980 assassination of Archbishop Oscar Romero), and General José Alberto Medrano (the founder of ORDEN and called the "founder of the death squads" by José Napoleón Duarte). Noam Chomsky, *Turning the Tide* (Boston: South End Press, 1986), p. 98.; Allan Nairn, "Behind the Death Squads," *The Progressive,* May 1984.
58. Allan Nairn, op. cit.
59. *In These Times,* August 20, 1986.
60. Interview by authors, August 1986.
61. Representative Jim Leach, Representative George Miller, and Senator Mark Hatfield, *U.S. Aid to El Salvador: An Evaluation of the Past, A Proposal for the Future,* A Report to the Arms Control and Foreign Policy Caucus, February 1985.
62. In early 1987, Duarte, reacting to mounting pressure from the oligarchy, weakened state control over agroexport commercialization while at the same time withdrawing proposed taxes on business and affirming his government's support for the private sector.
63. AID Certification Cable, San Salvador, January 12, 1983.
64. Other AID-created business organizations include CONAES (National Commission of Salvadoran Entrepreneurs) and the Salvadoran Association of Nontraditional Agroexport Producers (ASPENT).

Chapter Eight:
The Destabilization of Nicaragua

1. Notes taken during a September 15, 1970, meeting between National Security Adviser Kissinger, Attorney General Mitchell, and CIA Director Helms. Included in *Senate Select Committee to Study Government Operations with Respect to Intelligence Activities,* Vol. 7, December 4–5, 1975, p. 96.
2. Jim Morrell and William Jesse Biddle, "Central America: The Financial War," *International Policy Report* (Center for International Policy) March 1983, p. 7.
3. Statement at presidential press conference, February 21, 1985.
4. AID, *Agency for International Development, FY 1978 Congressional Presentation,* 1979.

5. The *Financial Times* (October 1, 1975) reported: "Much of the disaster relief and development aid money to Nicaragua has been channeled into the multimillion dollar Somoza business empire which already dominated most sectors of private as well as public life. Certainly the only visible government expenditure has been on roadbuilding using cement blocks made by the family's Mayco firm with cement from the National Cement Company."

6. *Human Rights in Nicaragua, Guatemala, and El Salvador: Implications for U.S. Policy,* hearings before the House Subcommittee on International Relations, July 8 and 9, 1976, p. 13.

7. Additional cause for concern stemmed from the role played by Robert Culbertson, the AID Mission director in Nicaragua at the time, who previously administered AID's counterinsurgency programs in Peru, Guatemala, and South Vietnam. After a stint at the Ford Foundation, Culbertson became AID director in Peru in the early 1960s, where he helped develop programs combining military civic action programs with rural development. From 1966 to 1968, he was associate AID director in Saigon, and then he became the Deputy Assistant Secretary of State for Social and Civic Development in Washington (where he oversaw civic action programs worldwide). Before being appointed to the new trouble spot of Nicaragua, Culbertson served as AID director in Guatemala. See NACLA's *Latin America and Empire Report,* February 1976.

8. Jaime Biderman, "The Development of Capitalism in Nicaragua: A Political Economic History," *Latin American Perspectives,* Winter 1983.

9. Jaime Wheelock and Luis Carrion, *Apuntes sobre el desarrollo económico y social de Nicaragua,* (Managua: Centro de Publicaciones Silvio Mayorga, 1980). Cited in *Centroamerica—Más allá de la crisis* by Donald Castillo Rivas (Mexico City: Sociedad Interamericana de Planificación, 1983), pp. 203–04.

10. Ibid.

11. Report by Penny Lernoux included in: *Foreign Assistance and Related Agencies Appropriations for 1978,* hearings before a Subcommittee of the House Committee on Appropriations, House of Representatives, April 5, 1977, "Report on Human Rights." Part 3, 1977, p. 551–56.

12. The $32.5 million includes development assistance and food aid.

13. "A Secret War for Nicaragua," *Newsweek,* November 8, 1982.

14. See Jeff McConnell, "Counterrevolution in Nicaragua: the U.S. Connection," in *Nicaragua Reader* (New York: Grove Press, 1983), p. 176.

15. Description of FY 1981 program in *AID Congressional Presentation for Fiscal Year 1982.*

16. Jeff McConnell, op. cit. p. 183.

17. Cleto Di Giovanni, "U.S. Policy and the Marxist Threat," *The Heritage Foundation Backgrounder,* No. 128, October 15, 1980, pp. 1–3.
18. This announcement extended the temporary suspension of this aid by the Carter administration during its last several weeks.
19. Statement of Otto J. Reich before Subcommittee on Foreign Operations, House Committee on Appropriations, June 23, 1982.
20. Ibid.
21. Department of State, *Foreign Assistance and Related Programs, Appropriations for FY 1983,* hearings before a subcommittee of the House Committee on Appropriations, Part 7. Reprogramming for the Nicaraguan Private Sector, June 23, 1982.
22. Jeff McConnell, op. cit, p. 183; *The Guardian,* December 2, 1981.
23. *Washington Post,* September 4, 1982; *Update,* Central America Historical Institute, April 1, 1985. Most of the $5.1 million, however, did get through to the intended private sector beneficiaries. AID reports that $4.8 million of that grant was expended. Of the original $7.5 million grant (scaled down to $5.1 million in June 1982), $1.6 million was expended in FY 1981; $3.0 million in FY 1982; $208,000 in FY 1983; $76,000 in FY 1984; and $12,000 in FY 1985. Information from interview by authors with Tom Stukel, AID, August 1986.
24. James Ridgeway, "Iran or Bust," *Village Voice,* December 9, 1986.
25. Knight-Ridder Newspapers release, August 11, 1985.
26. *Washington Post,* March 21, 1986.
27. NED, *Statement of Principles,* December 1984.
28. Pan American Development Foundation (PADF) and Nicaraguan Development Institute (INDE), *Nicaragua: The Informal Sector in Transition,* June 1985; CIPE, "CIPE Achievement in Latin America"; CIPE, *Report on 1985 Program Activities.*
29. USIA, Description of Operations in Central America, 1985.
30. Ibid.
31. Jacqueline Sharkey, "Back in Control," *Common Cause Magazine,* September–October 1986.
32. See the excellent study: *Electronic Penetration in Low Intensity Warfare: The Case of Nicaragua* by Howard H. Frederick, Ph.D, School of Communications, Ohio University, Athens, Ohio. This study was presented at the Fourteenth Annual Telecommunications Policy Research Conference at Arlie House in Arlie, Virginia (April 29, 1986).
33. Ibid.
34. *New York Times,* November 5, 1986.
35. *Washington Post,* September 11, 1984.
36. Report by the Committee of U.S. Citizens Resident in Costa Rica, May 1985.

37. The Nicaraguan Ministry of Planning in 1980 began a trade diversification campaign. At that time, the United States accounted for more than 30 percent of the country's total imports and exports. By the 1985 announcement of the embargo, that figure had dropped to less than 15 percent as Japan, Western European countries, and socialist nations substantially increased their trade with Nicaragua.

38. Tony Jenkins, "The U.S. Embargo Against Nicaragua: One Year Later," Center for International Policy and Overseas Development Council, May 1986; *Central America Report,* June 27, 1986.

39. Ibid (Jenkins).

40. Jim Morrell and William Jesse Biddle, "Central America: The Financial War," *International Policy Report* (Center for International Policy), March 1983, pp. 7–11.

41. IDB, "Nicaragua: Programa Global de Credito Agropecuario," p. 25.

42. See: Jim Morrell, "IDB Writes Negative Loan," *Aid Memo* (Center for International Policy), December 20, 1985.

43. Jim Morrell, "Redlining Nicaragua," *International Policy Report* (Center for International Policy), December 1985.

44. *Central America Report,* October 10, 1985.

45. Caleb Rossiter, "The Financial Hit List," *International Policy Report,* (Center for International Policy), February 1984.

46. World Bank, *Nicaragua: The Challenge of Reconstruction,* October 1981; Morrell and Biddle, "Central America: The Financial War," op. cit.

47. World Bank/International Finance Corporation, "Office Memorandum: Nicaragua—Urban Reconstruction Project, Credit 965-NI, Project Completion Report" (mimeo, June 24, 1983), p. 16; Cited in CIP, "Nicaragua's War Economy," *International Policy Report,* (Center for International Policy), November 1985.

48. World Bank, "Office Memorandum: Nicaragua—Urban Reconstruction Project, . . ." p. 1.

49. Jim Morrell, "Nicaragua's War Economy," *International Policy Report* (Center for International Policy), November 1985.

50. Statement of Jaime Belcazar, United Nations Development Program, April 12, 1985.

51. Information from Ministry of External Cooperation compiled by Richard Stahler-Sholk in *Nicaragua: Through Our Eyes,* Vol. 1, No. 5.

52. This estimate is based on per capita assistance from IMF, World Bank, and IDB. Between 1982 and 1985, Nicaragua received $81 million in IFI loans while neighboring countries each received from $380 to $600 million.

53. Mark Hansen, *U.S. Banks in the Caribbean Basin: Towards a Strategy*

for Facilitating Lending to Nations Pursuing Alternative Models of Development (paper prepared for conference of Policy Alternatives for the Caribbean and Central America (PACCA)), October 1983.

54. Sylvia Maxfield and Richard Stahler-Sholk, "External Constraints," in Thomas W. Walker, ed., *Nicaragua: The First Five Years* (New York: Praeger, 1985), p. 259. Despite Nicaragua's compliance with its debt schedule, the U.S. government's Inter-Agency Country Exposure Review Committee downgraded the country's status from "substandard" to "doubtful." The prestigious business organization, the Group of Thirty, found that some bankers believed these rankings to be less than fully objective: "An assertion made by several commercial banks was that U.S. supervisors were politically influenced by the State Department in their assessment of claims held on sovereign borrowers by American banks."

55. Figures from Henry Ruíz, Minister of External Cooperation; *New York Times,* October 27, 1985.

56. *The Electoral Process in Nicaragua,* the Report of the Latin American Studies Association Delegation to Observe the Nicaraguan General Election of November 4, 1984, p. 6.

57. Central American Historical Institute, "The Economic Costs of the Contra War," *Envio,* September 1985.

58. Economic Commission for Latin America (ECLA), "Nicaragua: repercusiones económicas de los recientes acontecimientos políticos," September 1979.

59. Speech by President Daniel Ortega to National Assembly, February 21, 1986; Nicaragua Ministry of Foreign Trade; evidence submitted to the International Court of Justice by the Secretariat of Planning and Budget; *Envio,* September 1985.

60. AID, "Northern Zone Infrastructure Development Project Paper," #515–0191, 1983.

61. The population is 74 percent native Costa Rican, 15 percent Nicaraguan, and 11 percent Costa Rican by naturalization.

62. AID, "Northern Zone Project Paper," op. cit.

63. Carlos Granados and Liliana Quezada, "Los intereses geopolíticos y el desarrollo de la zona norte nor-atlántica costarricense," *Primer Encuentro Centroamerico-Mexicano Sobre Problemas, Perspectivas, y Planificación Para El Desarrollo de las Regiones Fronterizas* (SIAP: November 1984), p. 22.

64. Ibid. p. 14.

65. Ibid. p. 21; *El Debate,* September 3, 1984.

66. The two lawmakers, Senator Jeremiah Denton (R-AL) and Representative Robert Livingston (R-LA), responsible for getting additional AID

funds for the project, are friends of the directors of Friends of the Americas (FOA), which has an office in the very area where AID funds are targeted. Calling the Nicaraguan border region "the most strategic place in the world," FOA asked its supporters for money to assist in the "struggle between freedom and slavery." (FOA fund-raising letter, October 27, 1986.) The money that FOA raises is used to support contras and their families with social services and supplies. Along the border, it distributed "Shoeboxes for Liberty," which among various items contain a U.S. flag and a note saying, "We hope the small things in this box are useful in your struggle for freedom."

67. Catholic Relief Services (CRS), "Nicaraguan Miskito and Sumo Indian Refugees in Honduras: A Report," March 14, 1985.

68. *International Trip Report: Nicaragua Indian Refugees in Honduras,* Center for Disease Control, Atlanta, October 12, 1984.

69. Judy Carnoy and Louise Levison, "The Humanitarians," in Steve Weissman, ed., *The Trojan Horse* (San Francisco: Ramparts Press, 1975), pp. 117–35.

70. *National Catholic Reporter,* January 1, 1985.

Chapter Nine:
AIFLD: Agents and Organizers

1. Two other regional labor institutes were created in the 1960s. In 1965, the African-American Labor Center (AALC) was established and Irving Brown was appointed its first director. Three years later, the Asian-American Free Labor Institute (AAFLI) was set up to support U.S.-backed regimes in South Vietnam, the Philippines, South Korea, and Turkey.

2. For more information on the CIA's use of AFL-CIO's international operations, see the following: Sidney Lens, "American Labor Abroad: Lovestone Diplomacy," *The Nation,* July 5, 1965; Dan Kurzman, "Lovestone's Cold War: The AFL-CIO Has Its Own CIA," *New Republic,* June 25, 1966; Henry W. Berger, "Lovestone, Meany & State: American Labor Overseas," *The Nation,* January 16, 1967; Daamon Stetson, "Meany Opposes CIA Aid to Labor," *New York Times,* February 21, 1967; Richard Dudman, "AID Funds for CIA Projects," *St. Louis Post-Dispatch,* April 13, 1969; Richard Dudman, "The AFL-CIO as Paid Propagandist," *New Republic,* May 3, 1969; Sidney Lens, "Partners: Labor and the CIA," *The Progressive,* February 1975; Michael J. Sussman, *AIFLD: U.S. Trojan Horse* (Washington: EPICA, July 1983).

3. Warner Poelchau, *White Paper Whitewash: Interviews with Philip Agee on the CIA and El Salvador* (New York: Deep Cover Books, 1981), p. 42.

4. J. Peter Grace, "A Consensus in Action—The AIFLD," AIFLD Pamphlet, 1965.

5. *AIFLD Report,* June 1966.

6. *AIFLD Report,* May–June 1981.

7. The numbers of in-country AIFLD students in 1985 were as follows: Costa Rica: 604; El Salvador: 1,834; Guatemala: 1,721; Honduras: 1,803; Panama: 249. Total in-country students for all of Central America between 1962 and 1985 was 111,627. Information from AIFLD's *Annual Progress Report 1962–1985.*

8. "Agrarian Union Development Department 1986–1987," (budget proposal submitted to AID by AIFLD).

9. In 1968, the U.S. Comptroller General did undertake a cursory review of AIFLD finances and programs but found that grants from AID often could not be traced to specific projects. It also reported that there was little accountability and an almost complete lack of evaluation of AIFLD by AID. See: *Survey of the Alliance for Progress: Labor Policies and Programs* U.S. Congress, July 15, 1968.

10. The AFL-CIO's 1984 budget for international affairs was $2.7 million, most of which is for affiliation fees and contributions to its own regional institutes. This $2.7 million constitutes about 6 percent of the organization's total budget. Each year, the AFL-CIO contributes about $200,000 to AIFLD. Information from the *30th Anniversary: Report of the AFL-CIO Executive Council,* 1985.

11. Interview by authors, September 1986.

12. A June 1980 evaluation by the U.S. embassy said that the task facing AIFLD was to "increase participation among labor moderates and to some extent stem the tide of those shifting to the radical left." But the report admitted that "trying to develop an education program which calls for moderation and democratic practice under conditions such as these is, to say the least, difficult." Richard F. King, LAB/POL Officer at U.S. embassy, "AIFLD in Guatemala," June 9, 1980.

13. Labor Attaché, *Labor Trends in Guatemala, 1983* (U.S. embassy, Guatemala).

14. Ibid.

15. AIFLD, *Country Labor Plan, 1977–1981; NACLA Report on the Americas,* November–December 1981, p. 24.

16. William Bollinger, "Organized Labor in El Salvador," in *Latin American Labor Organizations* (forthcoming from Greenwood Press).

17. Philip Wheaton, *Agrarian Reform in El Salvador: A Program of Rural*

Pacification (Washington: EPICA), p. 2; See Bollinger's historical profile of UCS in *Latin American Labor Organizations,* op. cit.: "During its first four years as a legal organization, UCS was AIFLD's main vehicle for 96 training courses and 39 regional meetings. The U.S. government channeled funds to 45 UCS-affiliated rural cooperatives and provided $671,000 for a UCS chain of savings and loan coops. By 1977, UCS claimed to have helped 5,000 formerly landless peasants purchase land farmed through 20 production cooperatives."

18. In 1973, AIFLD assigned a Nicaraguan lawyer Torres Laso to be its director in El Salvador. Salvadoran intelligence regarded Laso, who had fallen out of favor with the Somoza regime, as a CIA agent and expelled AIFLD from the country.

19. Twelve dissident unions walked out of its national congress in 1972 and founded the National Federation of Salvadoran Workers (FENAS-TRAS). By the end of the decade, FENASTRAS was the country's largest industrial federation.

20. The CIA declined to comment on whether Hammer and Pearlman were acting as undercover agents, and AIFLD said it had "no knowledge" about any relationship the men may have had with the CIA. John Kelly, "AIFLD: Secret Plan for El Salvador," *CounterSpy,* January 1982; Edward S. Muskie, Secretary of State, Petitioner, *v.* Philip Agee, Respondent, No. 80–83, Oral Argument, Supreme Court of the United States, January 14, 1981, pp. 21–22.

21. *NACLA Report on the Americas,* November–December 1985, p. 31.

22. *Miami Herald,* April 20, 1985.

23. The three founding organizations of UNTS were the UPD, the Confederation of Cooperative Associations of El Salvador, and the May First Committee (which included CST and CCTEM).

24. AIFLD and Freedom House, "The Captured Documents: Guerrilla Penetration of Salvadoran Trade Unions", April 30, 1986.

25. CISPES, *The Alert,* May–June 1986.

26. *Labor Report on Central America,* May/June 1986.

27. For a discussion of AFL-CIO links with SDUSA, see: Tom Barry and Deb Preusch, *AIFLD in Central America: Agents as Organizers* (Albuquerque, N.M.: Resource Center, 1986), pp. 58–59.

28. *Washington Post,* June 1, 1986

29. *AFL-CIO Free Trade Union News,* September 1984, p. 8.

30. Ibid.

31. The document, dated August 3, 1983, also stated: "We need to examine how law and Executive Order can be made more liberal to permit covert action on a broader scale, as well as what we can do through substantially overt political action."

32. John Kelly, "National Endowment for Reagan's 'Democracies,' " *The National Reporter,* Summer 1986.
33. Ibid.
34. *New York Times,* February 15, 1987.
35. *Washington Post,* February 9, 1983.
36. PRODEMCA, *Statement of Purpose.*
37. Among those signing these ads were several representatives of labor unions and institutes, including William Doherty (AIFLD), Sol Chaikin (ILGWU), Albert Shanker (AFT), Frank Drozak (Seafarers International), and John Joyce (Bricklayers Union).
38. Kai Bird and Max Holland, "Capitol Letter," *The Nation,* May 24, 1986.

Chapter 10:
Conclusion

1. For further discussion of this theme, see: Teresa Hayter and Catherine Watson, *AID: Rhetoric and Reality* (London: Pluto Press, 1985).

Glossary

AID (Agency for International Development): U.S. Government agency that distributes and manages most U.S. foreign economic assistance.

AIFLD (American Institute for Free Labor Development): AFL-CIO's branch for organizing labor in Latin America, which receives 96 percent of its funding from the U.S. government.

CABEI (Central America Bank for Economic Integration): Regional bank founded with AID funds in the 1960s that promotes U.S. investment and trade by funding infrastructure and communications projects.

CACM (Central America Common Market): Regional common market established in 1961 under rules set by the United States supposedly to promote regional industrialization, but which resulted in domination of the region by U.S. interests and capital.

CADO (Central America Development Organization): Regional organization proposed by the Kissinger Commission in 1984 to coordinate Central American economic aid and regional economic planning.

CBI (Caribbean Basin Initiative): Reagan-initiated economic aid and investment plan for Central America and the Caribbean passed by Congress in 1983.

CCAA (Caribbean Central America Association): Private business association funded by AID with 60 corporate sponsors that promotes U.S. investment in the Caribbean and Central America.

CCC (Commodity Credit Corporation): A U.S. government food program that guarantees U.S. agricultural exporters payment for commodities imported by foreign buyers.

CIPE (Center for International Private Enterprise): Branch of the U.S. Chamber of Commerce that receives funds from NED to promote private enterprise development in the third world.

Civic Action: Use of military forces on projects useful to the local population in such fields as health, public works, communications, agriculture, transportation, and education, that serves to improve the standing of the military forces with the population.

Counterinsurgency: Military, paramilitary, political, economic, psychological, and civic actions taken by a government to defeat insurgency.

ESF   (Economic Support Funds): U.S. government economic assistance, which usually takes the form of "cash transfers" to stabilize governments considered to be of strategic importance.

Eximbank: A U.S. government bank whose funds are used to finance and insure payment for U.S. exports.

LIC (Low Intensity Conflict):   A limited political-military struggle to achieve political, social, economic, or psychological objectives. It is often protracted and ranges from diplomatic, economic, and psycho-social pressures through terrorism and insurgency.

NED   (National Endowment for Democracy): Funded by USIA, NED is a private organization founded in 1983 "to contribute to the development of democratic values and institutions abroad."

NSC   (National Security Council): A top-level interagency body that advises the president on national security and foreign policy matters. It is responsible only to the president, and its activities are, therefore, routinely shielded from congressional oversight and public scrutiny.

OPIC   (Overseas Private Investment Corporation): OPIC is the U.S. government's insurance company for U.S. corporations investing in foreign countries.

Pacification: In coordination with counterinsurgency campaigns, civic action and rural development programs are designed not to gain territory but to capture the hearts and minds of rural communities and to isolate guerrillas from their bases of popular support.

PL480   (Public Law 480, or Food for Peace): Congress founded the PL480 food program in 1954 "to increase consumption of U.S. agricultural commodities, improve the foreign relations of the United States, and for other purposes."

PRE   (Bureau for Private Enterprise): An office of AID, PRE sponsors programs to promote joint ventures between U.S. and third world investors.

PRODEMCA (Friends of the Democratic Center in Central America): Private organization that receives funding from NED and the conservative Smith-Richardson, Olin, and Carthage Foundations to promote right-wing causes in the name of democracy.

PVOs (Private Voluntary Organizations): Nonprofit, private organizations, many of which receive AID funds for their humanitarian and development projects.

Stabilization: Financial aid in the form of generous trade credits, insurance, balance-of-payments assistance, and budget deficit relief to help stabilize weak economies of friendly governments.

SOUTHCOM (Southern Command): U.S. military command responsible for the southern half of the Western Hemisphere.

TCIP (Trade Credit Insurance Program): Created in 1984 under Eximbank, TCIP uses AID funds to offer special guarantees to U.S. exporters to certain countries in Central America.

USIA (United States Information Agency): Propaganda department of the U.S. government. USIS is the foreign information service of USIA.

Index

Acul, 117–18
Adams, Gary, 120–21
Aderholt, Harry, 89, 136
Aesculapius International Medicine, 104
AFL, 229–30, 236–37
AFL-CIO, 208, 229, 230, 231, 232, 235, 237, 238, 241, 246, 286n; International Affairs Division of, 228, 248, 253, 254–55; NED and, 228, 248, 250, 253. (See also American Institute for Free Labor Development)
Agee, Philip, 231
Agency for International Development (AID), 3, 5, 18, 140, 247, 270n; agrarian reform and, 53–55, 125, 146, 149–52, 155; agricultural programs of, 52–67, 71, 125, 130; Alliance for Progress and, 9, 10, 12, 13–14, 15, 16–17; business associations supported by, 41–43, 125, 187–88, 198, 201, 204, 280n; conditions specified in agreements with, 18, 25–27, 124, 259; in destabilization of Nicaragua, 200, 201–2, 204–5, 208, 220–24; evaluation of, 256–61; in Guatemalan pacification, 115, 117, 118, 119, 120–27, 128–32, 134, 136–37, 275n, 276n; labor organizations and, 231, 233n, 235–36, 238, 239, 240, 243, 255; in LIC, 81, 83–84, 87, 88, 92, 96, 97, 98, 101, 102, 103; private-sector programs and, 33–39, 41–44, 49, 50, 88, 266n–67n; in Salvadoran pacification, 145–47, 149–52, 154, 155, 158–59, 161, 163, 168, 173–74, 175–76, 177–79, 180–82, 185, 186–91, 277n, 279n; security forces and, 180–82, 263n–64n; Somoza regime and, 195–99, 205; stabilization programs of, 19, 21–32, 185, 190–91, 256–57, 259. (See also Economic Support Funds; Public Law 480 food aid)
agrarian reform, 9, 53–55, 60, 137; in El Salvador, 55, 88, 146, 148, 149–56, 186, 243, 244, 245–46, 277n; in Guatemala, 108, 109, 125, 140; in Nicaragua, 55, 197; rural development and, 64, 65–66
Agrarian Union Development Department (AUDD), 234
Agribusiness Development program, 125

293